S0-FBM-595

Journalistic Advocates and Muckrakers

Journalistic Advocates and Muckrakers

Three Centuries of Crusading Writers

by
Edd Applegate

McFarland & Company, Inc., Publishers
Jefferson, North Carolina, and London

British Library Cataloguing-in-Publication data are available

Library of Congress Cataloguing-in-Publication Data

Applegate, Edd
    Journalistic advocates and muckrakers : three centuries of crusading
writers / by Edd Applegate.
      p.   cm.
    Includes bibliographical references and index.
    ISBN 0-7864-0365-9 (library binding : 50# alkaline paper) ∞
    1. Journalists — United States — Biography.   2. Journalism — United
States — History. I. Title.
PN4871.A56   1997
070'.92'273 — dc21
  [B]   97-11662
                                                     CIP

—— ACKNOWLEDGMENTS ——

A book of this kind is a major undertaking in the sense that the author has to select who should be included and then locate information about the numerous individuals. The latter, of course, takes the most time, and an author is usually indebted to several people who have helped.

For this book, I am indebted to several reference librarians and interlibrary loan librarians at the Edmon Low Library, Oklahoma State University, and at the Todd Library, Middle Tennessee State University. I wish to thank them for their time and their expertise.

TABLE OF CONTENTS

INTRODUCTION

Advocacy and muckraking journalism have been practiced for a long time — the former for several hundred years, the latter since the late 19th century. Yet when they became popular in mainstream newspapers and magazines during the 1960s and 1970s, they were considered forms of what was labeled "new journalism," an admittedly broad term generally applied to journalistic writing that expressed a personal perspective. With the growing popularity of new journalism, certain journalists became celebrities for *what* and *how* they reported. Some writers who practiced new journalism began to explore the topic in articles and in panel discussions on college campuses. Eventually, a furor erupted between the new journalists and the traditional journalists. Articles denouncing the trend began to appear in numerous journals. As the furor subsided, certain journalists continued to write new journalism, while others began to write novels.

The Birth of New Journalism

Writing that was termed new journalism became particularly popular in the 1960s and 1970s because, as John Hellman claimed, reporters were "saddled with rules and formulas that made it impossible for them to deal adequately with their subjects" and hence revolted against the inverted pyramid.[1]

In essence, reporters believed that if the theory of objectivity were applied to every subject, the reader might be misinformed because of the subject's complexity. Michael Schudson claimed that the concept of objectivity could be attacked with three kinds of criticism: "[1] the content of a news story rests on a set of substantive political assumptions, [2] the form of the news story incorporates its own bias, [and 3] the process of news gathering itself constructs an image of reality which reinforces official viewpoints."[2]

As subjects were becoming more complex and the notion of objectivity was coming under question, journalists and writers began writing what was termed new journalism.

What Is New Journalism?

Books concerning new journalism were numerous in the 1970s, 1980s, and early 1990s. Most were compilations either of articles representing new journalism or of articles about new journalism. Some of these books identified the trend of new journalism explicitly, but few focused on the lives of the so-called new journalists.

The new journalism included literary journalism as well as advocacy and muckraking. Advocacy journalism is perhaps the oldest form of journalism because writers have been advocating ideas for hundreds of years. Muckraking journalism is not as old. Although examples of it appeared before 1900, the bulk of muckraking journalism appeared in magazines in the early 1900s, before World War I. Advocacy and muckraking were included under new journalism because each form concerned topics that had not been discussed for some time, if ever, particularly in the mainstream press, or each form was appropriately modified to provide emotional impact.

In 1971, Everette E. Dennis mentioned that the definition of new journalism had been expanded to include several kinds of journalism, including advocacy and alternative or muckraking journalism.[3] The same year Michael L. Johnson claimed that new journalism included what he termed "New Muckraking."[4]

In 1974, Everette E. Dennis and William L. Rivers discussed several kinds of new journalism, including advocacy and muckraking journalism.[5] The same year Charles C. Flippen claimed that new journalism was an umbrella term that included advocacy journalism, among other kinds.[6]

Advocacy New Journalism

In 1971, Everette E. Dennis claimed that certain newsmen argued against balanced news, objectivity, and the use of traditional sources of news. He wrote, "They sought and were granted opportunities for open *advocacy* in the news columns."[7]

In 1980, Ernest C. Hynds defined advocacy journalism in these terms:

> Advocacy journalism is based on the premise that the journalist has both a right and an obligation to become involved in the events that he reports. The advocate, or activist, says that since objectivity in reporting cannot be obtained, it should not be attempted. The reporter should instead tell the truth of the event or situation as he sees it.[8]

In essence, the writer presents his or her position when discussing a specific topic.

Since new journalism is an imprecise term, not everyone agrees on who should be categorized what way. It is interesting to survey writings on the subject to see what journalists have been identified by others as advocacy journalists.

In 1971, in his discussion of advocacy new journalism, Everette E. Dennis mentioned Nicholas von Hoffman, Jack Newfield, and Pete Hamill.[9]

In 1972, Jack Newfield discussed new journalism and mentioned Jack Anderson, Michael Arlen, James Baldwin, William F. Buckley, Eldridge Cleaver, Nat Hentoff, Seymour Hersh, Jeremy Larner, Karl Marx, H. L. Mencken, Ralph Nader, Jack Newfield, Thomas Paine, Robin Reisig, James Ridgeway, Lincoln Steffens, I. F. Stone, and Ida Tarbell, among others.[10]

In a 1974 discussion of advocacy new journalism, Everette E. Dennis and William L. Rivers mentioned William F. Buckley, Pete Hamill, Nat Hentoff, Jack Newfield, James Ridgeway, Gloria Steinem, and Nicholas von Hoffman.[11] The same year Jack Newfield discussed new journalism and mentioned Joseph Alsop, Jack Anderson, William F. Buckley, Eldridge Cleaver, Seymour Hersh, Jeremy Larner, Karl Marx, H. L. Mencken, Jack Newfield, Thomas Paine, James Ridgeway, Lincoln Steffens, I. F. Stone, and Ida Tarbell, among others.[12] The same year Nicolaus Mills discussed new journalism and mentioned Peter Collier, Vivian Gornick, Andrew Kopkind, Michael P. Lerner, Jack Newfield, and Robin Reisig, among others.[13]

In 1975 George A. Hough discussed new journalism and mentioned Ray Stannard Baker, Winifred Black, Elizabeth Cochrane, Lincoln Steffens, and Ida Tarbell, among others.[14] The same year Everette E. Dennis discussed new journalism and mentioned Jack Anderson, Nellie Bly, Seymour Hersh, and Ida Tarbell, among others.[15]

Muckraking New Journalism

In 1971, Michael L. Johnson claimed that new journalism included what he termed "New Muckraking."[16] But what is muckraking journalism?

In 1973, Harry H. Stein and John M. Harrison discussed muckraking journalism, writing:

> Muckraking is associated with four major press traditions in America. It bears closest resemblance to investigative journalism; less, to advocacy journalism. It has a distant relation to sensationalistic and to yellow journalism.... Muckrakers exercise a surveillance over a wider area than government and politics and so have probed the unique and the common in American society, the highest reaches of power and the everyday social patterns of the population. Also, muckrakers sometimes define as a removable evil a practice or view normally accepted as natural, inescapable, or beneficial. By helping to enlarge Americans' expectations of what is possible and desirable in their lifetimes, they illuminate fundamental intentions both to inform and to improve their fellows.[17]

In 1977, John C. Behrens discussed muckraking journalism in these terms: "Investigative reporters, for the most part, are newsroom irregulars who volunteer for hazardous duty because they enjoy the excitement of going behind sensitive questions and issues of public interest and because by doing so, they believe the results will benefit society."[18]

In 1980, Ernest C. Hynds defined muckraking journalism as a form of "investigative reporting that began in small publications outside the establishment press and seeks to make the larger press responsive."[19]

In essence, muckraking journalism occurs when a reporter or writer suspects that there may be a potential problem in some field, investigates to determine if the problem actually exists, and then reports about the problem.

In 1932, C. C. Regier discussed muckraking journalism and mentioned Samuel Hopkins Adams, Ray Stannard Baker, Edward W. Bok, Benjamin O. Flower, Josiah Flynt (Willard), Will Irwin, Thomas W. Lawson, Alfred Henry Lewis, Charles Edward Russell, Upton Sinclair, Lincoln Steffens, Ida Tarbell, and George Kibbe Turner, among others.[20]

In 1971, Michael L. Johnson discussed "New Muckraking" and mentioned Seymour Hersh, Andrew Kopkind, Gene Marine, Ralph Nader, James Ridgeway, Upton Sinclair, and Ida Tarbell, among others.[21] The same year James Ridgeway discussed muckraking new journalism, particularly underground muckraking new journalism, and mentioned Ronnie Dugger, Seymour Hersh, Warren Hinckle, Andrew Kopkind, and Robert Sherrill, among others.[22]

In 1972, K. Scott Christianson discussed muckraking new journalism and mentioned Bob Greene, Seymour Hersh, William Lambert, and Carey McWilliams, among others.[23]

In 1974, Everette E. Dennis and William L. Rivers discussed alternative or muckraking new journalism and mentioned Ronnie Dugger, among others.[24]

In 1976 Leonard Downie, Jr., discussed muckraking journalism and mentioned Jack Anderson, Fred J. Cook, Robert W. Greene, Seymour Hersh, Carey McWilliams, Drew Pearson, and Robert Sherrill, among others.[25]

In 1977, John C. Behrens discussed muckraking journalism and mentioned Jack Anderson, Seymour Hersh, and Jack Nelson, among others.[26]

Other Forms of New Journalism

Other forms of new journalism exist, according to several writers and scholars who have explored the subject in articles and books.

In 1971, in addition to identifying advocacy and alternative or muckraking new journalism, Everette E. Dennis identified the new nonfiction, underground press, and precision journalism as forms of new journalism.[27] The same year Michael L. Johnson claimed that new journalism included the underground press, rock journalism, and underground radio, in addition to "New Muckraking."[28]

In 1974, Everette E. Dennis and William L. Rivers added journalism reviews and alternative broadcasting to the other forms of new journalism — literary, counterculture, precision, advocacy, and muckraking — that Dennis had mentioned previously.[29] The same year Charles C. Flippen claimed that literary journalism, underground journalism, democracy in the newsroom, and public access, like advocacy journalism, were new journalism.[30]

In 1977, Curtis D. MacDougall classified new journalism as activism and advocacy, impressionistic reporting, saturation reporting, humanistic reporting, and investigative reporting (stunts, crusading, muckraking).[31] The same year John Hollowell classified new journalism as dealing with (1) celebrities and personalities, (2) the youth subculture and the still-evolving "new" cultural patterns, (3) the "big" event, often violent ones such as criminal cases and antiwar protests, and (4) general social and political reporting.[32]

Most of the literature, however, concentrated on one form of new journalism: literary, which the above writers and scholars acknowledged. Literary journalism was explained by Tom Wolfe as a piece of nonfiction that had emotional impact. According to Wolfe, such emotional impact was derived from four devices: (1) scene-by-scene construction, (2) the use of dialogue, (3) third-person point of view, and (4) the use of status symbols.[33] John Hollowell discussed two additional devices that were used: interior monologue, to indicate a person's thoughts, and composite characterization, to indicate a person's behavior.[34] Today, most writers who have written about literary journalism agree with Wolfe's and Hollowell's definitions.

A Note on the Text

The primary purpose of this biographical dictionary is to present information about writers who have practiced advocacy or muckraking journalism. Coverage is heaviest of the United States over the last hundred years or so, but important writers are included from earlier centuries and other countries as well. Most, if not all, of these writers have been identified by more than one source as having written advocacy or muckraking journalism.

Each biographical sketch begins with the writer's name and dates of birth and death, if found. Then the writer's life is summarized chronologically, with information pertaining to his or her professional career and major works. In some cases comments by others about the writer's work have been included. Readers interested in learning more about a writer should begin with that writer's works listed at the end of each entry. Of course, the selected bibliography at the end of the book will also help.

NOTES

1. John Hellman, *Fables of Fact: The New Journalism as New Fiction* (Urbana: University of Illinois Press, 1981), p. 2.

2. Michael Schudson, *Discovering the News* (New York: Basic Books, 1978), pp. 184–85.

3. Everette E. Dennis, "The New Journalism: How It Came to Be," in *The Magic Writing Machine*, ed. by Everette E. Dennis (Eugene: University of Oregon Press, 1971), p. 2.

4. Michael L. Johnson, *The New Journalism: The Underground Press, the Artists of Nonfiction, and Changes in the Established Media* (Lawrence: University of Kansas Press, 1971), p. xii.

5. Everette E. Dennis and William L. Rivers, *Other Voices: The New Journalism in America* (San Francisco: Canfield, 1974).

6. Charles C. Flippen, "The New Journalism," in *Liberating the Media: The New Journalism*, ed. by Charles C. Flippen (Washington, D.C.: Acropolis Books, 1974), pp. 9–17.

7. Dennis, "The New Journalism," p. 2.

8. Ernest C. Hynds, *American Newspapers in the 1980s* (New York: Hastings House, 1980), pp. 173–74.

9. Dennis, "The New Journalism," pp. 1–10.

10. Jack Newfield, "Notes on the Art: Is There a 'New Journalism'?" *Columbia Journalism Review* (July-August, 1972): 45–47.

11. Dennis and Rivers, *Other Voices*, pp. 104–135.

12. Jack Newfield, "The 'Truth' About Objectivity and the New Journalism," in *Liberating the Media: The New Journalism*, ed. by Charles C. Flippen (Washington, D.C.: Acropolis Books, 1974), pp. 59–64.

13. Nicolaus Mills, ed., *The New Journalism: A Historical Anthology* (New York: McGraw-Hill, 1974).

14. George A. Hough, "How 'New'?" *Journal of Popular Culture* (Summer 1975): 114–21.

15. Everette E. Dennis, "Journalistic Primitivism," *Journal of Popular Culture* (Summer 1975): 122–34.

16. Johnson, p. xii.

17. John M. Harrison and Harry H. Stein, "Muckraking Journalism in Twentieth-Century America," in *Muckraking: Past Present and Future*, ed. by John M. Harrison and Harry H. Stein (University Park: Pennsylvania State University Press, 1973), p. 14.

18. John C. Behrens, *The Typewriter Guerrillas: Closeups of 20 Top Investigative Reporters* (Chicago: Nelson-Hall, 1977), p. xviii.

19. Hynds, *American Newspapers*, pp. 173–74.

20. C. C. Regier, *Era of the Muckrakers* (Chapel Hill: University of North Carolina Press, 1932), pp. 49–193.

21. Johnson, *The New Journalism*, pp. 144–145.

22. James Ridgeway, "The New Journalism," *American Libraries* (June 1971): 585–92.

23. K. Scott Christianson, "The New Muckraking," *Quill* (July 1972): 10–15.

24. Dennis and Rivers, *Other Voices*, pp. 51–81.

25. Leonard Downie, Jr., *The New Muckrakers* (Washington, D.C.: New Republic Book Co., 1976), pp. 1–49; 202–258.

26. Behrens, *Typewriter Guerrillas*, pp. xvii–xxvii.

27. Dennis, "New Journalism," pp. 1–10.

28. Johnson, *New Journalism*, pp. xi–xvi; 149–152.

29. Dennis and Rivers, *Other Voices*, pp. 1–13.

30. Flippen, "New Journalism," pp. 9–17.

31. Curtis D. MacDougall, *Interpretative Reporting* (New York: Macmillan, 1977).

32. John Hollowell, *Fact and Fiction: The New Journalism and the Nonfiction Novel* (Chapel Hill: University of North Carolina Press, 1977), p. 24.

33. Tom Wolfe, *The New Journalism*, with an Anthology edited by Tom Wolfe and E. W. Johnson (New York: Harper and Row, 1973), pp. 31–32.

34. Hollowell, *Fact and Fiction*, pp. 25–26.

THE JOURNALISTS

Louis Adamic
(1899–1951)

Louis Adamic was born in 1899 in Blato, in Carniola, Austria, before the region became part of Yugoslavia in 1918. Although he attended the gymnasium of Ljubljana, he was dismissed when he was 14 for mischievous behavior. He immigrated to the United States and found employment with a Slovene language newspaper, the *Glas naroda* of New York City. Adamic enjoyed his work, but the newspaper collapsed and he was tramping the streets within months. In order to live, he worked at odd jobs — from sweeping floors to waiting on tables. In 1916 he joined the United States Army and served during World War I. He traveled to Panama, Hawaii, France, and throughout the United States, and he became a citizen in 1918. When he was discharged in 1923, he made his home in California.

For the first few years, Adamic's writing consisted of translations of South Slavic writers. Occasionally, he would submit a short story or article to a magazine, but his devotion to nonfiction and fiction did not develop until his articles were published by Haldeman-Julius publications, including the company's Little Blue Book series. Eventually his efforts were published in H. L. Mencken's *American Mercury*, and Adamic's reputation as an important contributor to American literature was established. He became friends with Carey McWilliams, Robinson Jeffers, Upton Sinclair, George Sterling, and others. His writing concerned the frustrations of working Americans, particularly the working immigrants in this country, who he believed were suffering from feelings of insecurity and inferiority, feelings that were not unnatural for thousands who had fled from their families and homeland.

In 1931, Adamic returned to New York City and saw his first major book published. *Dynamite: The Story of Class Violence in America* was just that. Using his muckraking skills, Adamic recorded the senseless violence caused by American labor disputes. This book was followed by his part-fiction, part-fact autobiography *Laughing in the Jungle*, which was published a year later.

In 1932, Adamic visited his homeland, and in 1934 *The Native's Return: An American Immigrant Visits Yugoslavia and Discovers His Old Country* appeared. Instantly successful, the book catapulted Adamic's literary reputation even further, but not without some criticism. Certain segments of society wrongfully accused him of having endorsed Communism for Yugoslavia's welfare. Needless to say, such accusations affected him, but his determination to spread his beliefs resulted in *Grandsons: A Story of American Lives* and *Cradle of Life: The Story of One Man's Beginnings*.

In 1938 what was perhaps Adamic's best book was published. Titled *My America*, it told from an immigrant's perspective how the United States was striving for perfection.

For the rest of his life, Adamic devoted his time to books about Yugoslavia's problems and racial instability; the problems of immigrants linked one book to another. Unfortunately, his denouncement of the Yugoslavian government and his support of Marshal Tito increased criticism. He was labeled a Communist by the media. When Tito's relationship with Stalin ended in 1948, however, Adamic remained pro–Tito and after a six-month stay in Yugoslavia a year later, his attitude was strengthened. He then was criticized by Communist sympathizers.

In 1951, Adamic died from a gunshot wound; the authorities ruled that he had committed suicide.

Adamic's style, like Sinclair's and other muckrakers', was simple and direct, especially in *My America*, an exposé written from a personal perspective. In this work he raised several questions and then tried to provide answers through facts.

Adamic, perhaps more than any of his peers, awakened American society to the problems of immigrants living in the United States. Since he realized that their problems affected all Americans, he tried through articles and books not only to reveal those problems but to provide solutions. In this way he attempted to bridge the gap between people of various countries and backgrounds so that misunderstanding would cease to exist.

REPRESENTATIVE WORKS

Dynamite: The Story of Class Violence in America (1931)
The Native's Return: An American Immigrant Visits Yugoslavia and Discovers His Old Country (1934)
Grandsons: A Story of American Lives (1935)
Cradle of Life: The Story of One Man's Beginnings (1936)
My America: 1928–1938 (1938)

Samuel Hopkins Adams (1871–1958)

A muckraking journalist and novelist, Samuel Hopkins Adams was born on January 26, 1871, in Dunkirk, New York, where his father, Myron Adams, served as a minister in a Presbyterian church. His mother was Hester Rose Hopkins Adams.

Adams attended the Free Academy in Rochester, Union College, and then Hamilton College in Clinton, from which he graduated in 1891. Although he had considered a career as a physician, he was hired as a reporter for the *New York Sun*. Adams learned about journalism from the newspaper's famous editor, Charles A. Dana. Almost immediately he grasped the basic fundamentals for producing an interesting story. Soon he was assigned to cover various murders and other crimes.

In 1900, Adams was hired by S. S. McClure, the publisher of *McClure's*, to manage the McClure Syndicate. By 1903 he was a member of the magazine staff, at a time when muckraking exposés filled the magazine's pages. Adams, who worked in advertising, remained with the magazine until 1905, when he left to earn a living from writing articles and books.

That same year Adams' muckraking series on patent medicine and quackery was published in *Collier's*. Titled "The Great American Fraud," the series exposed the evils of patent medicine, including how numerous individuals had grown addicted to the various "tonics." *Collier's* introduced the series with the following statement:

> These articles, which have been written by Mr. Samuel H. Adams, after an investigation lasting several months, will not only describe the methods used to humbug the public into buying patent medicines through fake testimonials and lying statements published in the newspapers, but will show that a large number of the so-called "tonics" are only cocktails in disguise, and that many of these nostrums are directly responsible for the making of drunkards and drug fiends.*

Adams set the tone for the article in the first paragraph:

> GULLIBLE America will spend this year some seventy-five millions of dollars in the purchase of patent medicines. In consideration of this sum it will swallow huge quantities of alcohol, an appalling amount of opiates and narcotics, a wide assortment of varied drugs ranging from powerful and dangerous heart depressants to insidious liver stimulants; and, far in excess of all other ingredients, undiluted fraud. For fraud, exploited by the skillfullest of advertising bunco men, is the basis of the trade. Should the newspapers, the magazines, and the medical journals refuse their pages to this class of advertisements, the patent medicine

---

*"*Editorial Bulletin: Patent Medicine Frauds,*" Collier's, *September 30, 1905, p. 30.*

business in five years would be as scandalously historic as the South Sea Bubble, and the nation would be the richer not only in lives and money, but in drunkards and drug-fiends saved.*

First Adams had various medicines analyzed. Then he studied the advertisements' claims for the medicines. Then he presented the histories of those who had used the medicines. The series had a major impact on the reading public and, later, on the industry. Indeed, together with the work of Harvey Wiley and of Upton Sinclair, Adams' series was responsible for inspiring members of Congress to pass the Pure Food and Drug Act, which restricted labeling and controlled certain claims made in advertisements.

The American Medical Association sponsored the publication of the series in a book by the same title in 1906.

In 1907, with Stewart Edward White, Adams wrote *The Mystery*, which became a best-selling novel. Although he worked briefly as editor of *Ridgeway's Weekly* in 1910 and contributed a series of articles about deceptive advertising to the *New York Tribune* in 1915 and 1916, Adams spent the rest of his life writing short stories, novels, biographies, and books for children. He wrote about unscrupulous advertisers, corrupt politicians, and unethical journalists in *The Clarion* (1914), *Common Cause* (1919), and *Success* (1921). In 1923, using the pseudonym Walter Fabian, he wrote *Flaming Youth*, which realistically characterized the 1920s. Three years later he wrote *Revelry*, a fictionalized melodrama about President Warren G. Harding. The book was banned in Washington, D.C., and Philadelphia, but it became a best-seller. *The Godlike Daniel*, published in 1930, concerned Daniel Webster, while *The Gorgeous Hussy*, published in 1934, concerned Margaret O'Neill, Andrew Jackson's hostess.

In 1939, Adams wrote a detailed account of the Harding administration in the *Incredible Era*. Even though the book was based on information from various sources but not on Harding's presidential papers, it was favorably reviewed.

Adams returned to biography in 1945, when he wrote *Alexander Woollcott: His Life and His World*, which was an affectionate perspective about a friend. The novels of this period concerned New York and included *Canal Town* (1944), *Banner by the Wayside* (1947), and *Sunrise to Sunset* (1950). He reminisced about his family in a series of lively, colorful essays that appeared in the *New Yorker* and were collected and published under the title *Grandfather Stories* in 1955.

Adams died at his home in Beaufort, South Carolina, in 1958.

REPRESENTATIVE WORKS

The Great American Fraud (1906)
Revelry (1926)

*Samuel Hopkins Adams, "The Great American Fraud," Collier's, October 7, 1905, p. 14.

The Godlike Daniel (1930)
The Gorgeous Hussy (1934)
Alexander Woollcott: His Life and His World (1945)
Grandfather Stories (1955)

Robert S. Allen
(1900–1981)

Muckraking journalist Robert Allen was born in Latonia, Kentucky, on July 14, 1900, to Harry and Elizabeth Allen. With Drew Pearson, he founded the syndicated newspaper columns "The Washington Merry-Go-Round" and "Inside Washington."

Allen, who began his journalistic career by reporting local events while in grade school, worked as a copyboy for the *Louisville Courier Journal* before he served in the U.S. Army. Allen served in John J. Pershing's company when it punished Pancho Villa of Mexico and when it fought in Europe during World War I.

Upon his return to the United States, Allen attended the University of Wisconsin and worked part-time as a police reporter for the Madison *Capital Times.* When he earned his bachelor's degree in 1922, he was awarded a scholarship by his alma mater to continue his education, but he worked as a political reporter for the Wisconsin *State Journal* and the *Milwaukee Journal* for at least a year.

In 1923, after he had saved some money, Allen used the scholarship he had been awarded and attended the University of Munich in Germany. Allen witnessed Hitler's famous beer hall putsch and wrote about it for the *Christian Science Monitor.* As a result of his insightful reporting, the editors of the *Monitor* hired him as a correspondent and he toured Europe.

Allen returned to the United States in 1924. He worked briefly for the United Press Association in New York City before he moved to Washington, D.C., where he worked at the *Christian Science Monitor*'s bureau. Allen wrote about politics and politicians, including presidential campaigns and elections. He met Ruth Finney, a correspondent for Scripps-Howard, and married her in 1929.

In 1930, Allen became the *Monitor*'s bureau chief and started investigating the Hoover administration. Although he wrote reports that were enlightening, the editors at the *Monitor* refused to accept them for publication. Allen met Drew Pearson, who worked for the *Baltimore Sun.* Pearson, like Allen, had attempted to have certain kinds of information accepted by his editors.

Together they wrote the successful but extremely controversial book *The Washington Merry-Go-Round*, which was published anonymously in 1931. Allen and Pearson wrote *More Merry-Go-Round* in 1932. Another best-seller, it too was published anonymously. Readers eventually learned the identities of the authors and Allen and later Pearson were dismissed from their jobs. They were not defeated, however, and they approached United Features, a newspaper syndicate, with an idea for a daily column that the firm accepted. The muckraking column "The Washington Merry-Go-Round" began before 1933. Allen was responsible for gathering information about the House, the Senate, and the Supreme Court, while Pearson was responsible for the military, the State Department, and the Department of Justice. Their gossipy column penetrated certain subjects that various officials in Washington had tried to sweep under the carpet. Within seven years the column was published in more than 300 newspapers and was read by more than 20 million people. Although researching and writing the column demanded considerable time, Allen and Pearson collaborated on the books *The Nine Old Men* and *Nine Old Men at the Crossroads*, which were published in 1936 and 1937, respectively, and concerned the aging members of the U.S. Supreme Court.

In the mid–1930s, as a result of their column's popularity, Allen and Pearson produced a news program that was broadcast on radio by NBC, and they created the comic strip "Hap Hazard," which concerned the exploits of a correspondent based in Washington.

In 1942, Allen stopped contributing to the column when he enlisted in the U.S. Army. Allen served as an intelligence officer in General George S. Patton's Third Army as it made its way across Europe. Before the Second World War ended, he lost his right arm. Allen received numerous medals, including the Purple Heart and the Croix de Guerre.

Upon his return to the United States, Allen decided not to rejoin Pearson and the column. Instead, he wrote the informative account *Lucky Forward: The History of Patton's Third U.S. Army*, which was published in 1947. He also edited the books *Our Fair City* and *Our Sovereign State*, which were published in 1947 and 1949, respectively.

In 1949, Allen started the controversial muckraking column "Inside Washington," which was syndicated to newspapers by several organizations, including the North American Newspaper Alliance. The column, which was similar to "The Washington Merry-Go-Round," appeared in numerous newspapers until cancer forced Allen to retire in 1980.

Allen, whose wife had died in 1979, was despondent over her death as well as his own ill health. On February 23, 1981, he died from a self-inflicted gunshot wound.

REPRESENTATIVE WORKS

"Washington Merry-Go-Round" (syndicated newspaper column with Drew Pearson, 1931–1942)
The Washington Merry-Go-Round (with Drew Pearson, 1931)
More Merry-Go-Round (with Drew Pearson, 1932)
Why Hoover Faces Defeat (1932)
The Nine Old Men (with Drew Pearson, 1936)
Nine Old Men at the Crossroads (with Drew Pearson, 1937)
"Inside Washington" (syndicated newspaper column, 1949–1980)
The Truman Merry-Go-Round (with William V. Shannon, 1950)

Joseph Alsop
(1910–1989)

Political journalist and columnist Joseph Alsop was born on October 11, 1910, to Corinne and Joseph Alsop, in Avon, Connecticut. His parents, who were active in Connecticut politics, lived on a farm. Alsop spent several years learning about agriculture before his parents sent him to the Groton School in Massachusetts. In 1928 he enrolled at Harvard University, where he enjoyed learning the liberal arts.

Upon graduation in 1932, Alsop became a reporter for the *New York Herald Tribune*, where he received notable credibility for his comprehensive coverage of the Hauptmann trial. The editorial staff sent Alsop to Washington, D.C., to cover politics several years later. Within a year, Alsop met Robert Kintner, another *Herald Tribune* staff member, and they began the nationally syndicated political column "The Capitol Parade."

For three years the column clarified political issues. In collaboration with Turner Catledge, Alsop also wrote *The 168 Days*, which was published in 1938. This book discussed the crisis that surrounded the United States Supreme Court after President Franklin Roosevelt decided that the Court should be enlarged. In collaboration with Kintner, Alsop wrote *Men Around the President* in 1939 and *American White Paper: The Story of American Diplomacy and the Second World War* in 1940. These books concerned Roosevelt's administrative advisers and personal confidants and the president's foreign policy before World War II.

Alsop's partnership with Kintner ended in 1940 when he enlisted in the U.S. Navy. He resigned a year later and joined the U.S. Army, specifically General Claire Chennault's staff in China. Alsop was sent to Manila in 1941 and was captured and imprisoned by the Japanese for a year. When he was released, he returned to the United States, where he became a civilian official in the

Lend-lease Mission to Chunking. Subsequently, he returned to China, and General Chennault had him commissioned as an officer in the army air force. Alsop returned to the United States after the war and, together with his younger brother, Stewart, started the column "Matter of Fact" in 1946.

Syndicated through the *New York Herald Tribune*, the column concerned more than just politics in Washington. Indeed, it not only contained information about the political scene, but its writers often attacked or defended certain political actions or figures. Occasionally they would predict certain political or military actions. The Alsops denounced Soviet expansionism while they advocated a strong national defense. They condemned Senator Joseph McCarthy, who falsely accused certain citizens of being Communists or Communist sympathizers.

In 1954 the Alsops collaborated on the book *We Accuse! The Story of the Miscarriage of American Justice in the Case of J. Robert Oppenheimer*, in which they defended physicist J. Robert Oppenheimer, who had been charged by certain individuals to be a risk to national security.

The column contained both bylines until Stewart accepted an editorial position with the *Saturday Evening Post* in 1958, the year their second book, *The Reporter's Trade*, was published.

Alsop continued the column alone. When the *Herald Tribune* ceased publication, the column was syndicated through the *Los Angeles Times* Syndicate. Alsop, a defender of the Cold War and later the Vietnam War, married Susan Patten in 1961. This marriage, which did not produce any children, ended in divorce in the 1970s.

Joseph Alsop retired the column in 1974, the year his brother died of leukemia (Joseph had provided Stewart with blood). Alsop had grown tired of writing the column; he also had other interests, including archeology and art. Indeed, his book *From the Silent Earth: A Report on the Greek Bronze Age*, which had been published in 1964, had been praised for its keen insight into a period of ancient history about which little had been written. In 1982, after having conducted several years of research, he wrote *The Rare Art Traditions: The History of Art Collecting and Its Linked Phenomena Wherever These Have Appeared*, which explored the world of art and art collecting from a historical perspective. The same year his book *FDR: A Centenary Remembrance*, which was a text filled with more than 200 lavish photographs, was published. The book was praised for Alsop's revelations, which tended to make Roosevelt less enigmatic than other biographies.

Alsop died in August 1989.

REPRESENTATIVE WORKS

"The Capitol Parade" (column with Robert Kintner, 1937–1940)
The 168 Days (with Turner Catledge, 1938)

Men Around the President (with Robert Kintner, 1939)
American White Paper: The Story of American Diplomacy and the Second World War
    (with Robert Kintner, 1940)
"Matter of Fact" (column with Stewart Alsop, 1946–1958)
The Reporter's Trade (with Stewart Alsop, 1958)
"Matter of Fact" (column, 1958–1974)

Stewart Alsop
(1914–1974)

Born on May 17, 1914, in Avon, Connecticut, to Corinne and Joseph Alsop, Stewart Alsop learned about agriculture on his parents' farm before he attended the Groton School in Massachusetts.

Upon graduation from the prestigious preparatory school, Stewart Alsop entered Yale University, from which he received a bachelor's degree in 1936. Alsop was hired as an editor by Doubleday Doran and Company, publishers, and wrote articles for several magazines.

When the United States entered World War II, Alsop tried to enlist in the U.S. Army, but he was rejected for medical reasons. He persevered, however, and in 1942 joined the King's Royal Rifle Corps of England. Alsop was commissioned an officer and had been promoted to the rank of captain when he was transferred in 1944 to the U.S. Army's Office of Strategic Services. The same year he married Patricia Hankey, who was from England. Alsop parachuted into France and, on assignment, joined the French underground. When the war ended in Europe, he was awarded the Croix de Guerre with palm. Alsop then returned to the United States.

In collaboration with Thomas Braden, Stewart Alsop wrote *Sub Rosa: The O.S.S. and American Espionage*, which was published in 1946 and depicted realistically the intelligence unit's activities in certain campaigns of the war.

With his older brother Joseph, Alsop started the political column "Matter of Fact," which was syndicated through the *New York Herald Tribune*. By 1950 the column was published in more than 125 newspapers. The Alsops discussed not only national and international politics but provided various predictions, some of which came true. Occasionally filled with gossip, the column also advocated certain positions, especially when the Alsops' convictions about those positions were strong. Usually one brother stayed in Washington, D.C., primarily to conduct interviews with politicians and other officials, while the other brother traveled abroad to gather material. As a result, their column presented subjects that were current and topical, and they enjoyed a certain amount of credibility. The Alsops disagreed on certain topics, however, and these disagreements tended to strain their collaborating efforts. Before they separated in 1958, they had collaborated on the books *We Accuse! The Story of Miscarriage of American Justice in the Case of J. Robert Oppenheimer* and *The Reporter's Trade*, which were published in 1954 and 1958, respectively.

Alsop became the political editor of the *Saturday Evening Post*. This position lasted until the magazine ceased publication ten years later in 1968. His book *The Center: People and Power in Political Washington* was published the same year and explored several federal institutions, including the Central Intelligence Agency, the State Department, and the Pentagon. Alsop acknowledged that Washington contained "many Washingtons" but that his book concerned the Washington that political journalists like himself found intriguing. After leaving the *Saturday Evening Post*, he wrote a political column for *Newsweek*. Alsop, unlike his brother, Joseph, argued against the Vietnam War and advocated a volunteer military.

In 1971, Alsop was diagnosed with leukemia. Although he was given only a year to live, he continued to write his column for *Newsweek*. His brother Joseph provided him with numerous blood transfusions, which seemed to force the disease into remission. He wrote the memoir *Stay of Execution: A Sort of Memoir*, in which he explored his life and the disease that eventually killed him. The book was published in 1973, and Alsop died on May 26, 1974. Alsop and his wife had six children.

REPRESENTATIVE WORKS

"Matter of Fact" (column with Joseph Alsop, 1945–1958)
The Reporter's Trade (with Joseph Alsop, 1958)
The Center: People and Power in Political Washington (1968)

Jack(son) N. Anderson
(1922–   )

Born on October 19, 1922, to Agnes and Orlando Anderson who were Mormons, Anderson moved with his parents from Long Beach, California, to Cottonwood, a suburb of Salt Lake City, Utah, when he was two.

Anderson's interest in journalism germinated when he was a child. At 12, for instance, he edited the page for "Boy Scouts," which appeared in the *Deseret News*. The *News*, which was owned by the Church of Jesus Christ of the Latter-day Saints, provided Anderson with professional newspaper experience, and Anderson was hired to work part-time as a reporter with the *Murray Eagle*. Anderson learned how to investigate stories as well as write lucid prose.

When he was in high school, Anderson served as president of the student body and worked part-time for the *Salt Lake City Tribune*. Upon graduation, he enrolled at the University of Utah in 1940. In 1941, when he was 19, he served as a Mormon missionary in several southern states. Anderson completed his obligation two years later and then joined the merchant marine as a cadet midshipman in 1944. After a brief tour, he worked as a foreign correspondent in China for the *Deseret News*. Although Anderson learned that a civil war had erupted in China, he could not persuade any newspaper to buy a story about it.

In 1945, as World War II ended, Anderson was recruited by the U.S. Army, in which he served two years. He spent most of his time working as a reporter for military newspapers and military radio networks. When he was discharged in 1947, he moved to Washington, D.C., where he was hired as an assistant by Drew Pearson, whose muckraking column "The Washington Merry-Go-Round," which had been founded by Pearson and Robert S. Allen in 1932, exposed political corruption.

While tackling various investigative assignments, Anderson studied for about a year at Georgetown University. In 1948, he enrolled in a course in libel at George Washington University. He did not, however, allow his studies to interfere with his work for Pearson, who seldom credited Anderson in the column even though Anderson proved his reportorial skills several times.

Anderson married Olivia Farley in 1949. He worked diligently for Pearson for ten years and received few acknowledgments in print. Finally, in 1957, after having grown disgusted with Pearson, Anderson confronted him. Pearson realized immediately that Anderson was furious; to appease him, Pearson promised him that he would have more bylines and eventually the column itself. Anderson remained. One year later, in addition to his disclosing the unethical relationship between Bernard Goldfine and Sherman Adams, which subsequently created a scandal, he collaborated with Pearson on the book *U.S.A.: Second-Class Power?* which criticized the Eisenhower administration, specifically its policies that stymied scientific progress.

To supplement his income, Anderson became the Washington editor of the Sunday newspaper magazine *Parade* in 1954. In 1968 he became the chief of the magazine's bureau in Washington. In addition to his work for *Parade*, he collaborated with Pearson on the book *The Case Against Congress*, published in 1968, which examined the corruption on Capitol Hill.

After Pearson died in 1969, Anderson controlled the column. Together with his staff, he uncovered such stories as the Nixon administration's hypocritical bias against India in its war with Pakistan over Bangladesh. They uncovered the Justice Department's settlement of its antitrust suit against the International Telephone and Telegraph Corporation (ITT), the ITT's and Central Intelligence Agency's relationship in Chile, the Thomas Eagleton affair, and the Iran Arms deal.

Joseph Spear and Brit Hume both worked with Anderson. In 1985, Dale Van Atta helped Anderson with the column, and his byline appeared regularly until 1991, when he left to pursue other opportunities. Michael Binstein joined Anderson's staff about the time the column's appearance decreased from seven times a week to four. Anderson, who purchased part of the *Annapolis Evening Capital*, wrote several novels in the 1980s and 1990s. His books about his career as a muckraking journalist received more attention. In 1973, he wrote *The Anderson Papers* with George Clifford; the book contained insightful, critical pieces about the federal government. In 1979 he joined James Boyd in writing *Confessions of a Muckraker: The Inside Story of Life in Washington During the Truman, Eisenhower, Kennedy, and Johnson Years*, which concerned his formative years as a muckraking journalist under the tutelage of Drew Pearson.

Anderson became a popular spokesperson as well as a guest on several television programs in the 1970s, 1980s, and 1990s, primarily because of his numerous years of experience as a muckraking journalist who wrote a popular syndicated newspaper column.

REPRESENTATIVE WORKS

"The Washington Merry-Go-Round" (column with Drew Pearson, 1947–1969)
"The Washington Merry-Go-Round" (column, 1969–present)
U.S.A.: Second-Class Power? (with Drew Pearson, 1958)
The Case Against Congress (with Drew Pearson, 1968)
The Anderson Papers (with George Clifford, 1973)
Confessions of a Muckraker: The Inside Story of Life in Washington During the Truman, Eisenhower, Kennedy, and Johnson Years (with James Boyd, 1979)

Michael J. Arlen
(1930–   )

Michael J. Arlen was born in London, England, on December 9, 1930, but moved to the United States with his parents, Michael and Atalanta Arlen, when he was 10. He attended Harvard University from 1948 to 1952 and then worked as a reporter for *Life* magazine for four years. In 1966 he became a staff writer and television critic for the *New Yorker*, for which he wrote numerous reviews and articles. His criticism, which was not so much about television as it was about American culture or American society, discussed the weaknesses and possible effects of certain programs, including the evening news. His first book, *Living Room War*, which was a collection of critical articles, was published in 1969. In the book's introduction, Arlen explained the title:

I call this book *Living Room War* not because I especially like the piece I first attached the title to ... but because quite a number of the pieces *are* about the war and television — because during the period I was writing them the war seemed to be the central fact in American life, seemed to be there, whether one talked about it or not at first, whether one claimed to be bored by it or not, later offended, later outraged, later bored. It was a changing shape beneath everything else in American life in that period, in a way that no other war we'd experienced had been, and most of us knew about it, felt about it, from television.*

A year later *Exiles*, a memoir of Arlen's search for his father, was published. The book was a minor effort.

In 1973, Arlen turned his attention to the Hanrahan trial in *An American Verdict*. Using short direct sentences, Arlen told of the questionable shootings of two Black Panther party members by Chicago police officers and the subsequent trial of State's Attorney Edward Hanrahan of Cook County and the police officers involved in the shootings. According to Benjamin De Mott, Arlen's method of writing was impressionistic: "Scenes and snippets of testimony from the trial are interspersed with short takes on the character of Mayor Daley, the birth and history of the Panthers, developments in the culture of street gangs, a cop awards night, the Chicago Irish in fact and fiction, Campaign '72, and a number of other subjects."† Arlen attempted to connect the pieces even if some did not fit, much as he had in his collection of articles. The latter, however, contained a logical progression and consequently was better received by the critics.

In *Passage to Ararat*, which was published in 1975, Arlen searched his father's homeland, Armenia, and told of his heritage, including the brutality of Turkey toward the Armenian women and children at the turn of the century. The book exhibited, perhaps better than any other, Arlen's power of writing and earned the National Book Award in contemporary affairs in 1976.

Other collections of articles appeared. For instance, *The View from Highway 1* was published in 1976 and concerned different topics in television news and entertainment. Through the use of such literary techniques and devices as informal style, dialogue, questions and answers, and explanations, Arlen presented his subjects in an arresting fashion. *Thirty Seconds*, which was published in 1980, examined the six-month effort by advertising agency personnel to produce a 30-second television commercial for AT&T. Arlen not only observed the process of creating and producing a commercial, he interviewed those involved. The book presented a candid look at another aspect of television. *The Camera Age: Essays on Television* contained 25 reviews and articles. At least 13 concerned news or other "fact" broadcasting, while 8 discussed dramatic series or films. The book, which was published in 1981, was praised by critics, who appreciated the author's literary style as well as insight.

*Michael J. Arlen, Living Room War (New York: Viking, 1969), p. xi.
†Benjamin De Mott, "Alone in Cover-Up Country," Atlantic (October 1973): 117–18.

Arlen's unique style of writing was not limited to criticism for the *New Yorker*, however. His enlightening articles were published in the *Atlantic Monthly*, *Cosmopolitan*, *Esquire*, *Harper's*, *Holiday*, *New York Times Magazine*, *Saturday Review*, and other publications.

Say Goodbye to Sam, Arlen's first novel, was published in 1984 to mixed reviews.

Arlen's articles and collections were examples of advocacy journalism primarily because they criticized the various kinds of programs that were broadcast on a popular medium. More important, the same articles and collections criticized American society for allowing such a medium to dominate American lives.

Several of his collections were published with new introductions in the early 1990s.

REPRESENTATIVE WORKS

Living Room War (1969)
Exiles (1970)
An American Verdict (1973)
Passage to Ararat (1975)
The View from Highway 1 (1976)
Thirty Seconds (1980)
The Camera Age: Essays on Television (1981)

Ray Stannard Baker
(1870–1946)

Ray Stannard Baker was born in Lansing, Michigan, in 1870. He became not only one of the muckrakers but one of the best reporters in America. According to Louis Filler: "Baker had the gift of absorbing himself in his subject. For this reason he was able to give fascinating accounts of a wide variety of events, people, institutions and places."*

Baker's parents were devout Presbyterians who had attended college. They encouraged him to read various forms of literature, which all but guaranteed his entrance into Michigan Agricultural College (Michigan State University) after one year of high school. In 1889 he graduated and returned home to work. Three years later he attended law school at the University of Michigan, but he dropped out after one semester because his interest was in literature and

*Louis Filler, The Muckrakers (*University Park: Pennsylvania State University Press, 1976*), p. 87.

journalism. He traveled to Chicago, where he was hired as a reporter for the *Chicago News-Record*. According to C. C. Regier:

> One of his early assignments was to go to Canton, Ohio, to interview Coxey, who was leading his famous army to Washington. Baker stayed with Coxey's Army.... Interviewing each member, he learned how that strange horde had been assembled, and gradually he came to understand the minds and hearts of the poverty-stricken. He remembered the extravagant crowds that had gathered to enjoy the lavish spectacles of the World's Fair, and he contrasted with them the ragged cohorts straggling over the Alleghenies in the hope of forcing an indifferent government to come to their aid.†

Baker's coverage of Coxey's Army automatically influenced the stories he was assigned. Whenever the *News-Record* needed a reporter to cover a particular labor disturbance, Baker was there. When the Pullman Strike occurred, he was indignant about what he observed; although the company had constructed homes for employees, many of the occupants were starving. Baker's stories were read and taken to heart; eventually a relief bureau was established.

Baker's reputation as a reporter spread, and by 1898 he was working for *McClure's*. For five years Baker wrote positively about imperialism in the United States, including its expanding economy and latest innovations. He also wrote about Theodore Roosevelt's exploits, which solidified Roosevelt's image as an American hero. In 1903, however, Baker wrote his first of eight articles on labor for *McClure's*. According to Filler, "He made sure not to make it appear the entire fault of labor: capital, he averred, was as much to blame as labor for the damage inflicted upon the 'citizen' and the 'consumer.' ...Invariably both sides of the issue were presented, for Baker was by no means anti-labor."§

At first, Baker was skeptical of labor unions, but as he investigated further his attitude changed. In several articles he vehemently criticized employer abuse; such was the case in his piece on the New York clothing industry.

In 1905, Baker exposed railroad corruption in a series of articles. He learned that railroad companies were guilty of fixing rates for certain passengers or companies, using rebates, allowing the Beef Trust to have private cars, creating public opinion through bribery, and destroying competing companies through railroad consolidation. As a result of these and other muckraking articles, railroads were finally regulated when the Hepburn Bill became law.

In 1906, Baker, together with other muckraking journalists of *McClure's*, purchased what soon became the *American Magazine*. Using a pseudonym,he wrote two popular series titled "Adventures in Contentment" and "Adventures in Understanding," which were positive rather than negative in tone. In addition to these series, he wrote a third titled "Following the Color Line," in which

†C. C. Regier, The Era of the Muckrakers *(Chapel Hill: University of North Carolina Press, 1932),* pp. 147–48.
§Filler, Muckrakers, 1976, p. 88.

he attacked the race problem. According to Baker, the Negro had little hope in the United States unless he was helped.

The series continued for over a year and was collected and published in 1908. Baker's series "The Spiritual Unrest" began the same year. In these articles he investigated the conditions of the church — missions work, finances, and attendance. He disclosed the numerous ills and asked whether the fault lay with the ministers and leaders or with the congregations.

In 1911, Baker supported Senator Robert LaFollette and prepared LaFollette's *Autobiography*. When Theodore Roosevelt did not view LaFollette as a presidential candidate and therefore failed to support his efforts a year later, Baker's friendship with Roosevelt soon ended. Consequently, Baker supported Wilson and by 1914 was proud that he had.

In 1915, Baker resigned from the *American Magazine* and devoted his time to political ventures and Woodrow Wilson's writings. In 1918 he served in England for the State Department, and he was director of the American delegation's press bureau at the peace conference. A year later he wrote *What Wilson Did at Paris*, which presented Wilson's arguments concerning the Versailles Treaty.

Baker's three-volume *Woodrow Wilson and World Settlement* was published in 1922, and for the next five years, he edited the six-volume *The Public Papers of Woodrow Wilson* with William E. Dodd. When President Wilson designated him as his authorized biographer he devoted the next fifteen years to his eight-volume *Woodrow Wilson: Life and Letters*, which won a Pulitzer Prize in 1940.

Baker's autobiography appeared in two volumes in 1941 and in 1945. Titled *Native American* and *American Chronicle* respectively, each captured a part of America that was no more. After the second volume had been published, Baker died of heart disease in 1946.

REPRESENTATIVE WORKS

"Adventures in Contentment" (*American Magazine)*
"Adventures in Understanding" (*American Magazine*)
"Following the Color Line" (*American Magazine*)
"The Spiritual Unrest" (*American Magazine*)
What Wilson Did at Paris (1919)
Woodrow Wilson and World Settlement (1922)
Woodrow Wilson: Life and Letters (8 vols.)
Native American (1941)
American Chronicle (1945)

James Baldwin
(1924–1987)

Born in Harlem on August 2, 1924, James Baldwin became one of the fore-most essayists and novelists of the 1960s. Throughout his writing he explored and deplored the injustices committed against African Americans. His essays, which moved critics and politicians, appealed to the human conscience to look beneath the skin and to think in terms of equality.

Baldwin, whose stepfather was a minister from New Orleans, preached "hell fire and damnation" at Harlem's Fireside Pentecostal Church before he was 15. After three years, however, he resigned because of a growing interest in writing.

When he graduated from De Witt Clinton High School in 1942, Baldwin worked briefly in Belle Meade, New Jersey. Because the country was at war, employment was available to those who wanted jobs. He then moved from Belle Meade to Greenwich Village, where he worked during the day and wrote at night. He reviewed books about the black problem for such publications as the *Nation*, *New Leader*, and *Commentary*. Baldwin also wrote two books that earned two fellowships but were not published. Finally, after five years of frus-tration, he moved to France. Although his life in Paris was free in the sense that he experienced little or no discrimination, he often suffered from not earn-ing enough to live. Nonetheless, he remained in France for ten years.

Baldwin's first partly autobiographical novel, *Go Tell It on the Mountain*, which concerned a confused Harlem youth named John Grimes and his reli-gious family, was published in 1953. The book was critically acclaimed for its insight into the American racial problem. His next book, *Notes of a Native Son*, which appeared in 1955, was a collection of essays that had appeared in sev-eral magazines, including *Commentary* and *Partisan Review*. The essays vividly penetrated the social injustices and prejudices of American society. Immedi-ately, Baldwin was recognized as a humanitarian spokesman for the oppressed. *Notes* was followed by another novel entitled *Giovanni's Room*, which explored homosexuality.

While Baldwin continued to write novels, he contributed essays to such periodicals as *Harper's*, *Reporter*, *New Yorker*, *Nation*, *Esquire*, *Commentary*, and *Partisan Review*.

In 1961, *Another Country* was published. A novel, it concerned an African American woman and a white man who discarded the rules imposed on them by a basically white society and subsequently lived for themselves. Baldwin's second volume of essays, *Nobody Knows My Name: More Notes of a Native Son*, was published the same year. In 1963, in *The Fire Next Time*, Baldwin returned to the problems of racial prejudice with power and magnitude. In two essays, both of which were in the form of letters, Baldwin recounted his experience as a preacher in Harlem and examined the movement founded by the Black Muslims. Any white who read the book sensed the degradation that confronted most African Americans.

In addition to writing such novels as *Tell Me How Long the Train's Been Gone* (1968), *If Beale Street Could Talk* (1974), and *Just Above My Head* (1979) and such collections of essays as *No Name in the Streets* (1972) and *The Devil Finds Work* (1976), Baldwin also explored the black problem in the plays *The Amen Corner* and *Blues for Mister Charlie*. Although the plays were produced and Baldwin's messages were clear, neither play had the impact of his essays.

Baldwin died of cancer in 1987.

REPRESENTATIVE WORKS

Go Tell It on the Mountain (1953)
Notes of a Native Son (1955)
Nobody Knows My Name: More Notes of a Native Son (1961)
The Fire Next Time (1963)

Sid Bernard
(1918–   )

Sidney Bernard was born in New York City in 1918 and attended Columbia University before he became a reporter for the Standard News Association in 1947. From the late 1950s to the early 1960s, he worked as a public relations writer for Fenster Associates, and from 1963 to 1967, he served as the New York editor for the *Literary Times*. When he left the *Times,* he became roving editor for the *Smith* and the *Newsletter* of New York City, for which he wrote entertaining, informative articles. He also wrote more than 500 left-wing essays, articles, and poems for such magazines and newspapers as *Ramparts, Realist, Rogue, National Observer, New York Herald Tribune, Nation, Commonweal, Defiance*, and *Evergreen Review.*

In 1969 a collection of Bernard's writing was published under the title *This Way to the Apocalypse: The 1960's*. Eight years later another collection was published. Titled *Witnessing: The Seventies*, the compilation contained essays that chronicled the previous nine years and concerned certain ideas and movements, especially various individuals and interesting places.

In 1984, Bernard wrote *Metamorphosis of Peace*.

REPRESENTATIVE WORKS

This Way to the Apocalypse: The 1960's (1969)
Witnessing: The Seventies (1977)

Winifred Black
(1863–1936)

Winifred Sweet or "Annie Laurie" was born in Chilton, Wisconsin, in 1863. Perhaps the second most daring young woman to invent stunts and unusual situations in order to obtain information and write sensational exposés during the "yellow" journalism period, Sweet was educated at the Sacred Heart Convent in Chicago, the Lake Forest Seminary in Illinois, and Miss Burnham's Preparatory School at Northampton, Massachusetts.

Because of her interest in the theater, Winifred moved to New York City, where she learned quickly that the only roles she could play were minor ones. Frustrated and disgusted, she left New York City and traveled to San Francisco, where she changed careers. In 1889 she obtained a reporting position on the *San Francisco Examiner*. Two years later she married Orlow Black and became Winifred Black, a name she kept even though she divorced her first husband in 1897 and married Charles Allen Bonfils in 1901.

Black had to learn the techniques of journalism like many other reporters of this period; the old impersonal style that had filled newspaper columns for years was changing. Joseph Pulitzer and his *New York World*'s staff was using a more informal, lively, and hard-hitting style that attracted readers and mirrored the times. Apparently it took time for Black to learn how to write for newspapers. Her early stories were stilted and filled with too many adjectives. She was not writing for the average newspaper reader, which Sam S. Chamberlain, the *Examiner*'s managing editor, emphatically pointed out.

Nonetheless, Black persevered until she knew how to compose personal, vivid prose and how to investigate and obtain information of interest. For one of her exposés, she "fainted" on a San Francisco street in order to be taken to the receiving hospital. She observed that she, along with other patients, was neglected. Her story criticized the handling of patients and as a result the city was forced to dismiss several hospital employees and improve patient care.

Black's success arose from at least two factors: she knew what would make an interesting story and she knew that William Randolph Hearst desired stories with short sentences, short paragraphs, and direct quotes. Therefore, she abandoned the mid-Victorian prose. Instead, "she went in for startling effects — hard jolts in short paragraphs. She used adjectives, but not in such dizzy numbers. Her stories were highly charged with emotion."*

In addition to exposés, Black's articles on "Little Jim," a crippled boy born to a prostitute in San Francisco's prison hospital, helped launch a campaign that ultimately provided a ward for incurables at the city's Children's Hospital.

In 1892, Black somehow snuck aboard President Benjamin Harrison's campaign train and eventually was granted an interview. She was persistent, but she had to be in order to compete with her male counterparts. She interviewed other prominent people of the times such as Governor William S. Taylor, Sarah Bernhardt, Henry Stanley, and Henry Irving.

In 1895, Hearst purchased the *New York Journal* in order to compete against Pulitzer. Although he hired reporters who lived in New York City, he brought "Annie Laurie" with him. Within two years she had enough of New York and moved back to California and then to Denver, where she obtained an additional position with the *Denver Post*.

As a feature writer for Hearst, Black covered America and England. For instance, she went to England to investigate the suffragettes who went to any length for their cause. She went to Chicago to investigate the juvenile court system, to New York to investigate the Charity Organization Society, and to El Paso to investigate the so-called last prize fight in America. She wrote a controversial story about pigeon shooting that "brought an abrupt finish to this sport and resulted in her getting medals from the humane societies of Great Britain and America."†

When Galveston was devastated by a tidal wave in 1900, Black, disguised as a boy, was the first female reporter to see the 7,000 bodies. Immediately, the Hearst empire sent relief trains, and Black received word that she was to have a hospital ready. She directed the relief workers and distributed to the survivors thousands of dollars that Hearst and others had donated.

In addition to disasters that included the San Francisco earthquake of 1906, Black covered trials. When Harry Thaw was charged for the murder of Stanford White, she was one of the four female reporters who, because of their sentimental and charitable treatment of Evelyn Nesbit Thaw, were later termed the "sob sisters."

Black's second marriage to Charles Bonfils did not last because of her career. Bonfils, who had been managing editor of the *Kansas City Post* and was then a freelance writer in New York City, seldom saw her because she was constantly traveling and reporting. After 1917 their separation became permanent. Black was in Europe covering the war and later the Versailles peace conference.

---

*Ishbell Ross, Ladies of the Press: The Story of Women in Journalism by an Insider (New York: Harper and Brothers, 1936), p. 62.
†Ibid., p. 66.

Although Black remained a reporter until her death in 1935, her later work was less significant; in fact, except for covering World War I in Europe and the Versailles peace conference, her work was confined to a regular column for the *San Francisco Examiner*.

Edward W. Bok
(1863–1930)

Edward W. Bok, an advocating and muckraking editor, was born on October 9, 1863, in Helder, The Netherlands, to Sieke Gertrude Bok and William John Hidde Bok, who were prominent and highly respected. Unfortunately, the family fortune was lost as a result of misguided investments, and Bok's father brought his family to the United States in 1870.

Along with his brother, Bok attended school in Brooklyn. Because he could not speak fluent English, other students ridiculed him. Bok learned how to fight at a very early age. He also learned to work, and his first job was cleaning a shop window twice a week. Later he delivered the *South Brooklyn Advocate* to subscribers. Bok learned to write journalistically when he contributed a column about children's parties to the *Brooklyn Daily Eagle*.

When his father became a translator for the Western Union Telegraph Company, Bok ended his formal education and worked as an office boy in the same company, earning $6.25 a week.

Bok started collecting autograph letters when he corresponded with famous Americans, including James A. Garfield, Jefferson Davis, Ulysses S. Grant, Henry Wadsworth Longfellow, and Rutherford B. Hayes, among others. He journeyed to Boston when he was 18 and visited Oliver Wendell Holmes, Longfellow, Ralph Waldo Emerson, and Louisa May Alcott, among others. Bok was fascinated by those who had achieved success. He wrote 100-word biographies of famous Americans for Joseph P. Knapp of the American Lithograph Company. These biographies appeared on cards and Bok earned $10 for each one. Eventually, Bok had to hire his brother and several others to write while he edited the copy.

When his father died, Bok and his brother earned enough to support the family. Bok wrote about the theater, for instance, for the *Eagle* and edited the *Philomathean Review* for Brooklyn's Plymouth Church.

In 1882, Bok worked as a stenographer for the Henry Holt Company. He joined Charles Scribner's Sons two years later. The same year the *Philomathean Review* became the *Brooklyn Magazine*. Bok secured writing from nationally known writers. Bok, the editor, and Frederic L. Colver, the publisher, not only published a quality magazine but established the Bok Syndicate Press in 1886. Bok realized that few women read newspapers; thus he hired Ella Wheeler Wilcox and others to write about topics that catered to women. These features were offered to newspapers. Other features concerned books.

When *Scribner's* was published in 1887, Bok was put in charge of its advertising. It was Bok's feature syndicate to newspapers, however, that caused Cyrus H. K. Curtis, publisher of the *Ladies' Home Journal*, to offer Bok the position of editor in 1889.

In October 1889, Bok moved to Philadelphia, where the *Journal's* offices were located, and he began at the age of 26 one of the best jobs he ever had. First, Bok asked readers of the magazine what they desired to read. Thousands responded. Bok started the column "Side Talks with Girls" by "Ruth Ashmore." Bok gave the column to Isabel A. Mallon, who continued it for 16 years. The column was extremely popular, and Bok started "Heart to Heart Talks," which was directed to mature women, and "Side Talks with Boys." These columns advised girls about their personal problems, young mothers about child care, and mature women about their spiritual needs. The column for boys counseled them about women, success, and marriage. In addition to the columns, Bok secured writing by nationally known writers, including William Dean Howells, Mark Twain, Bret Harte, Rudyard Kipling, among others. He made certain that the magazine not only informed but thoroughly entertained readers. Fiction, for instance, had to entertain with humor and concurrently offer hope.

Under Bok's direction, the magazine espoused certain issues. For instance, in a series of editorials, Bok advocated sex education for children. Venereal disease was even discussed.

In 1892 the *Ladies' Home Journal* announced that advertisements for patent medicine would no longer be accepted. Later, in several editorials, Bok asked people to boycott patent medicine. He even printed the percentages of alcohol for several tonics, which caused the *Journal* to be sued. Apparently, the percentage for one of the tonics, "Dr. Pierce's Favorite Prescription," was incorrect, and Bok was forced to print a retraction. In an effort to avoid further problems, he hired Mark Sullivan in 1904, primarily as a legal adviser and as a contributor of articles. According to Frank Luther Mott, "It was Sullivan who discovered that Lydia E. Pinkham was not 'in her laboratory at Lynn, Massachusetts,' as the advertisements said, but in her grave in Pine Grove Cemetery near that city, and had been there, according to the date on the tombstone, for twenty years — and a picture of the tombstone, with inscription, was presented to *Journal* readers."*

---

*Frank Luther Mott, A History of American Magazines, Vol. 4: 1885–1905 *(Cambridge: Harvard University Press, 1957), p. 543.*

Bok editorialized for legislation that would force makers of patent medicine to list on the labels the ingredients, including alcohol. Eventually, the Pure Food and Drug Act was passed in 1906.

Bok and the *Journal* had other campaigns, most of which were less dramatic. For instance, the "Beautiful America" campaign exposed the "atrocious" decor of Pullman railroad cars, which had, ironically, become a standard of home furnishing. Bok then attacked outdoor advertising, which he thought defaced the landscape. As a result, numerous city governments passed ordinances regulating billboards.

The *Journal* opposed women's suffrage. To Bok, a suffragette was a dangerous woman who believed that her work was not necessarily in the home. This campaign against women's suffrage failed, however, as women realized that they were productive citizens of society.

Other campaigns included municipal renovation, a "safe and sane Fourth of July," and the protection of Niagara Falls against power company encroachment.

During World War I, Bok and the *Journal* were most active. He offered the government as much help as possible, while the magazine covered women's activities during the war. In 1918 he was a guest of the British government at the battlefronts in France.

In 1919, after 30 years of guiding the *Journal*, Bok retired. The last issue he edited, the October one, sold more than two million copies and contained in excess of $1 million worth of advertising.

Bok's autobiography, *The Americanization of Edward Bok*, was published in 1920. Affectionately written in the third person, the book received the Pulitzer Prize a year later. He wrote seven additional books, including a biography of his father-in-law, Cyrus H. K. Curtis, in 1923. (Bok had married Mary Louise Curtis in 1896.) All of his books were filled with common sense and a certain appreciation for what was good and worthy in man.

Before his death in 1930, Bok had established the Philadelphia Award for Community Service and the American Peace Award for the most practicable plan by which the United States could cooperate with other nations to preserve peace. Bok had donated more than $2 million to charities.

It is Bok's role as editor that has secured his place in literary history, however. His magazine attempted numerous campaigns primarily for the betterment of mankind. Some of these campaigns were popular and successful; others were not. As editor, Bok was responsible for the popular successes as well as the failures.

REPRESENTATIVE WORKS

Ladies' Home Journal (editor)
The Americanization of Edward Bok (1920)

Elias Boudinot
(1803–1839)

Elias Boudinot was a Cherokee Indian who advocated acculturation in the *Cherokee Phoenix*, a newspaper directed to Cherokees and whites.

Oo-watie, Boudinot's father, had taken advantage of the government's "civilization" program, which encouraged Cherokees to move away from traditional towns, and had left Hiwassee, Tennessee, and had settled with his wife, Susanna Reese, on a small farm at Oothcaloga in northwestern Georgia near the present-day town of Calhoun.

Gallegina or "Buck" (he later took the name "Elias Boudinot") was born in 1803 and was the first of nine children. His father enrolled him in the Moravian mission school at Spring Place, which had been accepting Cherokee children since 1804. Missionaries taught the children hoeing, chopping wood, weaving, cooking, plowing, sewing, and religion, linking the latter to civilization. As many children as possible were housed on the premises, primarily to prevent them from lapsing into "savage" ways.

Buck stayed at Spring Place until 1817. Elias Cornelius of the American Board of Commissioners for Foreign Missions, an interdenominational missionary society headquartered in Boston, invited Buck and several others from the mission to further their education at the American Board school in Cornwall, Connecticut. Buck and another boy accompanied Cornelius and Jeremiah Evarts on their return to New England. They visited Elias Boudinot, who had been a member of the Continental Congress and who advocated that the American Indians were the lost tribes of Israel. Buck was impressed with Boudinot and enrolled in the American Board school as Elias Boudinot.

The school provided academic as well as practical instruction. Of course, religion was also emphasized, so that students could promote Christianity as well as practice a particular profession.

In 1820, Boudinot converted to Christianity. The American Board made arrangements for him to study at Andover Theological Seminary so that he could preach to the Cherokees in their language. His health prevented him from attending, however. In 1822 he returned to the Cherokee Nation, where he exhibited responsibility for the welfare of his people.

When Harriet Ruggles Gold asked her father for permission to marry Boudinot, her father refused. Interracial marriages, although some had occurred, were not socially acceptable. Harriet became critically ill soon after her father's decision; eventually, he changed his mind. Cornwall's citizens grew outraged. They blamed the American Board school for the interracial marriage. After all, if it had not been for the school, white female missionaries would not meet American Indians. The school soon closed, but in 1826 Boudinot and Gold were married.

Boudinot continued to be an ardent advocate of "civilization." He believed that the progress of his people depended upon the preservation of the Cherokees as a corporate group. Boudinot was a founder of and corresponding secretary for the Moral and Literary Society of the Cherokee Nation. He traveled to various cities and appealed for contributions, always prefacing his remarks with a summary of his people's accomplishments. His trips were a success. At least $1,500 was spent on a press, and Boudinot was offered the editorship of the *Cherokee Phoenix*, which he eventually accepted. Subscribers were found as far away as Mobile, Alabama, and Troy, New York.

The paper first appeared in 1827. Boudinot borrowed copy from other newspapers. He also published official correspondence and documents of the Cherokee Nation, legislation passed by the National Council, notices of weddings, meetings of societies, and advocating editorials. The paper became a powerful propaganda tool for the Cherokee Nation, and it demonstrated to whites the remarkable accomplishments of the Cherokees.

Although Boudinot mentioned the superior achievements of his people, he never implied that other tribes could not achieve the same.

In 1829, Boudinot changed the name of the newspaper to *The Cherokee Phoenix and Indians' Advocate*. The title reflected the editor's scope. Boudinot defended his people from certain whites, who criticized them or their progress. For instance, when the U.S. senator from Georgia claimed that the Cherokees were oppressed and exploited, Boudinot wrote an editorial that refuted his charges:

> Many of the people of the United States, who think with Mr. Forsyth that the Cherokee are *poor devils*, may be surprised to learn that among them are several societies for the spread of religion and morality, and what is still more astonishing, the chiefs of these people, "who grind the faces of the poor" and "keep them under, in poverty and ignorance," that "their avarice propensity may be gratified," generally take the lead and support them by their example and contributions. They have Missionary Societies, Tract Societies, Sunday School Societies, Benevolent Societies, Book Societies and Temperance Societies.*

Boudinot confronted charges and accusations. Some whites refused to believe that an Indian could edit a newspaper, for instance. Boudinot assured them that the paper was published by an Indian for Indians and whites. Boudinot also published Cherokee judicial proceedings for the purpose of enlightening whites, who sometimes were reluctant in sentencing their own when they committed similar crimes.

The Cherokees were portrayed in the paper as a "civilized" people because Boudinot believed that the Cherokee Nation was progressing; he also realized that if whites considered Cherokees savages they might exterminate American Indians.

*Cherokee Phoenix, *October 8, 1830.*

In 1828 the state of Georgia annexed a large section of Cherokee territory. As a result, that part of the Nation came under the state. The National Council was prohibited from convening, and Indians could not mine gold discovered on Cherokee land near Dahlonega.

Whites flooded the Nation in search of gold and seized Cherokee property. Cherokee laws were not considered valid by the state of Georgia, and Boudinot criticized the Georgia legislature. Federal troops were sent in by President Andrew Jackson to maintain peace; then the governor of Georgia sent in the Georgia Guard. Members of this unit harassed the Indians. Boudinot reported on various encounters between the Cherokees and members of the Guard, and even criticized the latter. He was brought before the commander for printing "lies." Because he could prove that the articles were true, however, he was not arrested.

The Indian Removal Act was passed in 1830. This piece of legislation empowered the president to negotiate Indian removal. Treaty commissioners arrived in the Cherokee Nation soon after and faced a cold reception.

In 1831, Boudinot toured the United States to raise funds for the newspaper and the Nation. He returned about six months later, in 1832.

Several months later he signed a petition that favored removal. When his views became apparent to members of the Cherokee government, they prohibited him from expressing them in the paper. Boudinot resigned as editor the same year.

Three years later Boudinot and several other Cherokees signed the Treaty of New Echota, which negotiated an exchange of Cherokee land in the Southeast for territory in what is today the state of Oklahoma. This action, which would have saved the Cherokee Nation, was not accepted by the elite class that governed the Cherokee Nation. Boudinot was seen as a traitor rather than a patriot by most Cherokees. Indeed, they charged that he sought to destroy rather than save the Nation.

Chief John Ross and other leaders of the Nation attacked Boudinot and vice versa, until Ross realized that the settlement under the provisions of the treaty could be increased.

The Senate ratified the treaty in 1836; the Cherokees had two years to move. Although hundreds of Cherokees believed Chief John Ross would make it possible for them to remain, they were forced to leave their land in 1838.

Boudinot's wife died in 1836. He married Delight Sargent, a missionary, in 1837, and they moved to the new Cherokee Nation before the mass migration.

In 1839, Boudinot was building a new house when several Cherokees approached and requested medicine. They attacked him with knives and tomahawks, and he died soon after.

REPRESENTATIVE WORKS

Cherokee Phoenix (editor)
The Cherokee Phoenix and Indians' Advocate (editor)

Paul Brodeur
(1931–   )

Born in Boston on May 16, 1931, to Paul and Sarah Brodeur, investigative journalist Paul Brodeur graduated from Phillips Academy in 1949 and from Harvard University four years later. He served in the U.S. Army's Counter Intelligence Corps for three years before he became a staff writer for the *New Yorker* in 1958. Topics Brodeur wrote about for the magazine's "Talk of the Town" included Charles de Gaulle's death, Robert F. Kennedy's funeral, and Werner Heisenberg, the German physicist. He also wrote several novels, including *The Stunt Man*, which was published in 1972. This work depicted a young soldier who, after deserting his regiment, became a stunt man in a film that resembled his own life.

Brodeur gained respectability as a muckraking journalist when his study of the asbestos industry appeared in the *New Yorker* and then in a book in 1974. Titled *Expendable Americans*, the book focused on the dangers of asbestos fibers, which cause asbestosis, a disease that eventually kills its victim, and the refusal of executives of asbestos-producing companies to correct the problems inside their plants. Brodeur, who spent six years investigating the problem and writing the book, learned that the relationship between business and government officials was one of cordiality; the worker's life was often overlooked by both parties.

In 1977, *The Zapping of America: Microwaves, Their Deadly Risk, and the Cover-Up* appeared. Like Brodeur's previous study, this work was also based on a series of articles that had appeared in the *New Yorker*. Brodeur not only explained what microwaves were and how they were produced but pointed out that invisible microwaves could possibly kill thousands of people. Since microwaves can be found in communications systems, weapon systems, video display terminals, burglar alarm systems, microwave ovens and automatic garage door openers, to mention a few sources, every person is exposed to them.

Brodeur exposed the ill effects of microwave radiation — from physical and mental disorders to blindness and bleeding from the eyes and ears — and he criticized the government's failure to enact legislation to control microwaves and other forms of electromagnetic radiation. Indeed, according to Brodeur, branches of the federal government such as the Department of Defense covered up certain findings by stamping them SECRET.

In *The Asbestos Hazard*, which was published in 1980, Brodeur reiterated the hazards of asbestos. Five years later he adapted a series of *New Yorker* articles into *Outrageous Misconduct: The Asbestos Industry on Trial*, which concerned the increased number of asbestos-disease-related lawsuits that had been filed against major corporations. The Johns-Manville Corporation was specifically mentioned because of its attempts to stifle information about asbestos and cancer. Brodeur also revealed that company executives had tried to prohibit employees and others from suing the company. According to Brodeur, lawyers who sought outrageous sums for their clients were responsible for revealing the asbestos industry's manipulative practices and irresponsibility.

The same year, in a series of articles and later the book *Restitution: The Land Claims of the Mashpee, Passamaquoddy, and Penobscot Indians of New England,* Brodeur explored an interesting subject. It was not a subject readers would associate with him, however. After all, he was known for examining cancer-causing products, not societal or minority issues.

In 1989, Brodeur's investigation into electromagnetic waves and ill health was presented in *Currents of Death: Power Lines, Computer Terminals, and the Attempt to Cover Up Their Threat to Your Health.* Brodeur reported that the federal government and the electric industry had conspired to keep certain information about electric lines and some kinds of household electronics, specifically the computer, and their harmful effects from consumers. Brodeur believed that electromagnetic fields caused cancer.

In 1993, Brodeur explored this subject again in *The Great Power-line Cover-Up: How the Utilities and the Government Are Trying to Hide the Cancer Hazard Posed by Electromagnetic Fields.* Brodeur claimed that utility company executives, government officials, and even members of the press were hiding the truth about the connection between electromagnetic fields and cancer. The book's credibility was questioned by some reviewers, but Brodeur cited study after study — at least 12 — that supported his thesis. Public officials, however, disagreed with his analysis.

Brodeur taught writing at several universities, including Columbia and Harvard. Although he and his wife have lived in Manhattan for years, they also have homes in California and Cape Cod.

REPRESENTATIVE WORKS

Expendable Americans (1974)
The Zapping of America: Microwaves, Their Deadly Risk, and the Cover-Up (1977)
The Asbestos Hazard (1980)
Outrageous Misconduct: The Asbestos Industry on Trial (1985)
Restitution: The Land Claims of the Mashpee, Passamaquoddy, and Penobscot Indians of New England (1985)
Currents of Death: Power Lines, Computer Terminals, and the Attempt to Cover Up Their Threat to Your Health (1989)
The Great Power-line Cover-Up: How the Utilities and the Government Are Trying to Hide the Cancer Hazard Posed by Electromagnetic Fields (1993)

Heywood Broun
(1888–1939)

Born in 1888 in Brooklyn, newspaper columnist Haywood Broun attended Harvard University for four years, but he failed to graduate because of his grades in French. When he left the campus in 1910, he joined the staff of the *New York Morning Telegraph*, a newspaper he had worked for during the summer of 1908. Two years later he asked for an increase in salary and was dismissed.

Broun became a sports writer for the *New York Tribune*. According to Irving Dilliard, "No sports writer before him had conveyed to the reader so much of the game's excitement or interlarded the facts with such graphic allusions."*

Eventually Broun served as the newspaper's drama critic. In 1917 he served as one of the newspaper's war correspondents in France, where his critical dispatches about the United States military were sometimes censored. When the war ended, he returned to the *Tribune* as drama critic and began a column on books and authors that not only expressed his opinions but captured hundreds of readers. Consequently, in 1921 he was lured to the *New York World* and began the column for which he is known — "It Seems to Me," in which he presented his opinions on major issues. The column was severely criticized by certain prominent members of New York society, particularly when he demanded that Eugene Debs be released. Broun demanded equal justice for all. When he vehemently attacked Governor Alvan T. Fuller's and Harvard president Lawrence Lowell's recommendations not to allow Nicola Sacco and Bartolomeo Vanzetti a new trial, Ralph Pulitzer, the *World*'s editor and publisher, demanded that he write on another topic. Broun refused, and Pulitzer suspended him. Broun was not deterred, however. In an article for the *Nation*, he criticized the *World* for its reversed philosophy and lack of responsibility. Of course, after the article appeared, Broun was no longer wanted by the *World*. Because he was a writer of high caliber, however, he was hired by Roy W. Howard's *New York Telegram*, which eventually purchased the *World*. The Scripps-Howard *World-Telegram* published and syndicated Broun's column until 1939, when Broun complained of how some of his columns had been altered or deleted.

In addition to his column for the *World-Telegram*, Broun wrote another for the *Nation* and then for the *New Republic*. He also helped organize the American Newspaper Guild in 1933.

Broun died of pneumonia in 1939.

"Sacco and Vanzetti," one of Broun's most bitter columns, exhibited a style that was direct and emphatic. With the quotation "It is death condemning

---

*Irving Dilliard, "Broun, Heywood Campbell," in Dictionary of American Biography: Supplement Two, vol. 22, ed. Robert Livingston Schuyler (New York: Charles Scribner's Sons, 1958), p. 67.

life!" Broun began his argument. Sacco and Vanzetti stood out in society; thus they had to be killed. They were life, and those who killed them were death. Broun argued that what happened in the courtroom, specifically the sentencing, was not an isolated ruling. Rather, in the American system of justice, particularly when American jurors judged defendants of another country or race, prejudices interfered much too often. Broun condemned not only the system but certain individuals such as Governor Fuller who had the courtroom and subsequently the verdict in their hands. Broun questioned whether those in high places should have the power to condemn others.

Broun's form of advocacy journalism was more inclusive, thought-provoking, and literary than other forms of advocacy journalism practiced at the time. Broun, who could criticize as well as praise a position, a decision, or an individual, had few rivals.

REPRESENTATIVE WORK

"It Seems to Me" (newspaper column)

William F. Buckley, Jr.
(1925–   )

Conservative editor, columnist, best-selling author, and host William F. Buckley, Jr., was born to William Frank and Aloise Buckley, both of whom were Roman Catholic and wealthy, in New York City in 1925. As a child, he attended private schools in England and France. When he returned to the United States, he attended the Millbrook School in New York, where he prepared for college. Upon graduation in 1943, he entered the University of Mexico. After a semester, he entered the U.S. Army and served in the infantry during World War II. Although he attained the rank of second lieutenant, Buckley realized that a career in the military was not for him. Consequently, when he was released in 1946, he attended Yale University, where he studied economics, history, and political science and developed a strong interest in the university's newspaper and forensics team.

Buckley received his bachelor's degree in 1950 but remained at the university as an instructor in Spanish. A year later he wrote the controversial book *God and Man at Yale: The Superstitions of Academic Freedom*, which attacked the anti–Christian, pro-liberal ideas taught by certain faculty members at Yale. Buckley's book caused a stir among reviewers. Some believed that Buckley was naive; others believed that he was incorrect in his assessment. Buckley left Yale and worked for a year as an agent for the Central Intelligence Agency.

In 1952, Buckley became an associate editor of the *American Mercury*, an iconoclastic magazine founded by H. L. Mencken and George Nathan in 1924. The magazine was sold to several people, one of whom was Clendenin J. Ryan. Ryan's editor, William Bradford Huie, an archconservative who enjoyed exposés, purchased the publication from Ryan and then sold it to J. Russell Maguire in 1952. Huie, however, remained editor until Maguire's anti–Semitic philosophy caused him to resign. Buckley resigned too and worked during the next several years as a freelance writer. In 1954 he collaborated with his brother-in-law, L. Brent Bozell, on *McCarthy and His Enemies*, which defended what McCarthy and men like him had tried to accomplish in American society. A year later he raised almost $300,000 from friends and launched the largest selling periodical devoted to conservatism, the *National Review*. Primarily a journal of political essays, Buckley's publication became the most important periodical on the American right. Indeed, Buckley recruited such writers and editors as John Chamberlain, Frank Chodorov, L. Brent Bozell, Suzanne LaFollette, Max Eastman, Whittaker Chambers, Priscilla Buckley, Russell Kirk, James Burnham, Ralph de Toledano, Joan Didion, Frank Meyer, Renata Adler, Eugene Lyons, Garry Wills, and John Leonard.

The publication received considerable criticism. Certain critics claimed that it was not truly conservative. Nonetheless, the *National Review* surpassed the circulation of its liberal competitors the *Nation* and the *New Republic* by a sufficient margin. In 1957 approximately 16,000 copies per issue were published. In 1980 the number of copies had increased to almost 100,000 per issue.

Buckley devoted time to the periodical, but his desire to write books continued. In 1959, for instance, he wrote *Up from Liberalism*, in which he denounced liberalism and its ruination of society.

In the 1960s, Buckley initiated or was a proponent in initiating several conservative activities. In 1960, for example, he helped establish Young Americans for Freedom, which was organized to attract young conservatives. A year later he, together with other conservatives, formed the New York Conservative party. In 1962 he began a syndicated newspaper column that was written for the sole purpose of presenting his conservative points of view on major issues. The column, filled with wit as well as information, attracted thousands of readers of some 350 newspapers by 1990. In 1966 the weekly program "Firing Line," on which Buckley discussed with guests a sociological or political issue, aired on WOR-TV. Five years later the Public Broadcasting System purchased the program and Buckley became a national celebrity.

Buckley, who devoutly supported such political figures as Senator Barry Goldwater, Richard Nixon, and Ronald Reagan, was appointed by President Nixon in 1969 to the five-member advisory board of the U.S. Information Agency. He resigned in 1972, however, when he disagreed with the Nixon administration's policies toward the Agency. In 1974, in the aftermath of Watergate, he, together with his brother, Senator James L. Buckley, another conservative, called for the president's resignation for the good of the nation.

Buckley, who wrote in the 1960s against the extreme right-wing organization called the John Birch Society, also condemned wage and price controls, American-Chinese relations, détente with the Soviet Union, abortion, the welfare-state, and injustice. His articles for the *National Review, Esquire, Harper's, Saturday Review,* and *Atlantic Monthly,* among others, were collected and published in several volumes in the 1960s and 1970s. For instance, *Execution Eve and Other Contemporary Ballads,* which was filled with political satire, was published in 1975. *A Hymnal: The Controversial Arts* was published in 1978 and, like the previous book, contained columns and essays that promoted the conservative spirit or chastised the liberals.

In 1976, Buckley wrote his first successful spy novel, *Saving the Queen,* which combined an intriguing story with his conservative propaganda. The hero, Blackford Oakes, appeared in other novels, including *A Very Private Plot,* which was published in 1993.

Buckley also presented his personal life in several books. For instance, in 1971 he wrote *Cruising Speed: A Documentary,* which reported a typical week in a diarylike format — from his numerous activities to the social functions in which he found himself. *Overdrive: A Personal Documentary,* which was published in 1983, was similar. He also discussed his fascination with sailing by chronicling three expeditions in *Airborne: A Sentimental Journey* (1976), *Atlantic High: A Celebration* (1982), and *Racing Through Paradise: A Pacific Passage* (1987).

In addition to writing books about conservative politics, Buckley edited several, including *Keeping the Tablets: Modern American Conservative Thought* (1988), which was a revision of *Did You Ever See a Dream Walking?: American Conservative Thought in the Twentieth Century* that was published in 1970.

In 1986, Buckley examined Mexico, Poland, and Spain, as well as certain figures such as Karl Marx, Pope Paul VI, and Henry Kissinger, in the compilation *Right Reason.* Four years later he outlined five reasons for a national program for young people in *Gratitude.* Buckley believed that this program would (1) help build character, (2) allow youth to repay a social debt, (3) mix the various classes of society in a common endeavor, (4) provide needed services, and (5) salvage those less fortunate.

A collection of columns, essays, and other writings that opened windows on history was published in 1993. Titled *Happy Days Were Here Again: Reflections of a Libertarian Journalist,* the collection's articles were divided into attitudinal categories such as "Assailing," "Playing," and "Celebrating" and concerned such luminaries as Jesse Jackson, Mario Cuomo, John Kenneth Galbraith, Carl Sagan, and others.

Even though Buckley continued to practice advocacy journalism to promote his conservative views in the early 1990s, it was his magazine that allowed others to advocate certain conservative beliefs.

REPRESENTATIVE WORKS

National Review (founder)
God and Man at Yale: The Superstitions of "Academic Freedom" (1951)
Up from Liberalism (1959)
Execution Eve and Other Contemporary Ballads (1975)
A Hymnal: The Controversial Arts (1978)
Right Reason (1986)
Gratitude (1990)
Happy Days Were Here Again: Reflections of a Libertarian Journalist (1993)

Rachel Carson
(1907–1964)

Rachel Carson was born May 27, 1907, in Springdale, Pennsylvania, and was raised in Springdale and nearby Parnassus. Maria McLean Carson was instrumental in her daughter's interest in nature and the environment.

Carson attended public schools of both communities and exhibited an interest in writing. When she was 10, she contributed a short story to *St. Nicholas Magazine*, which was published by the St. Nicholas League. The story was accepted and won the prestigious Silver Badge.

Upon graduation from Parnassus High School, Carson enrolled at the Pennsylvania College of Women (now Chatham College) at Pittsburgh. Although she had intended to major in English because of her desire to write, she changed her major to zoology after completing a course in biology. She graduated magna cum laude in 1929 and then enrolled in a master's program at Johns Hopkins University.

In 1930, Carson began teaching during the summer at Johns Hopkins University; this position continued for seven summers. In 1931 she became a member of the zoology staff of the University of Maryland and completed her master's degree in 1932. She gained additional scientific knowledge by working at the Marine Biological Laboratory in Woods Hole, Massachusetts.

In 1936, Carson was offered a position as aquatic biologist with the United States Bureau of Fisheries in Washington, D.C., which she accepted. Carson wrote and edited pamphlets, booklets, and radio scripts. She also contributed articles as a freelance writer to periodicals. One of these articles, "Undersea," which was published in the *Atlantic* in 1937, was the basis for her first book, *Under the Sea-Wind: A Naturalist's Picture of Ocean Life*, a novel that was published in 1941, a year after the Bureau of Fisheries and the Bureau of Biological Survey were merged into the United States Fish and Wildlife Service. The novel, which captured the Atlantic coastal area through descriptive narratives, achieved considerable success.

Carson postponed work on her second book because of World War II as well as new and revolutionary developments in the science of oceanography. In 1949 she was promoted to editor-in-chief of the Fish and Wildlife Service. Nonetheless, she continued to conduct research as well as to write. *The Sea Around Us* was published in 1951. The book described in poetic detail the history, geography, chemistry, and biology of the sea. Certain chapters of the book had appeared in the *Yale Review* and the *New Yorker*. Critics praised the book. Harry B. Ellis, for instance, wrote: "In *The Sea Around Us*, Rachel Carson has achieved that rare, all but unique, phenomenon — a literary work about the sea that is comparable with the best, yet offends neither the natural scientist nor the poet. Her book is a translation of the science of the sea into terms so imaginative and stirring as to evoke thoughts of those masters of the sea tale, Conrad and Melville."*

Sales topped 300,000 within months, and RKO made a documentary film based on the book. Fame and fortune came to Carson, even though she was not seeking either.

In 1952, Carson resigned from her position at the Fish and Wildlife Service so she could devote her time to conducting research and writing. Three years later *The Edge of the Sea* was published. Certain critics believed the book suffered as a result of its narrowly defined subject, the tidal zones and shallow waters of the East Coast. Most critics enjoyed the writing, however. Jacquetta Hawkes, for instance, wrote: "Miss Carson succeeds admirably in conveying a sense of the richness and intricate interrelatedness of the life she describes. No jeweler could create a work so delicately interlocked and encrusted."†

In a letter addressed to Carson, Stuart and Olga Huckins told of the destruction that aerial spraying had caused to their two-acre private sanctuary at Powder Point in Duxbury, Massachusetts. Carson read the letter and was dismayed that pesticides had destroyed her friends' birds and other wildlife. For the next four years, Carson investigated pesticides and other chemicals used by farmers and governments and subsequently wrote a disturbing indictment about the indiscriminate use of chemicals in our society. From her perspective, poisonous chemicals had been used for a number of reasons but posed many problems, including pollution of the planet. Consequently, life as we know it was affected.

*Harry B. Ellis, "Science and Literature of the World's Vast Seas," Christian Science Monitor, July 5, 1951, p. 11.
†Jacquetta Hawkes, "The World Under Water," New Republic, January 23, 1956, pp. 17–18.

Silent Spring was published in 1962, although parts of the book had appeared in the *New Yorker* several months before. Certain critics, including chemical manufacturers, claimed that Carson distorted the facts. Other critics came to her defense. Robert C. Cowen wrote: "Miss Carson does not suggest that modern pest control be abandoned. She urges that dangers be assessed and misuses curbed. She is pressing for a thoroughgoing research program to enable men to learn to use pesticides safely and effectively and to reduce their use to a minimum by developing alternative means of keeping bugs in check."§

Because she had presented a cautionary tale based on more than 50 pages of sources, the public and the federal government believed that Carson was on to something. The Life Sciences Panel of President John F. Kennedy's Science Advisory Committee investigated the issue and released its pesticide report in 1963; the report warned against the indiscriminate use of pesticides and requested that further research into potential health hazards be conducted.

Carson was vindicated. Indeed, her book, perhaps more than any other, forced the federal government to acknowledge that something was amiss in the environment. Eventually, legislation was enacted, and the Environmental Defense Fund and later the Environmental Protection Agency were created.

Carson was writing *The Sense of Wonder* when she died from cancer in 1964. The book was published posthumously in 1965.

REPRESENTATIVE WORKS

The Sea Around Us (1951)
The Edge of the Sea (1955)
Silent Spring (1962)

John Jay Chapman
(1862–1933)

Although he did not consider himself a muckraking journalist, John Jay Chapman influenced the muckrakers who came later. Primarily an advocate who wrote critical essays on politics and society's mores, he was born in New York City in 1862. He became an abolitionist and held a service in Coatesville, Pennsylvania, for a black who had been tortured and burned to death a year earlier. Chapman's extreme religious views were not particularly accepted by

§*Robert C. Cowen, "Yevtushenko in English-Housewifery — Miss Carson's 'Silent Spring,'"* Christian Science Monitor, *September 27, 1962, p. 11.*

some people. According to M. A. DeWolfe Howe, when Chapman attended St. Paul's School in Concord, New Hampshire, he "carried to such personal extremes the religious tendencies of the place that both masters and boys thought him 'queer,' and his parents took him home."*

Chapman ultimately attended Harvard, from which he graduated in 1885. He traveled throughout Europe for a year. When he returned home, he met Minna Timmins, whom he fought over at a social function. Chapman, who temporarily disregarded his religious convictions, beat the man who had been courting Minna and later, because of guilt, burned his own left hand, which had to be amputated. Chapman married Minna in 1889.

Chapman and his bride lived in New York City, where he practiced law, which he disliked. His interest in politics increased, and he became president of the Good Government Club, which had been founded by Edmond Kelly for the purpose of fighting Tammany Hall and had drawn upon the membership of the City Reform Club. Chapman had been a member of the latter for several years. According to Edmond Wilson, "Chapman and another Harvard man assumed the leadership of the Good Government movement, and from 1895 through 1900 he had an odd and very interesting career as a non-socialist political radical."†

John Jay Chapman campaigned against Tammany and in the process spoke against Joseph Choate and Edwin Godkin of the *New York Evening Post*. Chapman became one of the leaders of the Independent party. In 1898 he persuaded Theodore Roosevelt to allow the party to nominate him for the governorship of New York. Roosevelt accepted the offer, but he reneged when Tom Platt, the leader of the Republicans, offered the Republican ticket to him. According to Wilson:

> Chapman knew very well what Roosevelt had promised him. ... He observed that Roosevelt presently persuaded himself that he had never understood the original proposal; and that he thereafter became very vociferous over the damage done progressive movements by fanatics on their "lunatic fringe." Chapman had been publishing since March, 1897, a review called *The Political Nursery* ... and he now used it to attack Roosevelt's subsequent activities and those of the reformist mayor, Seth Low, formerly a candidate of the Independents.§

The review lasted until January 1901, but Chapman contributed more than his *Nursery*. In 1898 a collection of his essays entitled *Emerson and Other Essays*, which critiqued the popular writers of the day, was published. The same year Chapman published *Causes and Consequences*, which criticized the absurd

---

*M. A. DeWolfe Howe, "Chapman, John Jay," in Dictionary of American Biography, ed. Harris E. Starr (New York: Charles Scribner's Sons, 1944), p. 168.

†Edmund Wilson, "John Jay Chapman," The Triple Thinkers: Ten Essays on Literature (New York: Harcourt, Brace, 1938), p. 170.

§Ibid., pp. 172–73.

relationship between business and government. Two years later he published *Practical Agitation*, which declared that political reformation was impossible because of the times. He dismissed economics and proclaimed morality.

After the latter book was published, Chapman suffered from grippe and was bedridden for a year. Insecurity set in, and when he was able to leave his bed, he required crutches.

For two years, until one of his sons by his first wife drowned (his first wife died in 1897 and he remarried a year later), he carelessly put life aside. Perhaps it was the tragedy that made him realize that life was to be lived. At any rate, he recovered and lived for the most part at his country home, taking time to write and travel.

Chapman died several days after an operation in 1933.

REPRESENTATIVE WORKS

The Political Nursery (1897-1901)
Emerson and Other Essays (1898)
Causes and Consequences (1898)
Practical Agitation (1900)

Robert Christgau
(1942–   )

Robert Christgau, senior editor of the *Village Voice*, was born in New York City in 1942 and graduated from Dartmouth College in 1962. In 1969 he contributed a column "Rock & Roll &" to the *Village Voice*; the column lasted until he joined *Newsday* three years later.

Christgau, a music critic who reviewed not only the music but the artists and their particular characteristics that enhanced their music, returned to the *Village Voice* in 1974, a year after his colorful book *Any Old Way You Choose It: Rock and Other Pop Music, 1967-1973* appeared. This book contained witty and sometimes acerbic essays and columns about rock and roll's place within society. The essays and columns had been written for *Newsday* and other publications.

For the *Voice* Christgau wrote the column "Consumer Guide" and contributed features on music and musical personalities. He also contributed a "Consumer Guide" column to *Creem*, a popular music magazine, and a "Secular Music" column to *Esquire*. He reviewed films for other periodicals.

As Christgau noted in his guide to rock, *Christgau's Rock Guide: Rock Albums of the Seventies*, which was published in 1981, "When I became *Esquire*'s

'secular music' columnist in early 1967, I didn't know I'd found a vocation —
I was just staking my journalistic claim to a subject I'd been passionately analytic about since Alan Freed hit New York in 1954."*

Christgau, however, was unlike most critics who reviewed popular music.
He listened to the albums that were seldom played on the air and, as a result,
created the *Consumer Guide*, which provided prospective buyers ratings of particular albums. As he put it: "I conceived the CG as complementing my monthly
essay. It was criticism with an immediate, undeniable practical function — criticism in a pop form, compact and digestible."† Christgau's guide book was a
compilation of new as well as old commentary and ratings of several hundred
recordings from the 1950s, 1960s, and 1970s.

Indeed, it was an example of advocacy journalism.

In 1990, Christgau's collection of reviews from the *Village Voice* was published. Titled *Christgau's Record Guide: Rock Albums of the '80's*, the book contained reviews of some 2,500 albums. Christgau also included introductory
essays about the trends and developments in music that occurred during the
1980s.

In 1991, *Christgau's Record Guide: The '80s*, which rated certain recordings, was published.

REPRESENTATIVE WORKS

Christgau's Record Guide: Rock Albums of the Seventies (1981)
Christgau's Record Guide: Rock Albums of the '80's (1990)
Christgau's Record Guide: The '80s (1991)

(Leroy) Eldridge Cleaver
(1935–   )

Eldridge Cleaver was born in Wabbaseka, Arkansas, in 1935. His father,
Leroy Cleaver, worked as a waiter and piano player in a nightclub; his mother
was an elementary school teacher. When his father got a job as a waiter on the
Super Chief, a train running between Chicago and Los Angeles, the family
moved to Phoenix, Arizona, one of the cities in which the train stopped.

Eldridge Cleaver shined shoes when he wasn't in school. The job lasted
about two years, until the family moved to Watts, a section of Los Angeles.

---

*Robert Christgau, Christgau's Record Guide: Rock Albums of the Seventies *(New York: Ticknor
and Fields, 1981), p. 3.*
†Ibid., p. 4.

The Cleavers separated shortly thereafter, and Eldridge eventually was arrested for stealing a bicycle. He was sent to the Fred C. Nelles School for Boys in Whittier, California. Cleaver learned about crime from others. When he was released in 1953, he sold marijuana and was sent to another reform school. Eldridge Cleaver failed to learn from his mistakes, however. Several days after his release he was arrested for possession of marijuana. He was sentenced to the state penitentiary at Soledad, where he read works by Thomas Paine, Richard Wright, Voltaire, Karl Marx, Lenin, and Mikhail Bakunin, to mention a few. Cleaver also analyzed his predicament as well as that of black men in general. He had assumed that since the law had been written by whites for whites it had not applied to him. Now, he looked at white America through new eyes. As he wrote in *Soul on Ice*, "Somehow I arrived at the conclusion that, as a matter of principle, it was of paramount importance for me to have an antagonistic, ruthless attitude toward white women."* He considered himself to be an "outlaw" because he "had stepped outside of the white man's law," which he "repudiated with scorn."

Cleaver was finally released after two-and-a-half years. He sold marijuana and then became a rapist. First, he raped black girls who lived in the ghetto. Then he sought white women. As he wrote, "It delighted me that I was defying and trampling upon the white man's law, upon his system of values, and that I was defiling his women — and this point, I believe, was the most satisfying to me because I was very resentful over the historical fact of how the white man has used the black woman. I felt I was getting revenge."†

Within a year, Cleaver was arrested and sentenced to serve two to fourteen years. He was sent to San Quentin and then transferred to Folsom. Cleaver examined his actions and admitted that he was wrong. He could not approve the act of rape and wrote, "I lost my self-respect. My pride as a man dissolved and my whole fragile moral structure seemed to collapse."§ He started writing, primarily to save himself. Concurrently, he learned about Elijah Muhammad, who headed the Black Muslims, and the Black Muslim movement. Cleaver was converted and spent numerous hours reading the Bible. Later, he followed Malcolm X, who separated from Elijah Muhammad. When Cleaver learned about Malcolm's assassination, he defended his ideas and urged other inmates to support Malcolm's beliefs.

In 1965, Cleaver wrote his first letter to Beverly Axelrod, a lawyer, to ask her to handle his case. This letter began one of the most discussed love stories via letters in recent history. Axelrod responded to his letters and, after meeting him, became a devoted friend who encouraged the owner and editor of *Ramparts* magazine to examine some of what Eldridge had written. In June 1966, Keating published Cleaver's essay "Notes on a Native Son," in which he

*Eldridge Cleaver, Soul on Ice (New York: McGraw-Hill, 1968), p. 13.
†Ibid., p. 14.
§Ibid., p. 15.

criticized the work of James Baldwin, particularly the homosexuality theme that permeated *Notes of a Native Son.* Other articles by Cleaver appeared in the ensuing issues. As a result of his affiliation with *Ramparts* as well as the support he received from the intellectual elite, he was paroled in November 1966.

Eldridge Cleaver worked for *Ramparts* and was one of the founders of Black House, which appealed to youngsters interested in learning about black culture. In early 1967 he met Huey Newton and Bobby Seale, who founded the Black Panthers, a militant organization based in Oakland, California. He joined the organization shortly thereafter, primarily to protect blacks from being harassed by police.

In October 1967 a police officer was killed when violence erupted between the Black Panthers and the police. Huey Newton was arrested and sentenced for manslaughter. Cleaver, who had not touched a weapon, was not charged, but in April 1968 another confrontation between the police and Black Panthers occurred. Bobby Hutton, a young Black Panther, was killed, and Cleaver was wounded. He was sent to jail, but he only had to serve two months.

In the fall of 1968, Cleaver lectured on racism at the University of California at Berkeley. Later, he was the Peace and Freedom party's presidential candidate and received 30,000 votes. On November 27, 1968, he was ordered to return to jail, but he fled the country. He lived in or visited Cuba, Algiers, France, the Soviet Union, China, North Korea, and North Vietnam. While overseas, he was interviewed by reporters of *Time*, the *Washington Post*, and other magazines and newspapers.

After about eight years, in 1975, Cleaver returned to the United States to face prosecution. By pleading guilty to an assault charge, he was sentenced to 1,200 hours of community service. The system that he had despised was extremely lenient on him. Eldridge Cleaver had changed, and his rhetoric was no longer espousing hate. As he explained to one reporter: "I found the systems of dictatorships and communism to be absolutely unacceptable. Living in those countries put an end to my advocacy of communism."** In 1982 he became a Mormon. Critics complained that he had sold out. Rather than being an activist, he had become a passivist. Even his book *Soul on Fire*, which had appeared in 1978, was severely criticized for its languid style and syrupy subject matter. Many critics longed for the old Eldridge Cleaver, the one who would bite; they were not amused by the new one.

Eldridge Cleaver ran as a conservative candidate for Congress in 1984 but was not successful. During the late 1980s, he earned money from lecturing, making and selling ceramic objects, and writing.

Cleaver's book *Soul on Ice* was a personal indictment of the white man's world, and it revealed quite candidly how one black got caught in a system that he could not understand, let alone respect or appreciate. Perhaps no other

---

**"Whatever Happened to ... Eldridge Cleaver," Ebony* (March 1988):66.

book captured the animosity that many blacks felt toward whites as well as this one, and Cleaver's personal style added punch to each indictment discussed.

REPRESENTATIVE WORKS

Soul on Ice (1968)
Soul on Fire (1978)

Elizabeth Cochrane
(1867–1922)

Elizabeth Cochrane, or "Nellie Bly," as she was called, was born in Pennsylvania in 1867. Educated at home by her father until she was 13, she was then sent to a boarding school in Indiana, Pennsylvania, where she remained one year. In 1881 she moved to Pittsburgh, where she answered an article titled "What Girls Are Good For," which had appeared in the Pittsburgh *Dispatch*. Although he did not publish her letter, editor George A. Madden enjoyed her direct style and suggested that she contribute an article on girls and life. Immediately she started writing. One article followed another, and her article "Divorce," written at the suggestion of Madden, contained the pseudonym Nellie Bly.

Since this was the period of "yellow" journalism, which preceded muckraking, the newspapers were furiously competing for extraordinary investigative stories. By using a pseudonym, Nellie investigated practically any business or municipal operation she desired. She investigated factories and wrote indignant articles. She wrote articles about Pittsburgh society, including the theater as well as art. She traveled through the West and Mexico and wrote of her travels.

Upon Bly's return, Madden offered to increase her salary to $15 a week, but she had grown tired of Pittsburgh. She had seen part of the world and she was determined to see more. She moved to New York City and finally, through trickery, got a job on Joseph Pulitzer's *New York World*. Pulitzer allowed Nellie Bly to write whatever she wanted in order to prove herself. One of her first efforts was having herself committed to the insane asylum on Blackwell's Island, which resulted in two of the most sensational as well as controversial stories of that period. According to Ishbell Ross: "She told of the cold, the poor food and the cruelty to which the patients were exposed…. She charged the nurses with goading their patients. She saw demented and gray-haired women dragged shrieking to hidden closets, then cries being stifled by force as they were hustled out of sight."* As a result of these stories, Blackwell Island was investigated and subsequently improved. Immediately, Nellie Bly's name was known by thousands of readers.

Bly continued her investigations, exposing such political lobbyists as Edward R. Phelps of Albany, the conditions of city prisons, the mistreatment of invalids, the conditions of old women's homes, the mashers of Central Park, and male and female work relationships.

In 1889, Pulitzer finally allowed Nellie Bly to race Jules Verne's Phileas Fogg, which ultimately became her greatest feat. Sailing on the *Augusta Victoria*, she wired stories in which she tried to make the journey as interesting as possible. The *World* published her stories and added others. Comments on fog, storms, travelers, and food entertained readers every day for months. Bly wrote of her experience, including her visit with Jules Verne. She saw London, Boulogne, Brindisi, Port Said, Aden, and Colombo and wrote about the Cunnainon Gardens, the elephants, and the attractions of Kandy. She visited Singapore and Hong Kong, where she encountered a monsoon. Bly saw Canton, Yokohama, and Tokyo and sailed to the West Coast. On the West Coast, she boarded a special train that brought her to New York City, Brooklyn, and finally Jersey City, where crowds gathered. Her race was successful; she had completed the trip in 72 days, 6 hours, and 11 minutes.†

Although Bly had performed a remarkable feat, she returned to the *World* and continued to write exposés as well as articles that helped the Salvation Army.

In 1895, Bly married Robert L. Seaman, a wealthy businessman who was 72. They spent 15 years together, until his death in 1910. She had given up journalism and had become somewhat of a recluse. When her husband died, however, and the factory he had owned became bankrupt because of employee embezzlement, Nellie Bly opened another factory. Unfortunately, it too went bankrupt. She had little business sense, but she was unwilling to admit this fact. She tried yet a third, but it failed. Immediately, Bly traveled to Austria to visit friends. She could not face defeat and humiliation, nor the charge from her creditors of being fraudulent.

When Nellie Bly returned, she was hired by Arthur Brisbane of the *New York Journal*, for which she reported the execution of Gordon Hamby at Sing Sing. Although her article campaigned against capital punishment, it received little attention. Journalism had changed, and articles calling for reform were no longer popular among the reading public.

Nellie Bly died of pneumonia at the age of 56.

*Ishbell Ross, Ladies of the Press: The Story of Women in Journalism by an Insider (New York: Harper and Brothers, 1936), p. 51.
†Ibid., pp. 52–56.

Peter Collier
(1939–   )

Although he termed himself an advocacy journalist, Peter Collier was actually an investigative muckraking reporter and editor at *Ramparts*. Born in Hollywood, California, in 1939, Collier received both his bachelor's and master's degrees from the University of California at Berkeley. From 1964 to 1969, he was a member of the university's English faculty, and from 1967 to 1973 he was on the staff of *Ramparts*, where he advanced from writer to editor.

Peter Collier edited the books *Crisis: A Contemporary Reader* (1969) and *Justice Denied: The Black Man in White America* (1970), which included articles on blacks in a white man's world by such writers as Norman Podhoretz, Kenneth B. Clark, Le Roi Jones, Ralph Ellison, Jack Newfield, Tom Wolfe, Hunter S. Thompson, Norman Mailer, Paul Goodwin, W.E.B. DuBois, Richard Wright, William Bradford Huie, Martin Luther King, Jr., Claude Brown, Huey P. Newton, Tom Hayden, Malcolm X, Stokely Carmichael, and Eldridge Cleaver.

Collier, who contributed articles to such periodicals as the *Progressive* and *Esquire*, wrote the best-selling historical investigative narrative *The Rockefellers: An American Dynasty* in 1976. David Horowitz was the coauthor. To say the least, the book was a comprehensive examination of the Rockefeller empire.

In 1984, Collier and Horowitz collaborated on *The Kennedys: An American Drama*, which was loaded with anecdotal material that presented another side to the Kennedy clan. Another best-seller, the book discussed Joe Kennedy's passes at his son's weekend dates as well as the drug addiction of Bobby's son.

Three years later the authors wrote the controversial biography *The Fords: An American Epic*. Although the authors described an American dynasty, the book was severely criticized for its lack of anecdotal material to carry it along. Also, some reviewers complained that it was a mere retelling of history that many already knew. Other critics mentioned that the book focused on Henry Ford II, not on Henry Ford I, for too much of the book. The book involved muckraking journalism in the sense that it revealed thorny issues such as Ford's support for the Nazis and was a form of literary journalism in the sense that the individuals discussed came to life. Through the use of in-depth description, dialogue, and a colorful narrative, the authors presented an honest portrait of the characters involved.

In 1989, Collier and Horowitz examined *Ramparts* magazine in *Destructive Generation: Second Thoughts About the Sixties* and claimed that the publication's anti-establishment philosophy was wrong and that the authors' conservative philosophy of today was correct. The authors even mentioned that they supported Reagan and what he stood for. They examined the Left and were disgruntled at what it represented. The book was an indictment of the so-called "Sixties Generation."

Two years later Collier wrote *The Fondas: A Hollywood Dynasty*, which devoted too much space to Jane's successful film career, love affairs, and political naiveté and Peter's failed film career and drug experimentation and too little space to their father.

The Roosevelts: An American Saga, written by Collier and Horowitz, was published in 1994. This book focused on Theodore, Franklin, and Eleanor, as well as the division of the family into the Oyster Bay and Hyde Park branches. It was also about their children and grandchildren and their awkward, even estranged, relationships; the author presented the moles and warts of an American family.

REPRESENTATIVE WORKS

Crisis: A Contemporary Reader (1969)
Justice Denied: The Black Man in White America (1970)
The Rockefellers: An American Dynasty (1976)
The Kennedys: An American Dream (1984)
The Fords: An American Epic (1987)
Destructive Generation: Second Thoughts About the Sixties (1989)
The Fondas: A Hollywood Dynasty (1991)

Christopher Powell Connolly
(1863–1933)

C. P. Connolly was born at Wappingers Falls, New York, on December 23, 1863, to Jane and James Connolly. Primarily self-educated except for two years at a primary school, Connolly served as a clerk in the law office of William Gummere in New Jersey before he moved to Montana in 1884. In 1888 he married Mary Fallon.

Connolly studied law under Senator Thomas J. Walsh and gathered information about the controversial differences between the mining interests and the miners in Butte. Connolly was admitted to the bar, and in 1896 he became an assistant district attorney of Butte. Later he became the prosecuting attorney. In this capacity he prosecuted Dan Lucey, who had robbed and murdered a man. Lucey was the first man to be hanged by the state of Montana.

Connolly moved to Missoula and practiced law. He also incorporated the material that he had gathered while studying law into the informative but muckraking article "The Story of Montana," which started in the August 1906 issue of *McClure's*. The series continued in each issue for eight months. Connolly presented an early history of Montana, which was filled with lawlessness and vigilantism. Then he discussed the discovery of copper and the rise of the copper kings Marcus Daly and William Clark, who were commercial and political enemies. He also discussed the purchase of the Montana legislature, the attempt to bribe justices of the Montana Supreme Court, the controversial appointment of William Clark as a United States senator, and the struggle between F. Augustus Heinze and the Amalgamated Copper Company to control Montana. The editor of the magazine introduced the series with this statement:

> This is the first of a series of articles which will tell fully and accurately the story of the personal and political feuds, the legal and business wars which have kept the State of Montana in turmoil from the beginning of the rivalry between Marcus Daly and William A. Clark, in the early '90s, up to the compromise of the legal and commercial differences between the Amalgamated Copper Company and F. A. Heinze, in the early part of the present year. Of the motives and interests which lay behind this long fight, of the powerful and picturesque personalities who have led it, of the intrigue and plot which were always beneath the surface; the public has never had any knowledge — the only information has been fragmentary accounts of the more sensational incidents.*

The muckraking series was sensational, to say the least, except for readers living in Montana. To them, it was old news; after all, they had read about it in newspapers.

Connolly covered for *Collier's* the trial of "Big Bill" Haywood, who had been accused of murdering the former governor of Idaho. He also criticized the lawlessness of the Western Federation of Miners, which had been responsible for inciting violence.

In 1909, Connolly was hired by *Collier's* to investigate the Taft administration's Western land policy. The result was the explosive article "Can This Be White-Washed Also?" which was about the Ballinger-Pinchot controversy. Connolly compared the dispute to the Tea-Pot Dome scandal. The penetrating revelation harmed the reputation of the Taft administration.

Two years later Connolly covered the trial of the McNamaras, officers of a union in Indianapolis who had been accused of bombing the offices of the *Los Angeles Times* primarily because of the publisher's conservatism and anti-unionization policies. Clarence Darrow, the famous lawyer, defended the McNamaras until one brother confessed and both pleaded guilty. Connolly believed that Darrow had attempted to bribe one of the jurors before his

*C. P. Connolly, "The Story of Montana," McClure's Magazine (August 1906):346.

departure. Connolly described the crime for which the union had been responsible, but he refused to believe that the rank and file had supported the criminal activities of others.

By 1912, Connolly moved to New Jersey, where he became an ardent supporter of Theodore Roosevelt and Progressivism. The following year *Everybody's* published his series "Big Business and the Bench," which described the unethical relationship between business and the judiciary.

The same year Connolly supported Everett Colby, a Progressive who ran for governor of New Jersey, and he carefully examined corporate corruption by investigating certain public figures in Washington, D.C. For instance, in "Undesirable Senators" he disclosed that Senator Charles W. Fulton of Oregon had no sense of public trust because he had gained power by using a clever political machine. Senator Francis E. Warren of Wyoming had failed at business as a private citizen but had become a millionaire as a public servant. Senator Levi Ankeny of Washington had represented the lobbyists, not the citizenry of his state. Connolly described others who had served themselves by serving big business, especially the railroads, rather than their constituencies.

Connolly investigated the famous Leo Frank case for *Collier's*. Frank had been accused of murdering a young woman, and he was subsequently convicted and sentenced to death. Connolly informed readers that Frank, a Jew, had been convicted on the most circumstantial evidence because of religious prejudice. When Frank's sentence was commuted to life imprisonment, he was taken by force from the prison and lynched.

When the United States entered World War I, Connolly, like other muckrakers, stopped writing investigative articles. Instead, he traveled to France for the Knights of Columbus. Upon his return he practiced law in Newark, New Jersey.

Connolly died in 1933.

Although he was primarily a businessman and lawyer, Connolly's muckraking articles about big business corrupting state and federal judges and politicians not only performed a public service but enhanced his reputation as an ardent supporter of the penal provisions of the Interstate Commerce and Sherman Acts.

REPRESENTATIVE WORKS

"The Story of Montana" (1906-1907)
"Can This Be White-Washed Also?" (1909)
"Big Business and the Bench" (1912)
"Undesirable Senators" (1913)

Fred J. Cook
(1911–   )

Born to Frederick and Huldah Cook on March 8, 1911, Fred J. Cook graduated from Rutgers University in 1932 and began his journalistic career a year later as a reporter for the *Asbury Park Press*, Asbury Park, New Jersey. In 1936 he moved to Toms River as assistant editor, then city editor of the *New Jersey Courier*, where he remained until 1944. From 1944 to 1959, he served as a rewriteman for the *New York World Telegram and Sun*. Throughout the 1950s, 1960s, 1970s, and part of the 1980s, he wrote exposés and books that concerned corruption related to city governments as well as the federal government, big business, and certain prominent figures in society. He wrote extensively about murder, war criminals, syndicate figures, politicians, and the Ku Klux Klan. He crusaded against conglomerates and for the little guy.

Cook's writing during the 1950s and 1960s, especially the articles "The FBI" and "The Shame of New York," was acknowledged by his peers. His writing was recognized in 1980 for its crusading spirit, particularly the spirit exhibited in the article "Gambling, Inc.," which appeared in the *Nation*. His books included *The Unfinished Story of Alger Hiss* (1958), *John Marshall: Fighting for Justice* (1961), *The Warfare State* (1962), *The FBI Nobody Knows* (1964), *What So Proudly We Hailed* (1968), *The Nightmare Decade: The Life and Times of Senator Joe McCarthy* (1971), *Mafia* (1973), *Lobbying in American Politics* (1976), and *Mob, Inc.* (1977).

In 1984, Cook's autobiographical account of how he reported on the Alger Hiss controversy, the bungling of the FBI, and even religious broadcasting was published under the title *Maverick: Fifty Years of Investigative Reporting*. Although most reviewers believed the book was informative and should be read by journalists just starting their careers, a few reviewers criticized the author's seemingly self-congratulatory tone.

Five years later *The Ku Klux Klan: America's Recurring Nightmare* was reissued. Originally published in 1980, the book examined the early history as well as later events and provided clues as to why the group existed. Cook included the economic and political reasons as well as the obvious reasons. The book was well balanced even though it was about one of the worst hate groups in America.

REPRESENTATIVE WORKS

The Unfinished Story of Alger Hiss (1958)
The Warfare State (1962)
The FBI Nobody Knows (1964)

The Plot Against the Patient (1967)
The Nightmare Decade: The Life and Times of Senator Joe McCarthy (1971)
Mafia (1973)
Mob, Inc. (1977)
The Ku Klux Klan: America's Recurring Nightmare (1980, 1989)
Maverick: Fifty Years of Investigative Reporting (1984)

Geoffrey Cowan
(1942–   )

Geoffrey Cowan was born on May 8, 1942, in Chicago and was educated at Harvard and Yale universities, where he earned his bachelor of arts and his bachelor of law degrees, respectively.

From 1969 to 1972, Cowan worked as an attorney at the Center for Law and Social Policy in California; he then taught law for two years as an adjunct professor at the University of California, Los Angeles. In 1974 he became a lecturer of communications at the same university. Two years later he worked as an attorney at the Center for Law in the Public Interest, also in California. In 1979 he became a member of the board of directors of the Corporation for Public Broadcasting.

Besides his work as a lawyer and lecturer, Cowan contributed a column to the *Village Voice*, and, with Judith Colburn, he wrote an exposé on Operation Phoenix, a top-secret CIA and army intelligence operation that trained counterinsurgency teams to torture and assassinate members of certain groups. Cowan and Colburn's efforts were favorably received by those working in the print and broadcast media. In 1979, Cowan wrote *See No Evil: The Backstage Battle Over Sex and Violence on Television*, another insightful piece of investigative journalism.

Cowan's latest book, *The People v. Clarence Darrow: The Bribery Trial of America's Greatest Lawyer,* was published in 1993 and concerned Clarence Darrow, who was hired by Samuel Gompers, the president of the American Federation of Labor, to defend James McNamara and his brother John McNamara, who were arrested for the explosion that wrecked the building in which the *Los Angeles Times*, an aggressively anti-union newspaper, was housed. The case was airtight, however, and Darrow lost. The McNamaras changed their plea to guilty and consequently were sentenced to prison. Darrow was charged for attempted bribery of two jurors and had to defend himself.

REPRESENTATIVE WORKS

"The Seat of Government," *Village Voice* (1969–1972)
See No Evil: The Backstage Battle Over Sex and Violence on Television (1979).

Jennifer Cross
(1932–   )

Jennifer Cross was born in London in 1932 and received her bachelor's degree from King's College 21 years later. Upon graduation, she began a varied career in journalism as a subeditor at the London *Tattler*, as a secretary at two publishing companies, as a staff member at the *British Medical Journal*, and a public relations executive at an advertising agency. In 1963 she turned to freelancing and teaching. Her articles, which focused on subjects consumers desired, appeared in such periodicals as the *San Francisco Bay Guardian*, *London Times*, *Punch*, *New Statesmen*, and *Nation*.

In 1970, Cross's investigative study *The Supermarket Trap: The Consumer and the Food Industry* exposed the rise of the giant food companies and their corrupt advertising practices, which enticed shoppers to buy more than they ordinarily needed or items they did not need whatsoever. Some of the practices included the industry's use of gimmicks, including stamps, coupons, and games; promotion of new products; and improvement in the company's appearance — the inside and the outside of each store. The book received favorable criticism and rightly so, for Cross had thoroughly covered her subject and had presented her argument well.

Cross, who wrote other books in the 1970s, became a consultant to Consumer Action of San Francisco in 1975 and the editor of *California Consumer*.

REPRESENTATIVE WORKS

The Supermarket Trap: The Consumer and the Food Industry (1970)
California Consumer

Midge Decter
(1927–   )

Born in St. Paul in 1927, Midge Decter graduated from Central High School. She attended the University of Minnesota for a year and then transferred to the Jewish Theological Seminary of America in New York City, which she attended from 1946 to 1948. Although she never received a degree, she learned enough to survive.

When her marriage of seven years ended in divorce Decter became a secretary in the offices of *Commentary*, the American Jewish Committee's prestigious magazine. Two years later, in 1956, she remarried. The same year she became an assistant editor at *Midstream*. This position, which she held until 1958, was extremely beneficial to her. As an assistant editor, she learned the mechanics of the magazine industry.

Decter's husband, Norman Podhoretz, became editor of *Commentary* in 1960, and she joined the magazine as managing editor a year later. In addition to performing the duties of managing editor, she contributed articles that vituperatively discussed women's liberation. Denise Gattis described her views: "Decter argues that the feminists' goal is not freedom from sexual discrimination but freedom from all responsibility. Feminists, she contends, are unwilling to meet the challenges of freedom and equality."*

In 1962, Decter left *Commentary,* and for the next three years she did not work in the magazine industry. Instead, she became an editor at the Hudson Institute's national security and social issues research center. In 1966 she started hopping from one job to another. By 1971 she had worked at CBS Legacy Books, *Harper's, Saturday Review/World*, and Basic Books. She resigned her position at the latter in 1980 to begin the Committee for the Free World.

Decter's first book *The Liberated Woman and Other Americans*, a collection of critical essays that had appeared in such periodicals as *Harper's*, the *New York Review*, the *Atlantic, Commentary, Book Week*, and *Partisan Review*, was published in 1970. Reviewed by prominent critics from coast to coast, the book immediately propelled the author into national attention because of its controversial, rather conservative stand on the feminist movement.

Criticized by some, praised by others, Decter's second effort, *The New Chastity and Other Arguments Against Women's Liberation*, which appeared in 1972, was extremely critical of the feminist movement. Indeed, she asserted that the women's movement had not helped women in their careers. According to Decter, the women's movement had stifled women's efforts by refusing to acknowledge the new freedoms, including birth control.

In 1975, in her third book *Liberal Parents, Radical Children*, Decter ridiculed the youth of the 1960s and 1970s for not accepting responsibilities and for not facing the adult world. She placed the cause for the young people's indifference on the parents, who she maintained were ultimately responsible. To Decter, parents had been too permissive and had failed to show authority. The book was severely criticized by some reviewers.

Decter frequently contributed articles to *Commentary* during the 1980s and early 1990s.

---

*Denise Gattis, "Decter, Midge (Rosenthal)," in Contemporary Authors: New Revision Series, vol. 2, ed. Ann Evory (Detroit: Gale Research, 1981), p. 161.

REPRESENTATIVE WORKS

The Liberated Woman and Other Americans (1970)
The New Chastity and Other Arguments Against Women's Liberation (1972)
Liberal Parents, Radical Children (1975)

Ovid Demaris
(1919–   )

Ovid Demaris was born on September 6, 1919, in Biddeford, Maine, to Ernest and Aurore Desmarais (he changed the spelling of his birth name), and received his bachelor's degree from the College of Idaho in 1948 and his master's degree from Boston University in 1950.

From 1949 to 1952, Demaris worked as a reporter for the *Quincy Patriot Ledger* in Quincy, Massachusetts, and then for the United Press in Boston. In 1953 he moved to Los Angeles, where he worked for the *Los Angeles Times*. After six years of working on the advertising staff, he resigned to devote his time to other projects. He wrote magazine and book-length investigative exposés that thoroughly covered such topics as the Mafia, kidnapping, city politics and corruption, crime in America, the links between corporations and politics, and international terrorist groups and organizations. He also wrote biographies of John Dillinger, Jack Ruby, J. Edgar Hoover, and Jimmy Fratianno. For instance, *Dirty Business: The Corporate-Political Money-Power Game*, which concerned corporations funneling money to politicians, was published in 1974 and contained a simple, direct, and extremely forceful style of writing. Demaris' form of muckraking journalism was exciting; it seemed to grab readers by the lapels and shake them.

In 1986, Demaris wrote *The Boardwalk Jungle*, which examined the advent as well as the aftermath of legalized casino gambling in Atlantic City. Demaris, who learned as much as he could about the hotels, politicians, and Mafia, described in detail how elected officials had been corrupted by members of the Mafia.

Demaris also wrote several novels, including *Ricochet*, which was published in 1989.

Demaris' biography of J. Edgar Hoover was reissued in 1993 under the title *J. Edgar Hoover: As They Knew Him*. Demaris used personal interviews to piece together a scandalous portrait of the former chief of the FBI.

REPRESENTATIVE WORKS

Lucky Luciano (1960)
The Lindbergh Kidnaping Case (1961)

Dillinger Story (1961)
The Green Felt Jungle (with Ed Reid, 1963)
Jack Ruby (with Garry Wills, 1968)
Dirty Business: The Corporate-Political Money-Power Game (1974)
The Director: An Oral Biography of J. Edgar Hoover (1975)
The Last Mafioso: The Treacherous World of Jimmy Fratianno (1981)
The Boardwalk Jungle (1986)
J. Edgar Hoover: As They Knew Him (reprint with new title, 1993)

Raymond Dirks
(1934–   )

Born in 1934 in Fort Wayne, Indiana, Raymond Dirks received a degree from DePauw University in 1955. Dirks worked as an insurance analyst and later vice president for several firms in New York, including Bankers Trust, Goldman, Sachs and Company, G. A. Saxton and Company, Dirks Brothers Limited, and Delafield Childs, Inc., which purchased Dirks Brothers Limited.

Dirks earned the reputation of being an ethical, hard-working executive. Because of this reputation, a former employee of Equity Funding Corporation of America informed him that certain officials of the corporation had falsified records, created counterfeit insurance policies, and funneled millions of dollars into fraudulent assets. Of course, Dirks did not know whether the former employee was just disgruntled or whether the accusations against the insurance firm were true. He met with others who had worked at Equity Funding, and they confirmed the allegations. Dirks informed institutions that held large blocks of Equity Funding stock, and the institutions sold it. Within a brief period, the insurance firm was bankrupt.

In the book *The Great Wall Street Scandal*, which was written with Leonard Gross and published in 1974, Dirks explained his role in the downfall of the Equity Funding Corporation. Dirks admitted that when he learned of the scheme, he decided not to inform the authorities because an investigation would have taken too long, and if Equity Funding Corporation executives had found out about it they would have had time to cover it up. As he explained, he took it upon himself to expose the fraud, which caused Equity Funding's stock to plummet in value.

Although Dirks succeeded in exposing illegal activity by certain officials, he was accused by members of the New York Stock Exchange and the Securities and Exchange Commission of spreading rumors for personal profit. Dirks persevered against these accusations, however, and was recognized later as having performed a public service.

In 1979, Dirks wrote the informative *Heads You Win, Tails You Win: The Dirks Investment Formula*, which was a guide on how to invest in stocks.

REPRESENTATIVE WORKS

The Great Wall Street Scandal (1974)
Heads You Win, Tails You Win: The Dirks Investment Formula (1979)

Ronnie Dugger
(1930–   )

Muckraking journalist Ronnie Dugger was born in Chicago to William and Mary Dugger on April 16, 1930. He was educated at the University of Texas at Austin, from which he received his bachelor's degree in 1950, and Oxford University. Dugger worked as a newscaster and sports announcer before he joined the *San Antonio Express*. He broadened his experience later when he wrote political copy for the International News Service and served as a foreign correspondent for several Texas newspapers.

In 1954, after he had returned from Oxford, Dugger was offered full control of the newly developed weekly, the *Texas Observer*, that had been founded to serve as an alternative to the conservative metropolitan newspapers published in Austin, Dallas, Fort Worth, and Houston.

Dugger recruited such journalists as Willie Morris, Robert Sherrill, and Larry L. King and made the *Observer* one of the most insightful newspapers published in Texas. Indeed, the *Observer* not only provided in-depth political coverage, but it provided critical analysis of bills before the state legislature. Dugger was also a first-rate muckraker. He and his sparse staff uncovered corruption among Texas legislators as well as lobbyists. From state officials taking gifts and bribes to huge oil companies dodging taxes and polluting the environment, Dugger and his staff informed readers of the ills of Texas politicians and big business. The paper reported on Billy Sol Estes, the inhumane conditions in state mental hospitals, and the abuse of power at the University of Texas. Nothing was sacred, or so it seemed to the powerful who controlled or desired to control the state.

Although Dugger served as the newspaper's editor, editor-at-large, and publisher, he, like Morris, Sherrill, and King, resigned in the 1960s. He contributed exposés to various magazines and wrote several books, including the controversial *Our Invaded Universities: Form, Reform, and New Starts* (1974), which argued that colleges and universities had, because of their preponderant bureaucratic structures, become institutions that promoted capitalism and demoted any or all ideas to the contrary.

The *Texas Observer* continued under the guidance of Greg Olds, followed by Kay Northcott; Molly Ivins joined Northcott in 1970. Dugger returned to the *Observer* as publisher several years later, and Joe Holley became editor. Although the paper required much of his time, he wrote *The Politician: The Life and Times of Lyndon Johnson; the Drive for Power, from the Frontier to Master of the Senate* in 1982, which was a critical biography that traced Johnson's greed and crudeness from his early years to his rise in politics. The book was based on extensive research and on interviews Dugger had conducted with Johnson in 1967 and 1968. The book also interpreted the effects of Johnson's policies on American and world politics. Most critics applauded Dugger's efforts, even though a few acknowledged that he apparently did not like his subject.

Dugger wrote *On Reagan: The Man and His Presidency* in 1983, which examined the political philosophy that had guided Reagan's first term as president.

REPRESENTATIVE WORKS

Texas Observer (various positions)
Our Invaded Universities: Form, Reform, and New Starts (1974)
The Politician: The Life and Times of Lyndon Johnson; the Drive for Power, from the Frontier to Master of the Senate (1982)
On Reagan: The Man and His Presidency (1983)

Benjamin Orange Flower
(1858–1918)

Born on October 19, 1858, advocacy editor and muckraking journalist Benjamin Flower was reared in Albion, Illinois, by his mother, Elizabeth Orange Flower, and his father, Alfred Flower, who was a minister with the Disciples of Christ. Flower was educated briefly at the Bible School of Transylvania University. He had intended to become a Disciples of Christ minister like his father, but his religious beliefs changed; he became a Unitarian instead.

When Flower was 22, he founded the *American Sentinel*, a weekly newspaper in Albion that was devoted to the cause of temperance. He grew tired of small town life, however, and moved to Philadelphia, where his brother, Dr. Richard G. Flower, operated a successful mail-order business. His brother also had offices in Philadelphia and New York City. Flower worked as his brother's secretary. When his brother opened a sanitarium in Boston, Flower moved with him, and in 1886 he founded the *American Spectator*, which advertised his brother's elixir before his brother was charged for practicing medicine without the proper license.

Three years later Flower founded the *Arena*. Filled with articles about religious issues, including the effect of scientific discoveries on ideas about the nature of God, the magazine, under Flower's direction, soon turned to other issues. For instance, Flower explored the slums in Boston and consequently exposed the evils therein. As a result of the articles, laws were enacted to help the poor. The magazine also published articles about poverty, sweatshops, child labor, and unemployment written by social reformers and writers such as Frank Parsons, Edward Everett Hale, Helen Campbell, and, of course, Flower. The magazine also examined prostitution, birth control, and socialized medicine, among other topics.

One of the major campaigns waged by the magazine was to urge state legislatures to raise the age of consent to have sexual intercourse to 18. Eventually, laws were enacted in at least six states.

Topics such as the education of women, women as laborers, divorce, and the rights of women were also discussed in the magazine. Even articles about dress, including several by Flower, who claimed that tight lacing and long skirts were neither healthy nor practical, appeared in the *Arena*.

Flower also encouraged writers to examine political issues. For instance, writers proposed a single tax, free silver, primary elections, prohibition of liquor, and municipal government reformation, among other topics, in articles that bordered on editorializing. Flower favored the popular causes of the day, including agrarian reform. The *Arena*, if it did nothing else, reflected the populist movement, and articles revealed the various political reforms that were being developed or implemented throughout the nation.

The magazine published articles about criminal behavior, prison reform, and capital punishment, which Flower strongly opposed. Other articles examined psychic phenomena.

Issues concerning labor, such as unionism and strikes, were also discussed. Even socialism to a certain extent was advocated. Although the magazine was generally known for its candid, one-sided articles, some fiction was published in its pages, as well as literary criticism, including reviews of books.

In 1896, John D. McIntyre, who had earned a fortune in manufacturing, purchased the magazine. Flower, who had quarreled with his financial supporter, Mrs. Gideon Reed, was forced to resign.

Flower joined Frederick Adams and his *New Time*, another reform periodical, in Chicago. This relationship, however, soon ended. Indeed, within a year, Flower was contributing at least one article every month to the *Arena*.

In 1899, Flower coedited with Mrs. Calvin Kryder Reifsnider *The Coming Age: A Magazine of Constructive Thought*, which had offices in Boston. Although the magazine attracted several writers who had contributed to the *Arena*, it failed because it was not aggressive enough. Within a year, Flower returned to the *Arena* as managing editor.

Over the next several years, under Flower's guidance, the magazine captured as many readers as it once had. Other more popular and better financed magazines were publishing investigative articles that were truly muckraking, however. These magazines also published articles that were soundly researched; these articles were not just protests like those often found in the *Arena*. Thus, the *Arena*, which sold fewer than 30,000 copies, could not compete. Nonetheless, Flower and the *Arena* were responsible for initiating interest in a crusading-type of journalism, which was the forerunner to the in-depth exposé commonly known as the muckraking article.

The magazine was purchased in 1903 by Charles A. Montgomery, who then sold it to Albert Brandt. Brandt made Flower sole editor in 1904. The magazine published articles about socialism, trusts, direct legislation, and railroads. In 1905 and 1906, Flower published muckraking articles, primarily to compete with other publications, and articles that promoted certain reforms.

In 1909, Brandt filed for bankruptcy and the *Arena* ceased publication. Flower founded the *Twentieth Century Magazine*, another reform monthly, the same year. From 1916 until his death in 1918, he published the *Menace*, an anti-Catholic journal that lived up to its name, in Aurora, Missouri.

REPRESENTATIVE WORKS

Arena (editor)
The Coming Age: A Magazine of Constructive Thought (coeditor)
Twentieth Century Magazine (editor)
Menace (editor)

Sarah Margaret Fuller (Marchesa D'Ossoli) (1810–1850)

Born on May 23, 1810, in Cambridgeport, Massachusetts, Sarah Margaret Fuller, later Marchesa D'Ossoli, was the eldest of nine children. Her mother, Margaret Crane Fuller, a teacher, and her father, Timothy Fuller, a lawyer and politician, provided their daughter with a vigorous education. Indeed, her father taught her to read Latin and English before she was six. She read works by Horace, Ovid, Virgil, Shakespeare, Henry Fielding, Tobias Smollett, Molière, and Cervantes, among others. Fuller eventually learned Greek and other languages.

Fuller attended a school in Boston, which she enjoyed, and then Miss Prescott's School for Young Ladies in Groton, Massachusetts, which she did not enjoy. Most of her formal education, however, occurred at home. By the time she was 16, she was a brilliant conversationalist, and her friends included James Freeman Clarke, William Henry Channing, and later Frederick Henry Hedge, who introduced her to certain German writers as well as to philosophy.

Fuller studied and read most of the day. In addition to understanding several languages, she now understood mathematics, the Bible, and the works of Goethe, Madame de Staël, and George Sand.

In 1833, Fuller's father retired from public life and purchased a farm near Groton. He spent the next two years writing his memoirs but died unexpectedly in 1835. Fuller, who had been taking care of her younger brothers and sisters because her mother was ill, now was responsible for supporting the family.

In 1836, Fuller started teaching at Bronson Alcott's Temple School in Boston. Although the school was progressive, Fuller's salary was insufficient. To supplement her income, she taught several evenings a week in her Boston apartment and translated aloud the works of de Wette and Herder for Dr. William Channing, whose eyesight was poor. The same year she met Ralph Waldo Emerson. She also began working on a biography of Goethe, which was never published, and translations for John Dwight's edition of *Select Minor Poems, Translated from the German of Goethe and Schiller*. She moved to Providence, Rhode Island, in 1837, where she taught at the Hiram Fuller's Greene Street School and received a higher salary. The same year she joined the Transcendentalism Symposium Club; she was the first woman to be accepted as a member. Members would meet and discuss various issues pertaining to philosophy or literature.

Fuller translated Johann Eckermann's *Conversations with Goethe in the Last Years of His Life* in 1839, the year she left her teaching position at the Greene Street School. She moved to Boston and organized the famous "Conversations with Women," a series of meetings with educated women of the community. The first meeting's topic was Greek mythology. Fuller introduced the topic, presented a few ideas, then suggested a specific direction for the discussion. The meetings were so popular that she was asked to organize another series the following year. Eventually, men of prominence were invited to participate.

In 1840, Fuller was persuaded by Ralph Waldo Emerson to edit the *Dial: A Magazine for Literature, Philosophy, and Religion*, a journal that was about to be launched by the Transcendentalism Symposium Club. Fuller, who not only respected but admired Emerson, accepted. Unfortunately, members of the club believed in individuality, not teamwork, but a successful journal must have several supporters, if not staff members. Several prominent members, including her friend Frederick Henry Hedge, refused to write for the journal. To make matters worse, before the first issue was published, disagreement concerning the preface occurred between Emerson and George Ripley. Eventually, however, the first issue was published. Dated July 1840, the journal contained 136 pages and included "The Divine Presence in Nature and the Soul" by Theodore Parker, "Short Essay on Critics" by Fuller, "The Religion of Beauty" by John Sullivan Dwight, "Orphic Sayings" by Bronson Alcott, and other work, including poetry.

By the end of the first year, the journal had few subscribers. Fuller, who had worked extremely hard to put out a journal that did not pay its contributors, had not been paid either, even though she was supposed to earn an income as editor. The journal was sometimes criticized for its philosophy. Nonetheless, Fuller remained as editor of the journal for another year. Finally, Elizabeth Peabody, the new publisher, advised Fuller to relinquish her responsibilities because of her ill health. Fuller, who had been teaching, writing for other publications, and conducting "Conversations" to earn a living, left the *Dial* in March 1842. Emerson became the new editor. As Emerson and others admitted, however, had it not been for Fuller's sacrifices and tenacity, the journal would not have survived.

Fuller rested and visited relatives, as well as Brook Farm, which had been started by George Ripley in 1841. Fuller believed that Ripley's experiment in communal living was worth trying, but she never joined. She was a frequent visitor, however.

In November 1842, Fuller conducted another series of "Conversations" in Boston, from which she earned enough to travel to the Midwest with friends. Like other writers of the period, Fuller kept a diary of her journey, recording the places she visited as well as the individuals she met.

During this time, at the request of Emerson, Fuller contributed essays and reviews to the *Dial.* Her writing, which had concerned literature, painting, sculpture, and music, now concerned women. Her essay "The Great Lawsuit. Man *versus* Men. Woman *versus* Women" appeared as the lead article in the July 1843 issue and was the first major plea for women's rights in America to see print; it was read by both men and women around the world. Fuller became famous as a result of her advocating essay.

Upon her return from the Midwest, Fuller conducted another series of "Conversations" and started researching and writing *Summer on the Lakes, in 1843*, which concerned her experiences in the Midwest. She was the first woman to use the library at Harvard. *Summer on the Lakes, in 1843*, a travel book, contained an assortment of writing, including book reviews, translations, art criticism, short stories, and lengthy excerpts from other books. Fuller addressed various subjects — from the American Indians who inhabited the area to settlers who lived in peculiar surroundings. The book raised numerous questions about establishing a civilized society among so-called savages, and Fuller shared her insights and beliefs in an interesting mixture of writing styles. Nicole Tonkovich described the book in these terms:

> *Summer on the Lakes* ... demonstrates the multiplicity and simultaneity of several "phases of character." Therein "Margaret Fuller" takes up multiple and sometimes-contradictory positions, celebrating the West as a site of energetic and democratic expansion even as she condemns its cultural mediocrity, agitating for the betterment of the condition of western women even as she seeks to subsume them under the control of New England ideals of education.*

The book was published in 1844. Fuller then expanded the essay "The Great Lawsuit. Man *versus* Men. Woman *versus* Women" into the book *Woman in the Nineteenth Century*. Fuller focused her attention on the social disadvantages experienced by women by relying upon the lives of women in fiction rather than upon real people. In her commentary about these characters, she identified the works that she considered the most valuable as well as the figures that provided positive role models for real women. Fuller attacked the hypocrisy of men and pleaded for equality for women. She disliked the stereotypical roles in which men and women had been cast. Through discussing characters such as Margaret in *Faust*, Fuller impressed upon the female reader characters who had high moral principles. The book was published in 1845 and was without question her most important work.

Horace Greeley, the publisher of the *New York Daily Tribune*, offered Fuller a job as literary critic and social commentator. Greeley had been impressed by Fuller's ability to write. Accepting the offer, Fuller left New England for New York in 1844. Emerson and Transcendentalism were left behind. Instead of focusing on literary heroines and theories, she now focused on real life and became romantically involved with James Nathan. She produced at least two articles on literary subjects and at least one article on society every week. Fuller was also responsible for finding topics in the foreign press; these were discussed in editorials written by Greeley. She examined real women and sometimes the horrifying circumstances in which they found themselves — from serving time in prison to being committed to insane asylums. Fuller's observations reinforced her beliefs that society needed to be reformed.

Fuller's critical reviews were balanced, for the most part, in the sense that she presented the weaknesses as well as the strengths of a writer's work. She examined writers such as Elizabeth Barrett Browning, Ralph Waldo Emerson, Eugene Sue, Henry Wadsworth Longfellow, John Milton, Percy Bysshe Shelley, Caroline Kirkland, Lydia H. Sigourney, Henry R. Schoolcraft, Frederick Douglass, and Sylvester Judd.

In 1846, Fuller accompanied Marcus and Rebecca Spring to Europe, where

---

*Nicole Tonkovich, "Traveling in the West, Writing in the Library: Margaret Fuller's *Summer on the Lakes," Legacy (Fall 1993):96.

she met prominent writers and politicians and observed the working-class poor. Fuller recorded the places and people she saw and met and later expanded her notes into articles for the *Daily Tribune*. The same year a collection of some of her essays was published. Titled *Papers on Literature and Art*, the essays concerned American and European literature and art.

Fuller met Thomas Carlyle, Thomas de Quincey, and William Wordsworth in Great Britain and George Sand in France. In 1847 she and the Springs traveled to Italy, where she visited several cities, finally settling in Rome. Fuller met Marchese Giovanni Angelo D'Ossoli, a member of a prominent Italian family. Ossoli, who was considerably younger than Fuller, was nonetheless attracted to her. When Fuller returned from a trip to northern Italy, she and Ossoli became romantically involved. Although it is not known whether they married before Angelo Eugene Philip was born in 1848, most biographers assume they married. Fuller kept her involvement with Ossolia secret, but his family learned of it and grew so angry that they disinherited him.

Fuller and Ossoli became active participants in the Italian revolution, which was a struggle for self-rule and independence. Fuller mailed dispatches to the *Daily Tribune*, and Ossoli served in the Civic Guard. Guiseppe Mazzini, an Italian patriot, gained control in 1849. The French attacked Rome, however, and eventually gained control several months later. Fuller, in addition to submitting dispatches to the *Daily Tribune*, served as "Regolatrice" of the government's military hospital, where she spent days comforting the wounded. When the French gained power, she obtained passports for Mazzini and other leaders of the revolution; then she and Ossoli fled Rome for Rieti and Florence.

By this time Fuller was using the name "Ossoli." When Horace Greeley learned of her questionable relationship that had produced a son, he stopped publishing her columns. Suddenly Fuller and Ossoli had no income. She had almost finished a manuscript on the history of the Italian revolution, but it had not been shown to any publisher.

In 1850, Fuller borrowed money from friends so she and her family could sail to the United States. En route, the ship's captain died of smallpox, and their son almost died from the same disease. When the ship was near the United States, a storm forced it off course and it went aground off Fire Island and sank. Although some passengers and crew members were saved, Fuller, Ossoli, and their son were not. Some of Fuller's diaries and letters washed ashore, but her manuscript regarding the history of the Italian revolution was lost.

Fuller was a major force behind the *Dial*. Indeed, she was responsible for the publication's modest success during its first two years. For this she will always have a place in American literature. Although most of her writing was not representative of advocacy journalism, *Woman in the Nineteenth Century*, contained controversial ideas regarding women in society.

REPRESENTATIVE WORKS

Summer on the Lakes, in 1843 (1844)
Woman in the Nineteenth Century (1845)

Paul Goodman
(1911–1972)

Paul Goodman wrote short stories, poetry, novels, essays, and books that advocated New Left ideology, even though he considered himself a conservative. He became popular among the radical youth of the 1960s as a result of his book *Growing Up Absurd*.

Born September 9, 1911, in Greenwich Village in New York City, Goodman was the youngest of three children. His father deserted the family when Goodman was an infant. His mother and older sister worked to support the family; his older brother left home when he reached maturity.

Goodman attended a Hebrew elementary school and Townsend Harris High School, from which he received his diploma in 1927. He attended the College of the City of New York for four years, earning his bachelor's degree in 1931.

Metro-Goldwyn-Mayer hired Goodman to read screenplays. At night, he attended classes at Columbia University, even though he had not registered for the courses. One paper he wrote for one of the classes was published in the *Journal of Philosophy* in 1934; it concerned neoclassicism, Platonism, and romanticism. He published several short stories in the annual *New Directions in Prose and Poetry* and several essays in the *Symposium*.

Goodman contributed criticism and poetry to the *Partisan Review* in the late 1930s and later contributed to other publications, including *Poetry* and the *Nation*.

Although Goodman began work toward a doctorate before 1940 at the University of Chicago, he was dismissed for homosexual activity.

Goodman published several poems and an essay in 1941 and the first novel in *The Empire City* series a year later. A book of short stories followed in 1945. *Art and Social Nature*, a collection of essays, and *The State of Nature*, the second novel in *The Empire City* series, were published in 1946. Although *Kafka's Prayer*, an analysis of Kafka's writings, was published in 1947, it was overshadowed by *Communitas: Means of Livelihood and Ways of Life*, which was cowritten with his older brother, Percival. This book attempted to inform the serious reader in words and illustrations how metropolitan areas could be developed or improved through careful planning.

The third novel in *The Empire City* series appeared in 1950. Titled *The Dead of Spring*, it was for the most part unnoticed by critics and readers. The same year another collection of short stories appeared.

Goodman worked as a lay psychologist with the New York Institute for Gestalt Therapy, and in 1951, with Dr. Frederick Perls and Ralph Hefferline, he wrote *Gestalt Therapy*. Another novel was published a year later. Goodman was recognized by critics and scholars when his doctoral dissertation, *The Structure of Literature*, was published by the University of Chicago Press in 1954. Goodman finally earned his doctorate the same year.

Goodman suffered from an inferiority complex. His sexual orientation and his unsteady income put a strain on his marriage, and he grew depressed. The fact that publishers were not interested in his writing did not help either.

Although the novels of *The Empire City* were published as one work in 1959 and received favorable criticism, Goodman had not known financial success until his book *Growing Up Absurd: Problems of Youth in the Organized System* was published in 1960. Goodman, in this indictment against society, found society to be deficient in providing many of the most elementary opportunities and goals that could make growing up less difficult. The book appealed to thousands of young people who had grown disillusioned with the American dream. As Taylor Stoehr wrote: "*Growing Up Absurd* was a revelation. He pointed out how the wave of juvenile delinquency paralleled the beatnik subculture in the same urban centers, and he argued that both forms of rebellion were responses to the organized system, equally familiar territory mapped by everyone from George Orwell to Erich Fromm."*

According to Goodman, the young had a right to rebel. After all, if a society failed to provide them with meaningful work, sexual freedom, food for thought, and a community that they could be proud of, what purpose did it serve? Of course, the older generation dismissed Goodman, believing that he was naive about the world and perhaps life.

In 1962 a collection of Goodman's essays was published under the title *Drawing the Line*. One essay, "May Pamphlet," which he had written in 1945, explained why Goodman, a pacifist, disagreed with his draft board during World War II. There is little question that this essay encouraged hundreds of young people to dodge the draft in the mid to late 1960s. The same year Goodman focused on the problems confronting higher education in *The Community of Scholars*, criticizing the inflated bureaucratic administrations for caring more about dollars than students.

In 1964, Goodman explored the exploited class — students — and presented possible alternatives to the traditional forms of education. In this work titled *Compulsory Mis-Education*, Goodman suggested that the traditional forms of education had failed.

---

*Taylor Stoehr, "Growing Up Absurd — Again: Rereading Paul Goodman in the Nineties," Dissent (Fall 1990):487.

Goodman published several collections of short stories, essays, and poetry in the 1960s as well, but most critics dismissed his fiction and poetry, claiming that both were too political and sociological in tone.

Before his death on August 2, 1972, Goodman had served as an editor at *Liberation*, a New Left publication, for 12 years and had written several books of literary criticism.

REPRESENTATIVE WORKS

Communitas: Means of Livelihood and Ways of Life (1947)
Growing Up Absurd: Problems of Youth in the Organized System (1960)
The Community of Scholars (1962)
Drawing the Line (1962)
Compulsory Mis-Education (1964)

Vivian Gornick
(1935–   )

Vivian Gornick, a feminist who taught English at the State University of New York at Stony Brook and later at Hunter College of the City University of New York, was born in New York City in 1935. She attended City College of the City University of New York, from which she received her bachelor's degree in 1957, and New York University, from which she received her master's degree in 1960.

Gornick, who wrote explicitly about women in contemporary society and the frustrations they endured from forced stereotyped sex roles, worked as a staff writer for the *Village Voice* from 1969 to 1977. Her investigative, advocative essays were collected and published in 1978 under the title *Essays in Feminism*. In the Introduction, she explained that the collection seemed to be "a reflection of the manner in which American feminists — both as individuals and as a movement — have been coming of age in this past decade."* To Gornick, "The feminist perspective has grown measurably throughout American life because feminist consciousness has thrived and become ever more sophisticated whereas feminist dogma has shriveled and become ever more parochial."†

Gornick's essays, which explored such themes as liberation, lesbianism, feminist writers, the women's movement, Virginia Woolf, Dorothy Thompson,

---

*Vivian Gornick, Essays in Feminism *(New York: Harper and Row, 1978), p. 1.*
†Ibid., p. 2.

and Margaret Fuller reminded the reader that few, if any, progressive steps had been made since her essays had first appeared in the *Village Voice*.

"On the Progress of Feminism: The Light of Liberation Can Be Blinding" was indicative of Gornick's straight-forward style and her ability to advocate as well as inform. More personal, perhaps, than most of the advocacy reporting of the late 1960s and early 1970s, Gornick's piece revealed that she was extremely close to her subject. Although it would seem she would be in favor of feminists who revel in their verbal castration of men, Gornick's position was reserved, farsighted, and logical, for she looked ahead to the future. She realized that name-calling merely caused frustration, which ultimately drained the body — physically as well as mentally. Consequently, she encouraged her sisters to look ahead, to concentrate their efforts on tomorrow and on the end of the road. Although Gornick provided few, if any, facts to support her point, facts in this instance were not needed because her piece was spiritual in tone.

In 1983, after interviewing more than 100 women scientists, Gornick's book *Women in Science: Portraits from a World in Transition* was published. She presented an impressionistic, journalistic portrait of women who worked in science and disclosed their diverse problems and ambitions related to their chosen careers.

Four years later Gornick wrote *Fierce Attachments: A Memoir*, an autobiography that covered three years. According to Steven J. Rubin, the book

> is the compelling account of Gornick's lifelong struggle with her mother for independence, acceptance, and love. Within the context of that strife, Gornick reveals other aspects of her existence: efforts to succeed in her professional and personal life, relations with lovers and friends, and her own search for a meaningful existence. Her primary objective, however, is to elucidate fully the complex bond between an immigrant Jewish mother and a modern American daughter.§

Among the book's numerous literary devices, flashbacks depicted the characters at various stages in their lives.

REPRESENTATIVE WORKS

Essays in Feminism (1978)
Women in Science: Portraits from a World in Transition (1983)
Fierce Attachments: A Memoir (1987)

§*Steven J. Rubin, ed.,* Writing Our Lives: Autobiographies of American Jews, 1890–1990 *(New York: Jewish Publication Society, 1991), p. xxiii.*

Joseph C. Goulden
(1934–   )

Joseph C. Goulden was born to Joseph and Lecta Goulden on May 23, 1934, in Marshall, Texas. He attended the University of Texas in Austin from 1952 to 1956 and then served for two years in the U.S. Army. He began a career in journalism as a reporter for the *Marshall News-Messenger* in Texas. Two years later he moved to the *Dallas News*, where he worked as a reporter until he was offered a position with the *Philadelphia Inquirer* in 1961. Goulden, perhaps one of the most revered if not prolific investigative muckraking journalists who ever wrote an exposé article or book, remained with the *Inquirer* until he resigned in 1968 to devote his time to freelance writing.

Goulden's first book, *The Curtis Caper* (1965), was immediately followed by other investigative reports, including *Monopoly* (1968), which exposed the gigantic and most powerful corporation on Earth — the American Telephone and Telegraph Company; *Truth Is the First Casualty: The Gulf of Tonkin Affair, Illusion and Reality* (1969), which comprehensively presented the often complex Gulf of Tonkin incidents that catapulted the United States military into involvement in Vietnam; *The Money Givers* (1971); *Meany: The Unchallenged Strong Man of American Labor* (1972), which painted a different portrait of one of America's labor bosses; *The Superlawyers: The Small and Powerful World of the Great Washington Law Firms* (1972), which in traditional muckraking fashion disclosed the corruption of and the collusion between certain Washington law firms and members of the federal government; *The Benchwarmers: The Small and Powerful World of the Great Federal Judges* (1974), which disrobed the judges for their unlawful decisions; *The Million Dollar Lawyers* (1978), which examined the conduct of the most expensive legal representatives; *Korea: The Untold Story of the War* (1982), which revealed an undeniably accurate history of the Korean War; *Jerry Wurf: Labor's Last Angry Man* (1982); and *There Are Alligators in Our Sewers, and Other American Credos* (1983), which was written with Paul Dickson.

Goulden, who contributed incisive exposés to such periodicals as the *Texas Observer*, *Texas Monthly*, *Harper's*, and *Nation*, received praise from numerous critics for several of his in-depth studies, especially *Monopoly*, *Truth Is the First Casualty*, *The Superlawyers*, and *The Benchwarmers*.

In 1984, Goulden wrote *The Death Merchant: The Rise and Fall of Edwin P. Wilson* with Alexander W. Raffio. The book concerned the one-time intelligence officer who betrayed his country to Colonel Muammar el-Qaddafi. Wilson, who worked for the CIA until his contract was not renewed in 1971, was about to supply Qaddafi with explosives and personnel. The book penetrated the intelligence community and explained how it operated.

Four years later Goulden wrote *Fit to Print: A. M. Rosenthal and His Times*, which concerned the editor of the *New York Times*. Filled with anecdotal material, the gossipy biography was written primarily to titillate the reader, not to provide a well-balanced profile of the subject.

Goulden became a media critic for Accuracy in Media, Inc., in 1989. Goulden used a direct approach in his muckraking books. Seldom did he use excess words or sentences. He presented the facts and his observations based on those facts. Goulden exposed his subject by providing incidents or examples.

Like other muckrakers, Goulden informed the American people of wrongdoing. His book *Monopoly* undoubtedly influenced politicians to examine the American Telephone and Telegraph Company and its hold on the communications industry. Eventually this examination led to the company's breakup. His book *Truth Is the First Casualty: The Gulf of Tonkin Affair, Illusion and Reality* opened the eyes and minds of readers, including politicians, to the fact that the Gulf of Tonkin affair may not have happened as it had been reported. His other exposés had similar effects.

REPRESENTATIVE WORKS

The Curtis Caper (1965)
Monopoly (1968)
Truth Is the First Casualty: The Gulf of Tonkin Affair, Illusion and Reality (1969)
The Money Givers (1971)
Meany: The Unchallenged Strong Man of American Labor (1972)
The Superlawyers: The Small and Powerful World of the Great Washington Law Firms (1972)
The Benchwarmers: The Small and Powerful World of the Great Federal Judges (1974)
The Million Dollar Lawyers (1978)
Korea: The Untold Story of the War (1982)
Jerry Wurf: Labor's Last Angry Man (1982)
The Death Merchant: The Rise and Fall of Edwin P. Wilson (with Alexander W. Raffio, 1984)
Fit to Print: A. M. Rosenthal and His Times (1988)

Robert W. Greene
(1929–   )

Former investigative journalist Robert W. Greene was born in 1929 and attended Fordham University in the late 1940s. In 1949 he worked as a reporter for the *Jersey Journal*, a position he held until he was offered an investigative position with the New York City Anti-crime Commission a year later. In 1955 he moved to *Newsday*, a tabloid-sized Long Island newspaper, where he worked first as a reporter. From 1967 to 1973, he was the leader of the investigative team. He also became a senior editor in 1970 and an assistant managing editor in 1974.

Although Greene, together with other writers at *Newsday*, wrote the phenomenally best-selling novel *Naked Came the Stranger* in 1970, his work as an investigative journalist was unequaled. For instance, when the team was initiated in 1967, its first target was the unorthodox zoning practices in Long Island townships. The team reported that developers had bribed local officials to rezone certain areas to enable the developers to build on land they would not have been able to use otherwise. After two years of stories, at least seven persons were indicted and convicted, at least thirty public officials resigned their positions, and new legislation was enacted.

In 1969, Greene and another reporter at *Newsday* retraced Ted Kennedy's footsteps in Chappaquidick and wrote an inquisitive story that raised several questions about Kennedy's actions after his car went off the bridge. Greene, who had written about the Kennedys earlier in his career, had been a friend of Robert F. Kennedy before he was assassinated. Needless to say, his relationship with the Kennedys was severed after this story was published.

Two years later the team reported on Richard Nixon's lifestyle, investments, and friends in Florida. The Nixon White House reacted by putting the newspaper and its reporters on the White House enemies list.

Perhaps the team's most ambitious investigative work concerned the heroin trail from Turkey to New York City, which took months to unravel and present to the public because the team lived not only in Turkey, France, and Mexico, but in several cities in the United States. The series was worth the time and expense, however, because it won a Pulitzer Prize in 1974; more important, it set a goal for other newspapers to try to achieve.

When *Arizona Republic* reporter Don Bolles was killed by a car bomb, Greene headed a team of reporters and editors from around the nation who investigated what Bolles had been researching. The team worked tirelessly for five months and uncovered a link between organized crime and political corruption, land fraud, and illegal drugs in Arizona. According to Steven J. Stark: "The series, published in numerous newspapers and carried by the Associated Press and several radio stations, was controversial for the way it put together reporters from different newspapers to work with each other ... on the investigation. But it was a hallmark event in journalism — one of the most ambitious stories ever done. It became known as the Arizona Project — and Bob Greene became a legend."[*]

[*]Steven J. Stark, "Investigating Bob Greene: His Mighty Ax Felled Presidential Timber and Cub Reporters Alike," Quill (June 1993):17.

Greene's investigative power was seen again in 1981 in *The Sting Man: Inside ABSCAM*, a book which not only explained the FBI's operation in detail but presented quite candidly Greene's assessment of Melvin R. Weinberg, the principal participant.

Throughout the 1980s, Greene, primarily as a result of his position at the Suffolk County bureau, influenced numerous reporters and editors who worked at *Newsday*. Although he was demanding, he made certain that his team of reporters covered the lighter sides of life; he even had reporters write about Halloween by having them dress in costumes and go trick-or-treating. He was also instrumental in hiring female reporters out of college and teaching them the fundamentals of investigating and reporting hard news.

Greene retired from *Newsday* in 1992. He contributed an occasional op-ed column to the newspaper, however, and became an adjunct professor of journalism at the State University of New York at Stony Brook.

REPRESENTATIVE WORKS

Naked Came the Stranger (1970)
The Sting Man: Inside ABSCAM (1981)

Leonard Gross
(1928–   )

Leonard Gross was born in Chicago to Benjamin and Clara Gross on April 21, 1928. Upon graduation from high school, he attended the University of California at Los Angeles, from which he received his bachelor's degree in 1949. He attended Columbia University, where he received his master's degree in 1950 and then he served in the U.S. Army.

Gross entered the field of journalism as a reporter for the *Wall Street Journal* and was assigned to the San Francisco bureau. In 1952 he joined the staff of the *San Francisco Chronicle*, where he remained for two years. In 1955 he returned to New York City and joined the staff of *Collier's*.

Although Gross enjoyed working as a journalist for newspapers and magazines, he worked as a freelance writer from 1956 to 1959, the year he was hired by the editors of *Look* magazine. He served as a senior editor in New York City, as a Latin American correspondent in Rio de Janeiro, as a European editor in Paris, and as a West Coast editor in Los Angeles. He remained with the magazine for 12 years, until it ceased publication in 1976.

In 1972, Gross became a theater critic for *Westways* magazine, a position that lasted until 1980. Thereafter, he spent his time as a freelance writer between his home outside Los Angeles and his retreat in Bear Valley. His experiences, particularly those he had with *Look*, were incorporated into articles and books after he left the magazine.

Gross wrote about politics, journalism, fitness, history, social drinking, and, with Raymond Dirks, unscrupulous business practices. *The Great Wall Street Scandal*, which was written with Dirks in 1974, explained Dirks's role in the downfall of the Equity Funding Corporation (the entry on Dirks elsewhere in this book provides additional information).

In 1982, Gross wrote *The Last Jews in Berlin* in 1982. This book, based on numerous interviews with Jewish survivors who hid in Berlin during World War II, presented an emotional portrait of a courageous group of people who had been despised by the Nazis but nonetheless escaped the Nazi deathcamps.

Gross also wrote and cowrote several novels, including *The Dossier*, which was written with Pierre Salinger in 1984. Other novels as well as a few works of nonfiction followed.

REPRESENTATIVE WORKS

The Great Wall Street Scandal (with Raymond Dirks, 1974)
The Last Jews in Berlin (1982)

Michael Harrington
(1928–1989)

Michael Harrington was born on February 24, 1928, in St. Louis. After attending parochial schools, he enrolled in a Jesuit institution, Holy Cross College, in Worcester, Massachusetts. He received his bachelor's degree in 1947 and then entered Yale University Law School. Within a year, however, he was dissatisfied with law and with Yale University; he transferred to the University of Chicago, where he studied English literature. In 1949 he received his master's degree and returned to St. Louis, where he worked as a welfare worker until 1951.

Although Harrington was convinced that socialism was necessary to improve American society, he did not promote the idea until he moved to New York City, where he not only worked as a staff member of St. Joseph's House of Hospitality, which catered to derelicts, but also as an associate editor of the *Catholic Worker*. When he left the monthly publication in 1952, he joined the

Workers Defense League. Then he became a researcher for the Fund for the Republic. For most of the 1950s, he gathered information and wrote various Fund projects, including at least one report on blacklisting in the entertainment industry.

Harrington, who enjoyed stimulating conversation with other socialists in Greenwich Village, contributed articles to such periodicals as the *Nation*, *Commentary*, *New Republic*, *Commonweal*, *Reporter*, *Harper's*, *Atlantic*, *Dissent*, and *Village Voice*. From 1961 to 1962, Harrington edited *New America*. Throughout the 1960s, he was also associated with several socialist organizations, including the International Union of Socialist Youth, the League for Industrial Democracy, and the American Socialist Party.

In 1962, Harrington wrote the best-selling book *The Other America: Poverty in the United States*, in which he exposed the fact that while America was beginning to call itself the affluent society, some 40 to 50 million Americans were poor both physically and spiritually. To say the least, the book was an indictment of the so-called American dream. Harrington called for immediate action because he realized that only the larger society could implement socialized programs that would alleviate some of the problems. The book was respectfully received by critics, and President John F. Kennedy, who read it, requested congressional action.

The Accidental Century, which defended democratic socialism and severely attacked capitalism, appeared in 1965. In *Toward a Democratic Left: A Radical Program for a New Majority*, which was published in 1968, Harrington exposed and analyzed the problems of American society, including the technological innovations of the Western World, which he believed created additional problems rather than remedies for man. He failed, however, to provide an overall plan that would correct the problems he discussed.

In 1973, Harrington formed the Democratic Socialist Organizing Committee. The goal was to forge a coalition of environmentalists, feminists, peace activists, racial and ethnic minorities who belonged to the Democratic party, and trade unionists. The membership grew from 200 members in 1973 to 4,000 by 1980. In 1981 the Committee merged with the New American Movement to create the Democratic Socialists of America.

Harrington, who became editor of the newsletter *Democratic Left* in 1973, wrote additional books about America's problems and socialistic remedies throughout the 1970s and 1980s. For instance, he wrote two highly acclaimed books on political strategy in 1972 and 1976, respectively: *Socialism* and *The Twilight of Capitalism*. In 1977 and 1984, respectively, he returned to the subject of poverty in *The Vast Majority: A Journey to the World's Poor* and *The New American Poverty*. The last book discussed the structures that kept the underprivileged poor. According to Harrington, conservatism was the culprit, while socialism was the answer. The book was nominated for a National Book Award.

In 1980 and 1987, respectively, Harrington examined political issues in *Decade of Decision: The Crisis of the American System* and *The Next Left: The History of a Future*, which discussed how the nature of economic growth had changed. Investments, he claimed, could not create more jobs, but investments could create more national products. In three lengthy chapters, Harrington explained how the United States had progressed. He also explained how well-meaning social policies had actually harmed society.

In *The Next America: The Decline and Rise of the United States* and *The Politics at God's Funeral: The Spiritual Crisis of Western Civilization*, which were published in 1981 and 1983, respectively, Harrington described the cultural and spiritual crisis in American values and presented various versions of the country's future. He called for a public policy that would not only address American values but preserve them as well.

Harrington wrote two autobiographies — *Fragments of the Century: A Social Autobiography* (1973), which explored the reasons for his being a socialist as well as his life, and *The Long-Distance Runner: An Autobiography* (1988), which included the account of how he brought about the merger of the two major socialist organizations in America in 1981. He also collected some of the essays and articles that he had written between 1955 and 1983 for the book *Taking Sides: The Education of a Militant Mind* (1986). The essays covered various topics, including the politics of the peace movement, the political novel, and Disney World.

Harrington's last book, which was completed before he died of cancer on July 31, 1989, was titled *Socialism Past and Future* and was published in 1989. He called for reform such as state intervention in the form of retraining the work force and improving public education. He also requested that markets be pragmatically regulated and that leveraged buyouts be restrained.

In *The Accidental Century*, Harrington used simple words in simple sentences to make certain complex points comprehensible. Like other advocacy journalists, Harrington made his point and then supported it with facts. In one section, he argued that although corporations were no longer owned by any one person, the same out-dated philosophy underlined their purpose. To Harrington, this philosophy was not necessarily good for the corporation, its employees, or society, and he supported his thesis with substantial evidence.

REPRESENTATIVE WORKS

New America (editor)
Democratic Left (editor)
The Other America: Poverty in the United States (1962)
The Accidental Century (1965)
Toward a Democratic Left: A Radical Program for a New Majority (1968)
The Vast Majority: A Journey to the World's Poor (1977)

Richard Harris
(1928?–1987)

Richard Harris, who was probably born in 1928, was an investigative reporter for the *New Yorker* before he turned to the novel in the late 1970s. In 1964, after he had written about politics in America for the magazine for nine years, he wrote his first book-length exposé. In *The Real Voice*, Harris, in his characteristic advocacy style, analyzed Senator Estes Kefauver's investigation into the drug industry's unscrupulous practices of selling and overpricing products. In 1966, in *A Sacred Trust*, he vehemently attacked the American Medical Association for its uncaring politics concerning medical care for the aged. Three years later he expanded the article "The Turning Point," which had appeared in the *New Yorker*, into the informative, fully documented, advocative book *Fear of Crime*. Basically a critique of the Omnibus Crime bill of 1968, which had been passed by President Johnson in response to the fear of crime and not to an increase in criminal acts, Harris claimed that the bill, because of its nature, overturned the Supreme Court's decisions in the Wade, Mallory, and Miranda cases. According to Jean B. Elshtain's review of his book, the bill "provided powers for wire-tapping and bugging which were so broad that any investigative agency or law enforcement official who determined that an emergency involving national security or organized crime existed could tap or buy whoever he thought might be involved for 48 hours without even getting near a judge."*

A year later Harris wrote *Justice: The Crisis of Law, Order and Freedom in America*, which analyzed the operations of the Justice Department under Ramsey Clark and later John Mitchell. Although Harris admired Clark's refusal to politicize the Justice Department, he was severely critical of Mitchell and Nixon when they approved funds to be used arbitrarily by police departments. Harris also criticized the politicization of the Justice Department by Mitchell as well as his failure to stop illogical and immoral acts performed by various police departments across the country.

---

*Jean B. Elshtain, "Justice and The Fear of Crime *by Richard Harris," Commonweal, May 29, 1970, p. 274.*

In 1971, Harris wrote the scathing book *Decision*, a detailed, analytical account of President Nixon and John Mitchell's attempt to put an apparent racist, G. Harrold Carswell, on the Supreme Court. Harris noted:

> Of all the actions that President Richard Nixon took during his first two years in office, probably none more clearly revealed the character of his Presidency — the regional and class appeals that divided the nation, the disregard for the Constitutional separation of powers, the embittered relations between the Administration and the Senate, the apparent confidence that the people would sleep through even the noisiest raid on their liberties, and the belief that members of Congress could be counted on to put their own political interest above the public interest — than his nomination of George Harrold Carswell, of Florida, to be an associate justice of the Supreme Court.†

Harris revealed the political shenanigans that were deployed by the administration. Fortunately, Senator Birch Bayh of Indiana and others learned of Carswell's discriminatory record and persuaded loyal Nixon supporters to resist the pressures from the White House. Carswell was defeated, and Nixon never recovered.

Five years later Harris examined in traditional muckraking style three cases in which people's civil rights had been grossly overlooked by representative bodies of the government. Harris, who claimed that the federal government was unaware of people's needs and that the judiciary served the state in most cases, advocated that any representative body should obey the laws of the Constitution; if it failed to do so, then it should have to pay the consequences.

In August 1987, Harris fell from his apartment window and died. The police ruled that he had committed suicide.

REPRESENTATIVE WORKS

The Real Voice (1964)
A Sacred Trust (1966)
Fear of Crime (1969)
Justice: The Crisis of Law, Order and Freedom in America (1970)
Decision (1971)

Burton Jesse Hendrick
(1870–1949)

Muckraking journalist Burton Hendrick was born on December 8, 1870, in New Haven, Connecticut, to Mary Elizabeth Hendrick and Charles Buddington

†*Richard Harris,* Decision *(New York: E. P. Dutton, 1971), p. 10.*

Hendrick. Hendrick attended Hillhouse High School, where he edited the literary magazine. When he graduated, he worked at various jobs until he had saved enough money for college tuition; he then attended Yale, where he edited the *Banner* and the *Courant*. He earned the bachelor's degree in 1895.

Hendrick wanted to become a member of academe, but this desire required money for further study. After working as a reporter, he became the editor of the *New Haven Morning News* in 1896. Concurrently, he began graduate work in English at Yale. The same year he married Bertha Jane Ives, who had graduated from Mount Holyoke College. Hendrick ghost-wrote *Dragons and Cherry Blossoms*, a travelogue of Japan, for Alice Pamela Morris.

In 1897, Hendrick earned his master's degree. When the *Morning News* ceased publication the same year, he was unemployed. He attempted to procure an academic position but to no avail. Finally, he was hired as a reporter at the *New York Evening Post*, where he learned the necessary skills of a journalist from E. L. Godkin and Horace White. Hendrick wrote detailed accounts for the newspaper. To earn additional income, he contributed in-depth investigative articles to magazines. S. S. McClure, who published *McClure's*, read one of his stories and offered him a position at $100 a week. Hendrick accepted and joined other investigative writers, including Ida Tarbell, Lincoln Steffens, and Ray Stannard Baker, in making the magazine a national promoter of progressivism.

McClure realized that Hendrick was interested in investigating the insurance business, which had been discussed by other writers. No muckraking journalist had written about the subject, however. McClure was interested in Hendrick's version. As Louis Filler wrote, "Hendrick showed how the enormous surpluses which the companies collected were the basis for the corruption and degradation of the insurance principle."* Indeed, Hendrick explored the good and evil of the business. Through an in-depth study of Elizur Wright, the father of life insurance who had established a reserve for policyholders, Hendrick presented what was good about the industry. Through an in-depth study of Henry B. Hyde, the founder of Equitable who had employed scheme after scheme to acquire personal wealth, including a lottery that was masqueraded as insurance, and had brought disgrace to the entire industry, Hendrick presented what was evil about the industry. Needless to say, the series "The Story of Insurance" catapulted him to considerable fame.

McClure's introduced the series in an editorial announcement in April 1906:

> In the May number of *McClure's Magazine* will begin a series of articles telling the "Story of Life Insurance." Both the development of life insurance itself and the careers of the men who have most conspicuously contributed to it will be described in detail. With no attempt at sensationalism, and with the desire of relating simply and truthfully the actual facts, both the good and the bad will be given.

---

*Louis Filler, The Muckrakers *(University Park: The Pennsylvania State University Press, 1968),* p. 198.

On one hand will be described the work of the great men who made the American life insurance system one of our greatest claims to national distinction; and, on the other, the work of the corrupt men who have done so much to degrade it. For nearly a year Mr. Burton J. Hendrick has been working on these articles which will continue for many months.†

In the last paragraph from the introduction to the series, Hendrick discussed reputable insurance companies, what these companies did for their policyholders, and how they differed from their Manhattan counterparts:

If we wish mere life insurance unencumbered with modern improvements we must go to Connecticut, Massachusetts, New Jersey, and one or two other states. There we shall find great companies limiting their activities to one single end — the insuring of lives. They do not deal in investments, do not act as savings banks or lotteries. They collect from the insured during life certain stipulated sums, and, in the event of death, pay over to the widows certain equivalent indemnities. They collect from each member precisely the same pro rata price for the particular service rendered; and base this price upon certain well known mathematical laws which closely determine the exact cost. They treat all the insured upon a strictly "mutual basis," which, in the last analysis, means insurance at its actual cost and that actual cost to all. They furnish this article at a lower price than present quotations for the New York variety. They do it, too, without the elaborate machinery found so indispensable upon Manhattan Island. They have no subsidiary banks or trust companies; no string of office buildings stretched all over the civilized world; no alliance with captains of industry in Wall Street; no array of extravagantly salaried officers; no corruptionists in every important state capitol. They do not have enormous surpluses unjustly withheld from the policy-holders to whom they belong; do not pay in commissions for new business larger sums than that business is worth; do not write insurance in forty-five states and all foreign countries, including China, Japan, Borneo, and Malaysia; they remain quietly at home insuring only respectable heads of American families in good physical condition.§

The paragraph sets the tone and sums up what the remaining segments of the series focus on, including the corruption and graft.

When Steffens and other muckraking journalists left *McClure's* in 1906 to publish the *American Magazine*, Hendrick remained at *McClure's*; he was not, in his mind, in the same league. Indeed, to a certain extent, he secretly admired many of those about whom he wrote.

Although Hendrick stayed at *McClure's* until 1913, most of the articles he produced for the magazine paled in comparison to the series about insurance. "Great American Fortunes and Their Making" was the exception. In this article, Hendrick described the "trolleyization" of New York City through the exploitation of municipal utilities by the Widener-Whitney-Ryan syndicate.

†*"Editorial Announcements,"* McClure's Magazine *(April 1906):675.*
§*Burton J. Hendrick, "The Story of Life Insurance,"* McClure's Magazine *(May 1906): 36–37.*

According to David Mark Chalmers, the syndicate "showed no interest in providing service. It was all a great brokerage operation. Profit came from watered
stock, wasteful and dishonest construction, inadequate service, tax avoidance,
and the failure to provide even elementary safety precautions."** Hendrick
pointed out that the syndicate had been able to get away with this by corrupting the political and legal systems.

Hendrick became the associate editor of *World's Work* and commented
on politics and progressive reform. He supported Woodrow Wilson and Charles
Evans Hughes, among others.

In 1919, Hendrick wrote *The Age of Big Business*, which paled in comparison to his series on insurance. Indeed, Hendrick was not necessarily impar-
tial in his analysis. A sense of envy was evident in the book.

During the 1920s, Hendrick wrote several biographies, including *The Victory at Sea*, which was published in 1920 and recounted the war years of Admi-
ral William S. Sims; *The Life and Letters of Walter Hines Page*, which appeared
in three volumes from 1922 to 1925 and focused on Page's ambassadorship during World War I; and *The Training of an American*, which was published in
1928 and presented Page's earlier life. These three books earned Pulitzer Prizes.

In 1927, Hendrick resigned from *World's Work* because he needed more
time to devote to his writing. For the next five years, he researched and wrote
The Life of Andrew Carnegie, which appeared in 1932. The biography, which
had been subsidized by Louise Carnegie, Andrew's widow, was not objective
in its assessment of its subject. Hendrick, who had researched his subject at
length, failed to provide an in-depth critical evaluation. His style of writing,
however, reflected the many years he had worked as a journalist.

This biography was followed by *The Lees of Virginia* in 1935. Two years
later Hendrick wrote an unusual "biography" of the Constitution entitled *Bul-
wark of the Republic*. This was followed by *Statesmen of the Lost Cause*, which
was published in 1939 and discussed the Confederate leaders. *Lincoln's War
Cabinet*, which examined the individuals who lead the North during the Civil
War, was published in 1946.

Although Hendrick's books were well researched and movingly written,
most lacked in-depth analysis of the subjects discussed. Furthermore, none
could compare to his series on insurance.

Hendrick was working on a biography of Louise Carnegie when he died
in 1949.

REPRESENTATIVE WORKS

"The Story of Life Insurance" (1906)
The Age of Big Business (1919)

**David Mark Chalmers, The Social and Political Ideas of the Muckrakers (New York: Citadel,
1964), p. 43.

Nat Hentoff
(1925–   )

Nat Hentoff was born to Simon and Lena Hentoff on June 10, 1925, in Boston, and was educated at the Boston Latin School, Northeastern University, from which he received his bachelor's degree in 1946, Harvard University, and the Sorbonne in Paris. From 1944 to 1953, he worked as an announcer, writer, and producer for a radio station in Boston. In 1953, he became an associate editor of *Downbeat* magazine. He also wrote musical reviews for *Hi Fi Stereo Review*, *New York Herald Tribune*, *Book Week*, *Reporter*, and London's *Peace News*. In 1957 he became a columnist for the *Village Voice*, where his interest in jazz was replaced by an interest in sociological and political issues. An advocate, Hentoff wrote vehemently about such issues as civil rights, poverty, the draft, education, and police corruption.

In 1960, in addition to working for the *Village Voice* and contributing to such publications as *Inquiry* and *Liberation*, for which he once served as an associate editor, Hentoff became a staff writer for the *New Yorker*, where his interest grew more diverse. Several years later he also became a regular contributor to the *Progressive*.

Although Hentoff wrote several volumes on jazz, his advocacy journalism appeared in such books as *The New Equality* (1964), *Our Children Are Dying* (1966), and *Does Anybody Give a Damn?: Nat Hentoff on Education* (1977). In *The New Equality*, he criticized whites who, because of their guilt over the plight of African Americans, tried to guarantee civil rights reform. Such guarantees were preposterous to Hentoff, and he supported his thesis with credible evidence. In *Our Children Are Dying* and *Does Anybody Give a Damn?: Nat Hentoff on Education*, which were written more than 10 years apart, he explored the problems of the inner city schools and provided several possible solutions. In the former, for instance, he introduced Elliott Shapiro, a principal in Harlem who faced numerous problems every day — from a deteriorated school building to a public school system that discouraged change. Yet Shapiro had numerous ideas that, if implemented, could have helped countless students pass their courses and subsequently graduate. In the latter book, Hentoff examined the public school system again and learned that little, if anything, had been done to address the problems he discussed some ten years earlier.

Hentoff wrote *The First Freedom: The Tumultuous History of Free Speech in America* in 1980, which was inspired by his dismissal from the college paper staff at Northeastern University. As editor, he had been instrumental in having his staff write about anti–Semitism in Boston and question the administration of the university. In fact, Hentoff mentioned the authorities on the acknowledgments page of the book: "For my abiding concern with the First Amendment, I am particularly indebted to those officials at Northeastern University in Boston who tried to censor the writings of the staff when I was editor of the *Northeastern News* in the early 1940s.... I never lost my sense of rage at those who would suppress speech, especially mine. Those administrators truly helped inspire this book."*

In his book, Hentoff examined censorship in American society — from a libel case in 1735 to books being burned in 1973. He explored the subject of banning books in public and school libraries as well as the reasons for such actions, including obscenity. He discussed the Supreme Court's decisions and highlighted excerpts from the Court's printed opinions. The book's overall purpose was to inform the reader that most people involved in burning or banning books were not necessarily members of groups or members of Congress but were average citizens who questioned something they saw in print.

In 1986, Hentoff captured in a captivating autobiography the conflict between a first-generation orthodox Jewish youth and the varied ethnic communities that divided a city. Titled *Boston Boy*, the memoir covered his early years of growing up in an anti–Semitic Irish Catholic neighborhood. The book also chronicled Hentoff's emerging appreciation of jazz.

Hentoff wrote about John Cardinal O'Connor of New York City first for the *New Yorker* and then in the appropriately titled *John Cardinal O'Connor*, which was published in 1988. The biography detailed the life of the tough-minded defender of Pope John Paul II as well as the changing American Catholic church.

In 1992, Hentoff wrote about free speech in *Free Speech for Me But Not for Thee*. He presented numerous case studies to illustrate the ongoing struggle between the advocates of civil rights and the advocates of civil liberties. Hentoff claimed that the threat to free speech came from the Left, not from the Right.

In addition to his advocacy journalism, Hentoff wrote books for young people, including the popular *Jazz Country* (1965) and several novels for adults, such as *The Man from Internal Affairs* (1985), a mystery that featured Lieutenant Noah Green of the New York Police Department.

Does Anybody Give a Damn?: Nat Hentoff on Education exemplified Hentoff's simple, direct style that not only explained an important point regarding corporal punishment in the classroom but raised an unending question.

REPRESENTATIVE WORKS

The New Equality (1964)
Our Children Are Dying (1966)
Does Anybody Give a Damn?: Nat Hentoff on Education (1977)
The First Freedom: The Tumultuous History of Free Speech in America (1980)
Free Speech for Me But Not for Thee (1992)

*Nat Hentoff, The First Freedom: A Tumultuous History of Free Speech in America *(New York: Delacorte, 1980), p. 2.

Seymour Hersh
(1937–   )

He was born in Chicago on April 8, 1937, and graduated from the University of Chicago in 1958. He began his reporting career in 1959 as a police reporter for the Chicago City News Bureau. Within three years he moved to the United Press International, for which he worked as a correspondent. In 1963 he obtained a position with the Associated Press and he served as a correspondent in Chicago and Washington, D.C. Aggressive, brash, and eager to get a story, Hersh covered the Pentagon, where he eventually learned of chemical and biological warfare research, uncovering sensational pieces of information. From what he discovered, he wrote several articles that the Associated Press refused. Disagreeing with the editors' policies, Hersh quit his job and submitted the articles elsewhere. The articles first appeared in periodicals and then in the book *Chemical and Biological Warfare: America's Hidden Arsenal*, which was published in 1968. Hersh, like I. F. Stone to a degree, refused to accept press announcements from Pentagon officials. Instead, he roamed the building's corridors to find military brass and systems analysis personnel who had access to the truth. His articles on chemical and biological warfare, for example, described the development of chemical and biological warfare agents and identified the corporations and universities that produced them for the government. He even mentioned where they were stored.

When Senator Eugene McCarthy campaigned for president in 1968, Hersh worked for him as a press secretary until the Wisconsin primary, but politics was not for him. He returned to Washington and contributed articles to the *New Republic*, the *Progressive*, *Ramparts* and other magazines.

In 1969, Hersh investigated the My Lai massacre, which the Associated Press had disclosed. Although he was advised by various members of the U.S. Army as well as the federal government not to write about the incident, Hersh traveled across the United States to interview Lieutenant William Calley, who, according to army officials, had ordered the killing of 109 Vietnamese civilians. Hersh gave the story to the Dispatch News Service to sell to newspapers. He immediately followed up this story with another story concerning the men under Calley's command. Eventually, Hersh wrote of one veteran who had participated in the My Lai 4 massacre. The veteran, who was ashamed of what he had been ordered to do, appeared on the "CBS Evening News" and informed viewers of the atrocity. Hersh continued the series for the Dispatch News Service and wrote the book *My Lai Four: A Report on the Massacre and Its Aftermath*, which appeared in 1970 and depicted graphically what had occurred based on information provided by witnesses.

Hersh, who won the Pulitzer Prize for his stories, investigated other atrocities related to the Vietnam War. For example, he disclosed the apparent cover-up of My Lai and similar incidents by the army, a cover-up which involved officers of lower rank becoming scapegoats for carrying out orders that had been given by officers of higher rank. The reports, which first appeared in the *New Yorker*, were published in 1972 under the title *Cover-Up: The Army's Secret Investigation of the Massacre of My Lai Four*.

When Hersh joined the Washington bureau of the *New York Times* the same year, he revealed the secret bombing of North Vietnam and Cambodia. He also disclosed several important facts surrounding Watergate. For instance, he revealed that the burglars, although apprehended, were receiving money on a regular basis. In another story, he presented the persons responsible for the burglars' monetary support.

Hersh also disclosed that President Nixon, in order to learn who was leaking information concerning Watergate, authorized Henry Kissinger to have telephones wiretapped. In other stories, Hersh informed the citizenry of President Nixon's secret war in Cambodia, disclosed that agents from the Pentagon had stolen secret documents from Kissinger's office, revealed that Air Force general John D. Lavelle had ordered unauthorized bombings of North Vietnam, explained that the CIA had attempted to raise a sunken Soviet submarine in the Pacific, disclosed that the CIA had spied on certain private citizens in the United States, and revealed that the CIA had attempted to overthrow President Salvador Allende of Chile.

In the mid–1970s, Hersh moved to the newspaper's New York City offices, where he continued his investigative reporting. He left the paper in 1979, however, to devote his time to writing books.

In 1983, Hersh became a contributing editor to the *Atlantic*. The same year, after almost four years of conducting hundreds of interviews and gathering information, he wrote *The Price of Power: Kissinger in the Nixon White House*. A critical exposé, the book revealed Kissinger's calculated machinations. For instance, he straddled the political fence in 1968. Indeed, according to Hersh, Kissinger fed secret information about the Paris peace talks to members of the Nixon campaign; concurrently, he offered Nelson Rockefeller's files about Nixon to members of Humphrey's campaign. These actions were supposedly taken so he would have a position in the administration no matter who won the presidential election. Hersh also explained that Kissinger and Nixon had agreed on the overriding principle that guided the policies in Vietnam: South Vietnam had to remain non–Communist, no matter what. Secret massive bombings occurred in Cambodia primarily as a result of this principle. Of course, Hersh examined Kissinger and Nixon's so-called successes, such as the SALT treaty with the Soviet Union, with a critical eye and a sarcastic tongue. Although the book was praised for its insight by numerous reviewers, several critics claimed that many of those interviewed had been dismissed from their jobs or had been forced to resign. Nonetheless, the book earned Hersh a National Book Critics Circle award in general nonfiction a year later.

"The Target Is Destroyed": What Really Happened to Flight 007 and What America Knew About It was published in 1987. From countless interviews Hersh recounted the events and claimed that the passenger plane had merely flown off course unintentionally and that the Soviet Union had responded in haste. The book, packed with anecdotal material, revealed how officials in Washington, D.C., and Moscow interpreted the fragmentary data in terms of their own world views.

In 1991, Hersh wrote *The Samson Option: Israel, America and the Bomb*, in which he explored a topic that had been discussed by members of the media for several years. He exposed the top-secret Israeli nuclear-weapons program, describing how the Israelis had procured the bomb, how the American government had helped Israel, and why the Israelis had not actually needed America's help. The book examined the whole story — from the 1920s to the war with Iraq. Hersh claimed that he knew how many bombs were in Israel as well as where the bombs were stored, but several of his claims were undocumented. The book was intriguing and illustrated that Hersh had not lost his touch as a muckraking journalist.

REPRESENTATIVE WORKS

Chemical and Biological Warfare: America's Hidden Arsenal (1968)
My Lai Four: A Report on the Massacre and Its Aftermath (1970)
Cover-Up: The Army's Secret Investigation of the Massacre of My Lai Four (1972)
The Price of Power: Kissinger in the Nixon White House (1983)
"The Target Is Destroyed": What Really Happened to Flight 007 and What America Knew About It (1987)
The Samson Option: Israel, America and the Bomb (1991)

Warren Hinckle
(1938–   )

Born in San Francisco in 1938, Warren Hinckle graduated from the University of San Francisco in 1960. Primarily a writer of investigative exposés, Hinckle began his career in public relations. After two years he moved to the *San Francisco Chronicle*, where he was employed as a reporter.

Hinckle's best efforts in investigative reporting may have occurred when he became editor of *Ramparts* in 1964. The magazine, which had been founded two years earlier primarily as a forum for members of the Catholic church, aroused readers' interest under Hinckle's guidance. The magazine's circulation increased from 3,000 to 300,000. According to Leonard Downie, Jr., "Discussions about trends in Catholicism were replaced by revelations of American atrocities in Vietnam and the CIA's secret financing of supposedly independent student and labor organizations like the National Student Association."*

Unfortunately, Hinckle's high living eventually forced the magazine into the red. As a result, he moved to *Scanlan's Monthly*. In 1971 his first book, *Guerrilla Warfare in the USA*, was published. Hinckle, in his untiring style, discussed the numerous underground activities that had occurred across the United States. His best-known book, however, was published in 1974. Titled *If You Have a Lemon, Make Lemonade*, the book was a collection of articles, including the controversial essay about the investigation by James Garrison of the Kennedy assassination that had been published in *Ramparts*.

Hinckle, who contributed articles to such periodicals as *Playboy*, *Nation*, *Atlantic*, and *Esquire* edited the periodical *City of San Francisco* in the mid–1970s, before he became a columnist for the *San Francisco Chronicle* in 1977. In 1980 he collaborated with William Turner on the book *The Fish Is Red: The Story of the Secret War Against Castro*, which exposed the secret war against Fidel Castro and his Cuban regime. The book analyzed the CIA's useless, sometimes senseless, military as well as civilian efforts.

The *Fish Is Red* was characteristic of Hinckle's arresting style. The book exposed an unsettling, if not frightening, relationship between certain criminal factions and the CIA.

In 1986, Hinckle was lured away from the *San Francisco Chronicle* by the publisher of the *San Francisco Examiner*. He wrote a column about San Francisco and worked as an associate editor.

In 1993 the book *Deadly Secrets: The CIA-Mafia War Against Castro and the Assassination of JFK*, which he had written with William Turner several years before, was updated and reprinted. Hinckle and Turner contended that a melange of anti–Castro Cubans, Mafiosi, anti-communists, and operatives of the CIA played a major role in the Bay of Pigs, the assassination of John F. Kennedy, Watergate, and the Iran-Contra scandal, among other incidents. The authors claimed that George Bush, the former director of the CIA, was connected to drug traffickers in Latin America as well as to the murderers of Orlando Letetier. Unfortunately, as several reviewers noted, the book was riddled with holes; consequently, it lacked credibility.

REPRESENTATIVE WORKS

Ramparts (editor)
Guerrilla Warfare in the USA (1971)

*Leonard Downie, Jr., The New Muckrakers (Washington, D.C.: New Republic Book Co. 1976), p. 219.

If You Have a Lemon, Make Lemonade (1974)
The Fish Is Red: The Story of the Secret War Against Castro (1980)
Deadly Secrets: The CIA-Mafia War Against Castro and the Assassination of JFK (reprint, 1993)

Will Irwin
(1873–1948)

Will Irwin was born on September 14, 1873, to Edith and David Irwin, in Oneida, New York. When Irwin was five, his father, a bookkeeper, moved his family to Colorado, where he prospected for silver.

Irwin and his brother Wallace attended school in Leadville, which was located in the Rocky Mountains. Irwin enjoyed school, especially literature. While in school, he worked as a carrier at the *Herald-Democrat.*

Before 1890 the Irwins moved to Denver, and Irwin, because of his academic achievements, was encouraged by Sara Graham, a teacher at West High School, to attend college. Irwin graduated in 1892 and worked briefly before he matriculated at Stanford University, where he met Herbert Hoover, who became a loyal lifelong friend.

Irwin enjoyed college. He wrote poetry and fiction and became editor of the student newspaper. He also enjoyed socializing, particularly at parties. When he wrote questionable lyrics for a song that was sung by members of the baseball team, he was asked to leave the university; he left the campus in 1898. He attempted to serve during the Spanish-American War but was rejected because of his health.

Irwin married Harriet Hyde, who also attended Stanford. Then he obtained permission to complete his education at Stanford. Irwin received his degree in 1899 and moved to San Francisco, where he was employed by the *San Francisco Wave*, a weekly tabloid literary newspaper. Irwin interviewed celebrities and wrote reviews. He learned to interpret information quickly and precisely as well as to present information in an interesting manner. When J. O'Hara Cosgrave, the publisher, sold the paper in 1900, Irwin moved to the *San Francisco Chronicle*, where he covered trials, murder cases, and politics.

In 1902, Irwin became the editor of the Sunday edition. He also contributed articles to weeklies and short stories to magazines. He became a father when Harriet gave birth to their son, William Hyde Irwin, a year later.

Although Irwin earned enough to support his family, his friend Samuel Hopkins Adams helped him secure a job at the *New York Sun* in 1904. Irwin wrote stories about accidents, spiritual mediums, fires, demonstrations, and celebrities, among other subjects. In 1905 he reported the Portsmouth Peace Conference, which ended the Russo-Japanese War.

Even though his stories were occasionally edited, Irwin enjoyed writing for the *Sun*, one of the best newspapers in the country. In 1906, when San Francisco was devastated by an earthquake, Irwin wrote about the city he had grown to love and the destructive earthquake and ensuing fire that had toppled buildings and ended lives. His first story, which mixed the few facts he obtained about the quake with his knowledge of the city, was fourteen columns in length. For the next week, he wrote no fewer than eight columns a day, as additional facts about the devastation arrived at the newsroom. One of his stories, "The City That Was," vividly described the city that he remembered, including its hills, its surrounding water, its numerous restaurants, and its fascinating people. Irwin's colorful memories were revealed in the following excerpt:

> The old San Francisco is dead. The gayest, lightest hearted, most pleasure loving city of the western continent, and in many ways the most interesting and romantic, is a horde of huddled refugees living among ruins. It may rebuild; it probably will; but those who have known that peculiar city by the Golden Gate and have caught its flavor of the Arabian Nights feel that it can never be the same. It is as though a pretty, frivolous woman had passed through a great tragedy. She survives, but she is sobered and different.*

Irwin realistically described the fog that had engulfed San Francisco in the early hours. With words, he painted certain streets and certain areas of the city, as if the streets and areas were lost forever. Although the story contained no byline, readers learned that Irwin had been the author. The story was issued as a small book, which was circulated throughout the nation, and Irwin became famous as a result.

The same year Irwin left the *Sun* when S. S. McClure hired him as the managing editor of *McClure's*. Irwin now filled a supervisory position, not a writing or reporting one. He was promoted to editor after several months, but he and McClure disagreed over editorial matters. Irwin left the magazine within a year.

Norman Hapgood hired Irwin to write investigative articles for *Collier's*, another magazine that published muckraking articles. Irwin exposed spiritual mediums and discussed the illegal trafficking of liquor. While researching the latter, he learned that members of government were reluctant to regulate questionable activities primarily because their constituents had not demanded such legislation. Irwin learned that the press had failed to inform the citizenry of corruption involving the liquor trade. He believed it was up to the press to inform readers about the issue of possible prohibition of liquor sales.

---

*"The City That Was," New York Sun, April 21, 1906, p. 5.

In 1908, the year Irwin and Harriet divorced, Nicholas Butler, president of Columbia University, asked him to gather information from newspaper editors and publishers regarding Joseph Pulitzer's proposal for a school of journalism. Irwin collected opinions and studied journalism as it was being practiced at several major newspapers. He wrote several articles about certain newspapers, including the *Sun*, and journalism in general for the *American Magazine* and *Collier's* in 1909. His extensive series, "The Power of the Press," which criticized certain unethical practices by certain journalists, editors, and publishers, was published in *Collier's* from January to July of 1911. The 15 articles questioned the press, much like other muckraking articles had questioned the role of big business in society. Irwin recounted how he had researched the topic in *The Making of a Reporter*:

> I scoured the country, talking intimately with publishers ranging from the esteemed Clark Howell of the old Atlanta *Constitution* and Colonel William Nelson of the Kansas City *Star* who had proved how much government by newspaper can benefit a community, to a few virtual racketeers who laughed over the tricks they were playing on the public. And not only publishers, but editors and reporters who had been balked by newspapers in conspiracy with grafters. Some of this lot talked — off the record — with astonishing frankness.†

Irwin, like other muckraking journalists of the period, disclosed that certain problems existed in a particular industry and then attempted to provide solutions. "Press Agent, His Rise and Fall" appeared in *Collier's* the same year.

In 1914 Irwin contributed the articles "The United Press" and "What's Wrong with the Associated Press?" to *Harper's Weekly*. The same year, when Germany invaded Belgium, he traveled to Europe to cover World War I. His reports were published in *Collier's* and the *American Magazine*, as well as in publications in England. He returned to the United States and became a member of the executive committee of the Commission for Relief, which was chaired by his friend Herbert Hoover.

A year later Irwin returned to Europe to cover the war. His dispatches were published in the *New York Tribune* and several newspapers in England. For instance, "The Splendid Story of the Battle of Ypres," which depicted with incredible accuracy one of the greatest battles the British army had fought, was published in the *Tribune* and the London *Times* and *Daily Mail*. The story was praised for its realism, and Lord Northcliffe, the publisher of the London *Times* and *Daily Mail*, issued the story in a pamphlet that sold several hundred thousand copies.

Irwin, after inhaling poison gas that the German army had used in an attack, was hospitalized in London. When he recuperated, he returned to the United States, where in 1916 he married Inez Gillmore. They returned to

†Will Irwin, The Making of a Reporter *(New York: G. P. Putnam's Sons, 1942), pp. 164–165.*

Europe, however, where he covered the war for the *Saturday Evening Post*. Although Irwin was slightly injured during the war, he remained to witness the signing of the peace treaty.

When Irwin returned to the United States, he supported President Woodrow Wilson's League of Nations, which the publisher of the *Saturday Evening Post* did not like. Irwin wrote about the topic for *Collier's*.

For the remainder of his life, Irwin was not affiliated with any particular publication. Instead, he wrote articles about various subjects, including the press; short stories; novels; and nonfiction, including several biographies. For instance, he wrote *The Next War* in 1921, in which he called for the elimination of warfare. In 1925 he wrote the novel *Youth Rides West*, which concerned a young Easterner in the frontier West. In 1927, in *How Red Is America?*, he discussed certain questionable groups, including Communists, socialists, and anarchists and claimed that all the radical groups together would not total more than one percent of the nation's population. *The House That Shadows Built*, a biography of Adolph Zukor, specifically his role in the film industry, was published in 1929, the same year *Herbert Hoover: A Reminiscent Biography* appeared.

During the 1930s and early 1940s, Irwin contributed to the North American Newspaper Alliance as well as to numerous magazines. He also wrote an insightful account of publicity men and their methods in *Propaganda and the News*, which was published in 1936. His colorful autobiography, *The Making of a Reporter*, was published six years later and was favorably reviewed. In 1943, with Thomas M. Johnson, he wrote *What You Should Know About Spies and Saboteurs*, which disclosed how espionage and counterespionage agents worked.

Although Irwin had a productive career as a writer of nonfiction books, it was through his colorful story on San Francisco as well as his riveting series on the press that his reputation as an insightful and muckraking reporter was established.

Irwin died from a cerebral occlusion in 1948.

REPRESENTATIVE WORKS

"The City That Was" (1906)
"The Power of the Press" (1911)

Matthew Josephson
(1899–1978)

Matthew Josephson was born in Brooklyn in 1899 and attended Columbia University, from which he graduated in 1920. Attracted to European literature, especially the psychological literature of the French Symbolists, he traveled to Paris in 1921. According to David E. Shi, "Josephson was quickly drawn to the madcap Dadaists, especially Louis Aragon, Philippe Soupault, Tristan Tzara, and Paul Elward. He found them carefree, unpredictable, and totally without guile. They immersed themselves in literature and life and had no respect for their elders or entrenched literary conventions."*

Josephson tried to persuade his American friends Kenneth Burke, Malcolm Cowley, and Hart Crane to follow him to Paris. Unlike other writers he had met while living in Greenwich Village during the Bohemian period, Josephson changed his philosophy and form of writing when neither were in vogue. For instance, when he realized that Americanization of France was approved and actually encouraged by the Dadaists, his philosophy changed accordingly. According to Shi, "In Paris Josephson began promoting an artistic attitude that would accept the reality of modern life and use the machine and the modern idiom to aesthetic advantage."†

In 1922, Josephson and Gorham Munson founded *Secession*, a review that promoted his ideas and published such writers as Burke, Aragon, Soupault, Andre Briton, Cowley, and Marianne Moore. His ideas, although controversial, were accepted in Europe but criticized in the United States. That same year Josephson became an associate editor of *Broom*, another literary magazine, and for the next two years, until the magazine's demise, he criticized American writers for not taking the initiative to experiment. Perhaps if Josephson had not returned to New York City in 1923 to start an American edition of *Broom*, the parent magazine would not have failed. Nonetheless, among the avant-garde magazines *Broom* had no equal.

After a brief stint on Wall Street, Josephson returned to writing in 1926; once again his philosophy changed. This time he attacked the Dadaists for their refusal to write about societal ills. A year later Josephson returned to France to gather information on Emile Zola. The biography that resulted was well received, and he immediately realized his potential in this genre.

In 1928, Josephson became a contributing editor to *transition*, a magazine similar to *Broom*, except that its editors Elliot Paul and Eugene Jolas promoted Surrealism. His association with the magazine lasted for more than a year until he became so immersed in social and political issues that art and literature were no longer important. He was also gathering information for a biography of Jean-Jacques Rousseau, which was ultimately published in 1931.

During 1931 and 1932, Josephson worked as an assistant editor of *New Republic*, a left-wing magazine, and supported the efforts of the Communist party. His book *The Robber Barons: The Great American Capitalists, 1861–1901* examined the careers of such millionaires as Jay Gould, John D. Rockefeller,

---

*David E. Shi, "Matthew Josephson," in American Writers in Paris, 1920–1939, vol. 4, ed. Karen Lane Rood (Detroit: Gale Research, 1980), p. 232.
†Ibid., p. 233.

Henry Clay Frick, J. P. Morgan, Andrew Carnegie, and E. H. Harriman. Josephson noted: "They were aggressive men, as were the first feudal barons; sometimes they were lawless; in important crises, nearly all of them tended to act without those established moral principles which fixed more or less the conduct of the common people of the community.... These men were robber barons as were their medieval counterparts, the dominating figures of an aggressive economic age."§

Josephson's study was both factual and informative; every question raised was clearly answered. His book *The Politics, 1865–1896*, which was similarly researched and written, appeared four years later.

For the next three decades, Josephson wrote biographies, political and social histories, and several volumes devoted to his life. He also contributed articles to the *Saturday Evening Post, Nation, Outlook,* and *New Yorker.*

Josephson died in 1978.

REPRESENTATIVE WORKS

Secession (1922)
Broom (1923)
The Robber Barons: The Great American Capitalists, 1861–1901 (1934)
The Politics, 1865–1896 (1938)

Andrew Kopkind
(1935–   )

Andrew Kopkind, who was born in 1935, received his bachelor's degree from Cornell University in 1957 and his master's degree from the London School of Economics and Political Science in 1961.

Kopkind, an investigative muckraker, worked as a reporter for the *Washington Post* in the late 1950s and served as a correspondent for *Time* in the early 1960s, worked as an associate editor of the *New Republic* and as a foreign correspondent for the *New Statesman* in the late 1960s. He founded and edited *Hard Times*, a muckraking journal, in the late 1960s and early 1970s. Kopkind served as the editor of *Ramparts*, a similar muckraking journal, in the 1970s.

Kopkind also contributed articles to such publications as the *New York Review of Books, I. F. Stone's Weekly,* and *More.* For the latter publication, he

§*Matthew Josephson*, The Robber Barons: The Great American Capitalists, 1861–1901 (*New York:* Harcourt, Brace, 1934), p. vii.

wrote a scathing article that criticized the established press for not disclosing to the public various corrupt practices commonly perpetrated by American businesses.

Kopkind, an associate editor at the *Nation*, collected and published several of his articles in 1969 under the title *America: The Mixed Curse*. *Decade of Crisis* followed in 1972.

REPRESENTATIVE WORKS

Hard Times
America: The Mixed Curse (1969)
Decade of Crisis (1972)

Nick Kotz
(1932–   )

Nick Kotz was born to Jacob and Tybe Kotz on September 16, 1932, in San Antonio, Texas. He graduated from Dartmouth College in 1955 and attended the London School of Economics until he became a reporter for the *Des Moines Register* in 1958. A reporter who learned how to obtain information important to his readers, he wrote the revealing, penetrating *Let Them Eat Promises: The Politics of Hunger in America* in 1969. According to Kotz:

> I first saw the realities of extreme rural poverty through the eyes of my wife, Mary Lynn, on a 1960 trip to her native state of Mississippi. The insights she has given me are not ones about politics, racial conflict, or government programs, but rather the feelings of a sensitive woman on re-encountering the suffering of human beings whom she loves dearly. Working as a newspaper reporter, I saw similar suffering and injustice in Iowa, the golden breadbasket of this nation's prosperity. Returning to Mississippi and other parts of the rural South in 1967 as a Washington correspondent reporting on government programs supposedly designed to alleviate poverty, it seemed to me that the misery was worse than it had been seven years earlier.*

What Kotz presented was a disturbing piece of nonfiction, as Edward Weeks emphasized in his review:

> It strikes at the most persistent mismanagement in our federal system; it traces the root of the trouble to those agricultural states, particularly in the South,

*Nick Kotz, Let Them Eat Promises: The Politics of Hunger in America *(Englewood Cliffs, N.J.: Prentice-Hall, 1969), p. xi.*

where industrialization has driven the little farmer, black or white, off the land and into pauperism; it explodes the fallacy of paying a large landowner like Senator Eastland, who derives one profit from his fertile acres, a second for not planting other acres that might be productive. It traces the black migration north and west.†

Kotz contributed articles to various periodicals such as the *Progressive*, *Harper's*, *Look*, and *Nation*, and joined the *Washington Post* as a reporter in 1970. Two years later he and Haynes Johnson, another *Post* reporter, wrote the articles that appeared under the title "The Unions." The articles surveyed historically the problems between labor, business, and government. The articles were revised and published as the book *The Unions* in 1972.

In 1977, with his wife, Mary Lynn, Kotz wrote *A Passion for Equality: George A. Wiley and the Movement*. Eleven years later he wrote *Wild Blue Yonder: Money, Politics, and the B-1 Bomber*, which told the story of the failed attempts by the best engineers in the United States as well as Air Force strategists to design, produce, and deploy a state-of-the-art bomber. As Kotz pointed out, the reason for these failed attempts was the political bureaucratic process of procurement, not engineering. The book focused on three decades of military-industrial maneuvering — from President Eisenhower who said no to the concept to President Reagan who said yes. The muckraking book was thoroughly researched and superbly documented.

REPRESENTATIVE WORKS

Let Them Eat Promises: The Politics of Hunger in America (1969)
Wild Blue Yonder: Money, Politics, and the B-1 Bomber (1988)

Seymour Krim
(1922–1989)

Born in New York City in 1922, Seymour Krim attended the University of North Carolina for a year and then returned home, where he obtained employment as a reporter for the *New Yorker*, wrote publicity features for Paramount Pictures, and became a story editor for Otto Preminger Productions. Throughout the 1940s he earnestly desired to write the great American novel, but he realized that in the midst of intellectual giants such as Ernest Hemingway his talent as a writer could never propel him to such a height.

†*Edward Weeks, "The Peripatetic Reviewer," Atlantic (February 1970):120.*

Consequently, he became a book reviewer for the *New York Times Book Review* in 1947. This experience enabled him to move to the *Commonweal*, where he was given the opportunity to write longer, in-depth pieces. *Commentary* and the *Partisan Review* opened their pages to him. Although he did not care for writing reviews, he produced one after another until he was offered a position with the *Hudson Review*, a periodical respected by readers for its depth and quality.

Krim's experience broadened. He became an essayist of unusual merit, and a critic whose writing was published in such periodicals as the *Village Voice*.

From 1961 to 1965, Krim was the editorial director of *Nugget*, a men's magazine, and from 1965 to 1966, he was a reporter for the *New York Herald Tribune*. He taught at several universities, including the University of Iowa, Pennsylvania State University, and Columbia University. Collections of his essays appeared under the titles *Views of a Nearsighted Cannoneer* and *Shake It for the World, Smartass*.

"Revolt of the Homosexual," which Krim wrote in 1958, was quite distinct from most essays. Instead of employing the traditional form to explain his position toward the issue, Krim used what could be described as either an interview or a conversation between a heterosexual and a homosexual. By using this approach, he made his point strongly.

Krim died in 1989.

REPRESENTATIVE WORKS

Views of a Nearsighted Cannoneer (1961, 1968)
Shake It for the World, Smartass (1970)

William Lambert
(1922?–   )

Born in the early 1920s in Langford, South Dakota, William Lambert, the son of a machinist, attended public schools. When he was in high school, he moved with his parents to West Linn, Oregon. Lambert worked as a reporter for the high school newspaper and enjoyed the job so much that he desired to work as a reporter upon graduation.

Lambert realized, however, that he needed to attend college before he attempted to get a job in journalism. He found employment at a paper mill and had saved several hundred dollars — enough for at least one year of college — when World War II erupted in Europe. Lambert, a member of the

National Guard, went into the army when the National Guard was federalized in November 1940. Lambert, who entered the service as a corporal, was released five years later as a first lieutenant. He saw at least five major campaigns in the Pacific.

Upon his discharge from service, Lambert returned to Oregon, where he married his girlfriend from high school and went to work for the *Oregon City Banner-Courier*, later the *Enterprise-Courier*. Lambert was promoted to news editor before he left the paper in 1950. He joined the *Oregonian* as a police reporter the same year. Together with Wallace Turner, he wrote investigative stories, including a story about Dave Beck, the former president of the Teamsters Union who was involved with questionable individuals and businesses in the Northwest. Beck was investigated by authorities and sentenced to prison, and Lambert and Turner received the Pulitzer Prize. As a result, Lambert and Turner became witnesses before the Senate rackets subcommittee, which ultimately led to contacts in Washington, D.C.

Lambert received a Nieman Fellowship at Harvard University in 1959 as a result of the award-winning article. He attended several graduate classes in law, even though he had not attended college.

At the end of his fellowship, Lambert learned that the staff of the *Oregonian* was on strike and that Turner had gotten a job with Abraham Ribicoff in Washington, D.C. Although he was urged by Turner to get a job in Washington, Lambert went to work at a West Coast television station. Lambert realized almost immediately, however, that television was not for him. He moved to Washington, D.C., where he worked as a press agent with the Office of Education. Working on a per diem basis was not enough for him to support his family. He got a job in the Los Angeles bureau of *Time* magazine, but he was not happy there because *Time* expected precise and concise articles. He learned about *Life* magazine, specifically the freedom that its editors gave to writers who desired to investigate and report at length on controversial subjects. Lambert met with the editor and managing editor of the magazine and persuaded them to hire him as an investigative reporter.

The first major story Lambert was responsible for at *Life* was the article about Lyndon B. Johnson's fortune. Perhaps his biggest story was the incisive article that exposed the relationship between convicted stock manipulator Louis Wolfson and former U.S. Supreme Court justice Abe Fortas, which appeared in 1969. Fortas, who had been considered by President Johnson for chief justice, resigned from the Supreme Court as a result of the article.

Although Lambert received considerable accolades from his peers for the article, he continued to prowl the corridors of courthouses and state and federal buildings in search of another story.

REPRESENTATIVE WORK

Articles (*Oregonian* and *Life*)

Jeremy Larner
(1937–   )

Novelist and social reporter Jeremy Larner was born in New York City in 1937. Twenty-one years later he received his bachelor's degree from Brandeis University. He studied at the University of California at Berkeley until 1959. Although he wrote short stories and several novels, including the satirical social farce *Drive, He Said*, which was published in 1964 and ultimately made into a movie in 1970, his stories and novels had less effect on readers than his factual articles in *Dissent* on education in Harlem and poverty. These articles not only informed readers of the problems but inspired other writers to investigate the conditions and produce further findings. Some, like Larner, advocated that the problems be corrected.

In 1965, Larner's book *The Addict in the Street*, written with Ralph Tefferteller, appeared. Through interviews with certain heroin addicts, Larner and Tefferteller revealed how the addict conceived of himself and of the world in which he lived. The book was not an indictment, but an attempt to allow readers to understand the problems and conditions that addicts were forced to face. As Larner pointed out, each addict speaking was emphatically telling of his desire to be like any average middle-class American. Indeed, he longed for a wife, children, and a comfortable home, as Larner wrote: "Marriage is sacred to him; family is sacred to him; likewise God, church, and country. I'm basically a decent person, the addict insists, though the interviewer is not doubting him. This is the way I would lead my life … if only I weren't a drug addict. That's why I got to kick.— And he means it."*

Larner emphasized that society should change its methods as well as laws concerning addicts. He emphasized medical treatment and different attitudes by members of society so that the number of addicts would decline.

Larner contributed articles to such periodicals as the *Nation, Paris Review, New Republic, Partisan Review, Atlantic,* and *Evergreen Review,* among others. In addition to his essays, short stories, and novels, he wrote the insightful *Nobody Knows: Reflections on the McCarthy Campaign of 1968,* which was published in 1970.

Other books followed, including *Sex, Death and God in LA: Anthology,* which was a compilation of articles that was published in 1992.

Larner's article "Initiation for Whitey: Notes on Poverty and Riot" illustrated his forceful style of writing.

Jeremy Larner and Ralph Tefferteller, The Addict in the Street *(New York: Grove, 1964), p. 17.*

REPRESENTATIVE WORKS

The Addict in the Street (1964)
Nobody Knows: Reflections on the McCarthy Campaign of 1968 (1970)
Sex, Death and God in LA: Anthology (1992)

Thomas W. Lawson
(1857–1925)

Born on February 26, 1857, in Charlestown, Massachusetts, to Anna Maria and Thomas Lawson, who had emigrated from Nova Scotia several years before, Thomas W. Lawson was educated in public schools. When he was 12, he left school to work as an office boy in a brokerage firm in Boston. His father had died four years earlier, and his mother had struggled to keep food in the house.

Lawson learned about investing in stocks at a very early age. By the time he was 16, he was worth more than $50,000, but he lost this amount in another investment. By the time he was 20, however, he was worth several hundred thousand dollars.

When Lawson married Jeannie Augusta Goodwillie a year later, he became a broker and learned the art of dealing. He amassed a million dollars before he was 30. He also learned the importance of publicity. Lawson, who took pride in his command of the English language, was extremely influential. Although he lived and worked in Boston, he represented other financiers and corporations, including several located in New York City. In 1894 he assisted the Addicks in gaining control of the Bay State Gas Company from the Standard Oil Company. His ability at negotiation was recognized immediately by the barons of Standard Oil. For several years he was a productive ally to Standard Oil. He even became president of the Bay State Gas Company of Delaware.

In 1897, Lawson became associated with the promotion of Amalgamated Copper, which the barons of Standard Oil had created for the reorganized Anaconda mine and its related industries. The magnates of Standard Oil earned a considerable profit on the stock, which Lawson had helped sell. The stock's price soon declined, however, and thousands of investors suffered enormous losses.

Lawson's fortune was worth some $50 million by 1900, and he built "Dreamworld," a $6 million estate, outside Boston. A year later he attempted to compete against the New York Yacht Club's two vessels in the trials for the America's Cup race. His boat was almost barred by the Yacht Club. Lawson did not forget this embarrassing situation. In 1902, he joined Winfield M.

Thompson to write *The Lawson History of the America's Cup*, which disclosed his apparent grievance over how he was treated. George Warren Wilder, who was a silent partner in *Everybody's Magazine*, had learned of Lawson's unfortunate experience with the New York Yacht Club as well as his willingness to explain to the American people how business, specifically Standard Oil, Amalgamated Copper, and other companies, had manipulated and abused the system primarily for profits. Wilder mentioned Lawson to Erman Jesse Ridgway and John Adams Thayer, the other partners in *Everybody's*. The magazine's circulation was more than 150,000. A series of articles by Lawson, however, could increase circulation and attract advertisers, thus increasing the magazine's profits.

Lawson was persuaded by Ridgway and Thayer to write his articles for *Everybody's*, but he informed them that they would have to spend $50,000 in advertising the series, to which they agreed.

Before the series "Frenzied Finance" began, Lawson discussed his motives in an advertisement, which was published in the June 21, 1904, issue of the *New York Post*:

> I have unwittingly been made the instrument by which thousands upon thousands of investors in America and Europe have been plundered. I wish them to know my position as to the past, that they may acquit me of intentional wrongdoing; as to the present, that they may know that I am doing all in my power to right the wrongs that have been committed; and as to the future, that they may see how I propose to compel restitution.*

The series began in July 1904. Lawson explained how the Amalgamated Copper Company and the "system" operated in the first paragraph of the first article:

> There will be set down, in the series of articles of which this is the foreword, in as simple and direct a fashion as I can write it, The Story of Amalgamated Copper and of the "system" of which it is the most flagrant example. This "system" is a process or a device for the incubation of wealth from the people's savings in the banks, trust, and insurance companies, and the public funds. Through its workings during the last twenty years there has grown up in this country a set of colossal corporations in which unmeasured success and continued immunity from punishment have bred an insolent disregard of law, of common morality, and of public and private right, together with a grim determination to hold on to, at all hazards, the great possessions they have gulped or captured. It is the same "system" which has taken from the millions of our people billions of dollars, and given them over to a score or two of men with power to use and enjoy them as absolutely as though these billions had been earned dollar by dollar by the labor of their bodies and minds.†

Lawson later claimed that the system was at fault, not the men who had taken advantage of it, and therefore the system had to be changed. According

---

*Arthur and Lila Weinberg, The Muckrakers (New York: Simon and Schuster, 1961), p. 262.
†Thomas W. Lawson, "Frenzied Finance," Everybody's Magazine (July 1904):1.

to Lawson, the power of the system came from the money that it controlled, and insurance companies, corporations, banks, and stock exchanges had been corrupted by certain individuals. Lawson discussed his connection with the gas company wars in Boston and described the building of the copper trust. He recounted certain incidents and identified prominent men who headed businesses as wrongdoers. Lawson described midnight maneuvers as well as flights to avoid prosecution. To say the least, readers were captivated by the revelations. As a result, the circulation of *Everybody's* quadrupled; almost a million copies were selling every month in 1905.§

Lawson requested that an investigation be conducted. He also asked that legislation be enacted to regulate investment, especially between businesses. Lawson's articles were instrumental in influencing the governor of New York to appoint a committee to investigate several businesses, especially several life insurance companies. The committee was chaired by William W. Armstrong; its chief counsel was Charles Evans Hughes, who later became governor of New York and a U.S. Supreme Court justice. The committee held more than 50 public hearings in 1905 and disclosed that life insurance funds had been used improperly. A president, several vice presidents, and other officials of several companies were either indicted or forced to resign from their respective positions, and misappropriated funds were repaid by certain officials.

Eventually, changes in insurance practices occurred as a result of the committee's report. Some writers for newspapers and magazines questioned Lawson's actual motives, however. For instance, Denis Donohoe, who wrote "The Truth About Frenzied Finance" for *Public Opinion*, disclosed Lawson's unscrupulous career as a broker.

Several people who had been named in Lawson's series sued him, but when the cases went to court he was victorious.

On December 7, 1907, in various daily newspapers throughout the country Lawson, who had reveled in the publicity surrounding the series, informed readers: "Beginning January 1st, I shall allow the public to do their own reforming, and I shall devote my time and capital exclusively to my own business of stock "gambling" in Wall and State Streets — particularly Wall Street — for the purpose of recouping the millions I have donated to my public work."**

The series, which Lawson stopped writing, was published in book form and was followed in 1907 by a novel, *Friday, the Thirteenth*, which also lashed out against the stock market.

Lawson returned to making deals as a financier for the next several years. In 1912, Lawson returned to *Everybody's* as a muckraking journalist and wrote a series titled "The Remedy," which suggested certain solutions for the inherent problems found on Wall Street. Lawson believed that the distribution of

§*David Mark Chalmers*, The Social and Political Ideas of the Muckrakers (*New York: Citadel, 1964*), pp. 57–58.
**Thomas W. Lawson, "Why I Gave Up the Fight," Everybody's Magazine (February 1908):287.*

wealth in America, which was clearly uneven, was a result of the stock market. Thus, he believed that the stock market needed to be controlled so that individuals could not use it to gamble. The federal government needed to oversee the exchanges. This was his first solution. His second solution, unfortunately, was vague. Although he suggested that the real money, which was estimated to be $5 billion in savings banks, should be fairly divided, he did not necessarily explain how it was to be divided.

By this time the Pujo Committee had been formed primarily to investigate what Lawson had discussed, and Lawson's later articles in the series discussed the testimony that had been presented to the members of the committee.

Although the series did not attract as many readers as "Frenzied Finance," it attracted the interest of some members of the federal government. Indeed, a bill reflecting Lawson's suggestions was introduced into the United States Senate by Senator Henry Ashurst of New Mexico. Twenty years later, operating under the Securities Act of 1933, the Securities and Exchange Commission actually provided many of the safeguards that Lawson had requested.

The series was published in book form the same year. Other books such as *The High Cost of Living* and *The Leak* followed in 1913 and 1919, respectively. Lawson's series of articles caused numerous friends to become enemies, however, and by the time of his death in 1925 he had lost his fortune, including his estate and his car.

C. C. Regier wrote: "Lawson undoubtedly wished to pay off an old score, and it is possible that he used the sensation his articles caused to advance his personal interests in the stockmarket. On the other hand, there was a strange streak of altruism in the man, a sort of messianic eagerness to deliver the common people from what he regarded as their bondage."††

REPRESENTATIVE WORKS

"Frenzied Finance" (1904–1907)
"The Remedy" (1912)

Michael P. Lerner
(1943–   )

Born on February 7, 1943, in Newark, New Jersey, Michael Lerner was educated at Columbia University, from which he received his bachelor's degree

††C. C. Regier, The Era of the Muckrakers *(Chapel Hill: University of North Carolina Press, 1932),* p. 130.

in 1964, and at the University of California, Berkeley, from which he received his master's and doctorate in 1968 and 1972, respectively.

Active in New Left politics, Lerner was indicted as a member of the group identified by the media as the "Seattle Seven." The charges against him were dismissed, however.

In 1969, Lerner was an assistant professor of philosophy at the University of Washington in Seattle. In 1971 he wrote "Mayday: Anatomy of the Movement" for *Ramparts*, a magazine that frequently published his work. The article concerned the protest march in Washington, D.C. In particular, it concerned the divisions within the organizational structure of Mayday that affected the Mayday march of 1971. Lerner severely criticized the organizers for failing to organize a massive demonstration.

In 1972, Lerner accepted a position at Trinity College in Hartford, Connecticut; the same year he edited with David Horowitz and Craig Pyes co-edited the book *Counter-Culture and Revolution*. Lerner, an advocacy journalist as well as a professor of philosophy, believed that the New Left doctrine had not been presented coherently to the populace. Coincidentally, he believed and advocated that capitalism had to be explained more thoroughly before it could be replaced by socialism. He examined the issue in *The New Socialist Revolution*, for instance, which was published in 1973, the year he became a contributing editor to *Ramparts*, a position that lasted until the magazine folded several years later.

In 1986, Lerner founded the magazine *Tikkun* as a forum for liberal Jewish viewpoints, even though many Jews had become more conservative by the mid–1980s as a result of Israeli politics and Reagan becoming president. The journal published articles about relations between African Americans and Jews, AIDS, abortion, Israel, modernism, psychiatry, and Zionism. Contributors to the magazine included such luminaries as Annie Dillard, Jesse Jackson, Todd Gitlin, Woody Allen, Marge Piercy, and John Judis.

The same year Lerner wrote *Super Powerlessness*, in which he dealt with the "hidden" condition that inhibited Americans' fullest potential. According to Lerner, inequality existed among members of society primarily because of society's structure. For instance, most power in the United States was held by a few individuals, and most individuals had only a little power. This "powerlessness" on the part of the majority was real. "Surplus powerlessness" was the additional lack of power the majority imposed on itself; the majority of citizens did not exercise all of the options that were available to them and thus failed to gain power. In other words, most individuals, to a certain extent, failed to exert themselves; as a result, their lives at home and at work seemed monotonous or routine. This lack of hope on their part caused problems in the political arena as well, and, as Lerner pointed out, it was not power but powerlessness that caused corruption in society.

Tikkun ... to Heal, Repair and Transform the World: An Anthology, which Lerner edited, was published in 1992 and contained articles that had been published in his journal. The articles focused on various topics from AIDS to Israel.

In 1993, Lerner wrote *The Socialism of Fools: Anti-Semitism on the Left*, in which he explained that anti–Semitism existed because it was useful to those who wielded power, especially in exploitative or unequal societies. Lerner claimed that Jews had often appeared to have power over others because of their positions — from proprietors to physicians. He also claimed that anti–Semitism had never been a vital concern of the Left.

REPRESENTATIVE WORKS

Counter-Culture and Revolution (coedited with David Horowitz and Craig Pyes, 1972)
The New Socialist Revolution (1973)
Tikkun (editor)
Super Powerlessness (1986)
The Socialism of Fools: Anti-Semitism on the Left (1993)

Alfred Henry Lewis
(1857–1914)

Alfred Henry Lewis was born to Harriet Tracy and Isaac J. Lewis on January 20, 1857, in Cleveland, Ohio. He attended public schools and later studied for the bar examination, which he passed in 1876.

Lewis opened an office and quickly became involved in local politics. In 1880 he became the city's prosecuting attorney, a position he held until the following year, when he accompanied his family to Kansas City, Missouri.

Lewis eagerly worked as a cowboy on several ranches in the Cimarron region of Kansas. He enjoyed the freedom of the open spaces as well as the numerous stories that were told in front of a blazing fire. In addition to driving cattle to Dodge City and other towns, he explored the Southwest, including Texas and New Mexico, where he was hired as the editor of the *Mora County Pioneer*, a small newspaper. Lewis enjoyed journalism, especially writing. In Las Vegas, New Mexico, he served briefly as the editor of the *Las Vegas Optic*, in which he displayed an outrageous sense of humor.

After journeying to Arizona, Lewis returned to Kansas City to be with his parents. In 1885 he opened a law office and then married Alice Ewing, who was from Ohio. His brother, who was the city editor of the *Kansas City Times*, asked him to contribute a story to the paper. Lewis wrote an imaginary interview with an old cattleman who supposedly lived at the St. James' Hotel. The story, for which he was not paid, was extremely popular among readers. Lewis earned $360, however, for his next story. The old cattleman philosophized as he reminisced about his days in Wolfville, a mythical town that was actually based on Tombstone, Arizona. The stories were popular because they captured realistically the unusual characters who settled the West.

William Rockhill Nelson, the publisher of the *Kansas City Star*, hired Lewis as a reporter in 1890. A year later Lewis moved to Washington, D.C., where he worked as a correspondent for the *Chicago Times*. Lewis, a Democrat, learned about the federal government from Theodore Roosevelt, who became a close friend. In 1894 the *Chicago Times* was purchased by the *Chicago Herald*. Although Lewis was offered a position with the paper in Chicago, he accepted a job as head of the Washington bureau of William Randolph Hearst's *New York Journal*.

Lewis wrote interesting dramatic stories that resembled today's literary journalism. Indeed, those stories captured scenes, individuals, and incidents as if Lewis had been present when the events occurred. Most concerned the legislative process and how certain legislators had been manipulated by lobbyists. Lewis was not objective in his reporting; his position was quite clear and intentionally so. He was determined to reveal the truth to the reader. In addition to exposés and reform stories, he contributed investigative articles to *Cosmopolitan*, which was also published by Hearst.

Wolfville, which was published in 1897, was a compilation of "Old Cattleman" stories that had been published in various newspapers. The book, his first, was immediately successful.

A year later Lewis resigned from the Washington bureau and moved to New York City, where he edited the weekly Democratic paper the *Verdict* for more than a year. Lewis attacked the wealthy and demanded reform. He realized, as he became entrenched in New York City politics, that the corruption he had witnessed in Washington, D.C., was not isolated. Indeed, corruption was everywhere. According to David Mark Chalmers: "Lewis generally chose the 'robber barons' as his subjects. In his rococo style of extravagant hyperbole and classical references, he excoriated the Rockefellers and the Havemeyers, James Stillman, Elihu Root, Boss Platt, and the Senate of the United States."*

Lewis also knew that the common people were powerless, unless certain laws were enacted. If a particular law failed to eliminate the corruption that festered in cities, he believed that another law should be enacted, and so on, until corruption was eliminated.

When the *Verdict* ceased publication in 1900, Lewis continued his muckraking in articles for magazines. For instance, he examined the New York City Police Department and the New York City government, including Tammany

*David Mark Chalmers, The Social and Political Ideas of the Muckrakers (New York: Citadel Press, 1964), p. 35.

Hall. He investigated the corrupt politicians who had been purchased like any other commodity by the exceedingly wealthy, and condemned both in print. The information he gathered about New York City also filled several books, including *Richard Croker* (1901), *The Boss and How He Came to Rule New York* (1903), *The Confessions of a Detective* (1906), *The Apaches of New York* (1912), and *Nation-Famous New York Murders* (1914).

Lewis edited *Human Life* for about five years, until the magazine changed hands in 1911. *Human Life* published articles about muckraking journalists as well as articles that investigated the graft and corruption that routinely occurred between the barons of big business and the members of city, state, or federal government. Lewis also published fiction that entertained readers.

Before Lewis died in 1914, he had compiled five additional volumes of short stories about Wolfville and had written at least three dramatic biographies. These included *The Story of John Paul Jones* (1906), *When Men Grew Tall: The Story of Andrew Jackson* (1907), and *An American Patrician; or, The Story of Aaron Burr* (1908).

Although Lewis's reputation was based largely on his fiction, especially the "Old Cattleman" stories, his muckraking articles pleading for reform actually defined his character.

REPRESENTATIVE WORKS

Mora County Pioneer (editor)
Las Vegas Optic (editor)
Verdict (editor)
Human Life (editor)
Richard Croker (1901)
The Boss and How He Came to Rule New York (1903)

Benjamin Barr Lindsey
(1869–1943)

Judge and reformer Ben B. Lindsey was born to Letitia Anna and Landy Tunstall Lindsey on November 25, 1869, in Jackson, Tennessee. His father had served as an officer in the Confederate Army before he became a telegraph operator.

Lindsey lived in his maternal grandfather's home in Jackson until he was 11, when he moved with his parents to Denver, Colorado. His father was now a superintendent of telegraph operations. At first Lindsey attended an elementary school that was affiliated with Notre Dame University in Indiana. He returned to Tennessee two years later and lived with his maternal aunt and her husband while attending the Southwestern Baptist University, a preparatory school.

When Lindsey was 16 he returned to Denver, where his father had grown despondent over losing his job and not being able to support his family. He committed suicide, leaving Lindsey and his younger brother to care for the family. Lindsey worked at several jobs, including serving as an office boy, and read law books in his spare time, but the numerous jobs prevented him from attending high school.

Lindsey grew depressed and at 19 attempted suicide. It took several months for him to face life's many obstacles. With the assistance of one of his employers, a lawyer, he prepared for the bar examination. In 1894 he passed the examination and was subsequently admitted to the bar at the age of 24. His practice, which produced a modest income, was stimulated when he worked for the Democratic party, which in 1899 helped him secure the position of public guardian and administrator. Two years later he was appointed judge of a county court.

Judge Ben B. Lindsey became extremely well known for his untiring efforts on behalf of children and families. Indeed, his court evolved into the Juvenile and Family Court of Denver, the best-known court of its kind in the United States, if not the world, within five years. Legislators as well as reformers from all over the world wrote to him, seeking his advice.

Lindsey drafted revolutionary legislation for children's rights in Colorado. In 1903, for instance, he drafted the Colorado Adult Delinquency Act, which stated that adults who contributed to the delinquency of a minor were legally responsible. In 1904 he described the "Lindsey Bills" in the booklet *The Problem of the Children and How the State of Colorado Cares for Them*. This booklet, together with his ability to mobilize public opinion, led to the bills being adopted in various states, not just in Colorado. Lindsey believed that children were children and behaved accordingly, not like adults. Thus he was convinced that children who misbehaved deserved a second chance. He emphasized probation in his court, not confinement. From experience he knew that other reasons sometimes existed for children's unlawful behavior. For instance, he had learned from observation that economic injustice was the major cause of crime, especially by children. He believed, however, that children needed to be punished for committing crimes. For example, he would send an "incorrigible" youth to detention school, but he would not necessarily have an escort accompany the youth. He instead relied on the youth's word that he or she would attend detention school.

As word spread about Lindsey, numerous writers from national magazines traveled to Denver to observe him in court and to interview him about his revolutionary methods. These articles appeared in magazines such as the *Arena, Independent, Literary Digest, Outlook,* and *World Today.*

Lincoln Steffens, who was writing for *McClure's* at the time, arrived in Denver in 1906 and interviewed Lindsey at length. "The Just Judge," a series of three articles that applauded and endorsed Lindsey's efforts, was the result.

Perhaps as a result of the increasing publicity and his overwhelming popularity, Lindsey broke with the Democratic party to run for governor on the Independent ticket. Although he lost the election, he remained judge of the court. He realized that this position was now tenuous. After all, neither major party would endorse him for judge in the next election.

In 1908, before the election, Lindsey joined forces with Ellis Meredith, a professional writer, to write a booklet called *The Rule of Plutocracy in Colorado*, which explained that the public utilities corporations in the state had manipulated the Democratic and Republican parties. Needless to say, Lindsey, the muckraker, was not endorsed by either party, just as he expected, but he ran for the judgeship as an Independent and won the election.

The same year Upton Sinclair, a muckraking journalist who had written *The Jungle*, arrived in Denver on his way to California. Sinclair had read about Lindsey and desired to meet him. Lindsey gave Sinclair a copy of his booklet. When Sinclair had finished reading it, he told Lindsey that he would telegraph John O'Hara Cosgrave, the editor of *Everybody's*, and inform him about the booklet. Lindsey gave his permission.

In 1909, Harvey O'Higgins, who worked for Cosgrave, arrived in Denver and helped Lindsey expand and improve the booklet in two ways. As Charles E. Larsen wrote:

> First, the account was transformed from a rather tediously detailed record of backstairs political deals into a semi-autobiography of Judge Lindsey. In keeping with this new stress on human interest, the harmful influence of "the System" on the lives of children was also emphasized.... Secondly, with a view to appealing to audiences all over the country, the revised and expanded version forcefully reminded the reader that "the System" was a national evil and not merely a Colorado phenomenon.*

The series "The Beast and the Jungle" was published in *Everybody's* from November 1909 to May 1910, then in book form the same year. Some writers called the series and book the best piece of muckraking ever published. Walter Lippmann, for instance, praised Lindsey for relating the need for social reform to the protection of children in his *A Preface to Politics*, which was published in 1913.

Lindsey's belief that power had to be given to the populace in order for democracy to work led him to advocate specific reforms, including effective regulation of public utilities. The series appeared at a time when muckraking

---

Charles E. Larsen, Introduction to The Beast, *by Ben B. Lindsey and Harvey J. O'Higgins (Seattle: University of Washington Press, 1970), p. xix.*

journalists had revealed numerous abuses by corporations and readers were eager to learn about other wrongs.

Lindsey became concerned with child labor, women's suffrage, and prison reform, particularly the abolition of corporal punishment. In 1912 he aided in the formation of the Progressive party in Colorado and witnessed the state legislature enact a direct primary election law, an improved child labor law, and legislation that protected women who worked.

In 1913, Lindsey married Henrietta Brevoort, who helped him in his work.

A year later, with Edwin Markham and George Creel, he wrote *Children in Bondage*, which exposed how children had been exploited by employers. According to the authors, legislation was needed to protect children in the workplace. The book, which was based on muckraking articles that had been published in magazines, reflected the views of the National Child Labor Committee, which had been organized in 1904, primarily for the purpose of campaigning against the use of children in the workplace.

The authors pointed out that the Committee had been successful in obtaining the passage of certain laws. The authors had concerns, however, and wrote:

> The Committee does not look upon these legislative measures as ideal, for the laws thus far proposed would exclude children under 14 years from the ordinary gainful occupations, whereas all the evidence we have been able to gather during the past nine years supports the belief that children should not be employed in wage-earning occupations under 16 years of age, and that compulsory school attendance should uniformly be extended to 16 years.†

Before 1920, Lindsey had campaigned for Woodrow Wilson as well as for the reforms mentioned above. In the 1920s he encountered various problems in his court and consequently became engaged in the sexual revolution. Indeed, he advocated sex education in schools, birth control, and companionate marriages. Then, when his views were attacked by certain religious leaders, he countered by confronting religious fundamentalists and their antiquated beliefs.

In 1925, in collaboration with Wainwright Evans, Lindsey wrote *The Revolt of Modern Youth*, which was based on a series of articles that had been published in Bernarr Macfadden's *Physical Culture Magazine*. The book discussed the current laws and practices pertaining to divorce, alimony, and birth control. It also examined the age-old problem that young people faced: sexual intercourse before marriage. Lindsey discussed trial marriages. The book was criticized by members of the clergy for its apparent endorsement of trial marriages.

---

†*Edwin Markham, Benjamin B. Lindsey, and George Creel,* Children in Bondage *(New York: Arno and the New York Times, 1969), pp. 10–11.*

Lindsey and Evans wrote *The Companionate Marriage* in 1927. Based on a series of articles that had been written for *Red Book Magazine*, this book examined some of the issues that had been discussed in the previous book. Indeed, Lindsey advocated legal marriages with legalized birth control. He also advocated that married childless couples should have the right to divorce by mutual consent. He believed that alimony should not have to be paid in such divorces.

The book was criticized for its proposals, but it was translated into several foreign languages, and Lindsey debated the proposals all over the country. In 1927 his 1924 electoral victory was reversed when the supreme court of Colorado invalidated every vote in a Jewish precinct. Two years later he was disbarred for practicing law while serving as a judge.

Lindsey moved to California a year later, where he practiced law. In 1931, with Rube Borough, he wrote *The Dangerous Life*, which tied *The Companionate Marriage* and *The Revolt of Modern Youth* into an historical context. According to Lindsey,

> "The Dangerous Life" deals with the hazards which one man faced in opposing its reactionary elements of intrenched institutionalism — ecclesiastical, legal, economic. It is hardly necessary to point out that, though enemies were inevitable in such a struggle, I hold no personal bitterness toward them. After all, my war was not against people, individually or collectively. It was against the evils of a social system.§

Lindsey drafted new proposals, including the statute that established the Children's Court of Conciliation in 1939, which attempted to save marriages through professional counseling.

Lindsey was reelected to the bench in 1940 and presided over the court until his death three years later.

Even though he was first and foremost a judge, Lindsey was also a muckraker who advocated reform. He contributed investigatory articles to magazines and wrote controversial nonfiction books. Many of his ideas, some of which were considered too liberal for the times, were eventually adopted by state legislatures and enacted into law.

REPRESENTATIVE WORKS

The Problem of the Children and How the State of Colorado Cares for Them (1904)
The Rule of Plutocracy in Colorado (1908)
"The Beast and the Jungle" (1909–1910)
The Beast (1910)
Children in Bondage (1914)
The Revolt of Youth (1925)
The Companionate Marriage (1927)

§*Ben B. Lindsey and Rube Borough,* The Dangerous Life *(New York: Arno, 1974), p. xiv.*

H. D. Lloyd
(1847–1903)

Henry Demarest Lloyd preceded the muckraking days by several years. In fact, when he died in 1903, muckraking journalism was just beginning to excite readers of such magazines as *McClure's, Saturday Evening Post, Everybody's, Cosmopolitan, Munsey's, McCall's, American Magazine, Outlook, Century, Collier's Weekly, Ladies' Home Journal, Harper's,* and *Atlantic.*

Lloyd, who was born in 1847, received a master's degree from Columbia in 1869, was admitted to the New York bar, and for the next few years engaged in political reform. In 1871, for example, he campaigned against Tammany Hall; a year later he campaigned for free trade and against the liberal Republicans' nomination of Horace Greeley. When he realized that newspapers could help him in his crusades, he accepted a position at the *Chicago Tribune.* Immediately, his convincing arguments against monopolies were read by thousands.

William Dean Howells, the editor of the *Atlantic,* accepted in 1881 Lloyd's exposé of the Standard Oil Company, which preceded Ida Tarbell's investigative report by 22 years.

Four years later Lloyd left the *Tribune* and sailed abroad to study similar corporations in England. When he returned, he wrote *A Strike of Millionaires Against Miners,* which was published in 1890. Out of his convictions for the laboring class, he organized the Milwaukee street-car workers and then defended Eugene Debs, who had organized the 1894 Pullman strike. *Wealth Against Commonwealth,* his completely documented pronouncement against monopolies, appeared the same year.

From 1897 to 1901, Lloyd traveled throughout Europe. His findings and observations were explicitly incorporated in *Labour Copartnership* and *Newest England,* which were published in 1898 and 1900, respectively. *A Country Without Strikes,* which concerned New Zealand's laws on industrial management and labor confrontations, was published in 1900, and *A Sovereign People* was published posthumously in 1907.

Unquestionably, Lloyd paved the way for those journalists who were interested primarily in raising eyebrows or causing corporate leaders, politicians, judges, and others in comfortable positions to squirm. After all, as Chester McArthur pointed out, "Lloyd crusaded for untrammeled intellectuality, honest politics, against special privilege, for genuine business competition or government ownership where this was unrealizable, for ... social conscience, for industrial democracy and civil rights for the underprivileged, and for economic and social justice to be achieved by a new, positive democracy."*

*Chester McArthur, Henry Demarest Lloyd and the Empire of Reform *(Philadelphia: University of Pennsylvania Press, 1963), p. 1.*

REPRESENTATIVE WORKS

A Strike of Millionaires Against Miners (1890)
Wealth Against Commonwealth (1890)
Labour Copartnership (1898)
Newest England (1900)
A Country Without Strikes (1900)
A Sovereign People (1907)

Samuel Sidney McClure
(1857–1949)

Samuel Sidney McClure was born on February 17, 1857, to Elizabeth and Thomas McClure, in Frocess, County Antrim, Ireland. When McClure was eight, his father, a carpenter, fell to his death while working at a Clydesdale shipyard. His mother toiled on the small farm the family owned, but she was not able to feed four boys. A year later she moved her family to the United States and settled on a small farm near Valparaiso, Indiana, where two of her brothers and two of her sisters lived.

McClure, who had been an exceptional student in Ireland, attended public schools. In 1867 his mother married Thomas Simpson, another immigrant from Ireland. Although the family increased in number over the next few years, they did not live in poverty. McClure was sent to the high school in Valparaiso and worked when he was not attending classes. When his stepfather died of typhoid in 1873, McClure returned to the farm, which he and his brothers operated successfully.

In 1874, McClure was urged by an uncle to attend Knox College in Illinois. He enrolled in the preparatory school and then the college, where he exhibited not only his intellectual ability but his varied interests. He edited the *Knox Student*, published an intercollegiate news bulletin, and organized the Western College Associated Press. He also worked on a farm to earn enough to live.

McClure studied the classics as well as the sciences. He met Harriet Hurd, the daughter of a professor, and became infatuated with her beauty. Their courtship was discouraged, however, by Harriet's parents, who believed that McClure, the son of an immigrant, was not suitable for their daughter.

McClure's mother also was opposed to the relationship. She persuaded him to accompany her to Ireland, where she insisted he remain. McClure's love for Harriet was too strong, however, for him to remain in Ireland. When his mother returned to the United States, he found employment aboard a steamer. Within a few weeks he was in Illinois.

Harriet's father was determined to end the relationship. When Harriet graduated, she was sent to Massachusetts. McClure, who had another year of classes, remained in Illinois.

When he graduated in 1882, he immediately traveled to see Harriet, who was visiting friends in Marcy, New York. She explained to him that she did not love him and that their relationship was over. McClure, heartbroken, traveled to Boston, where he was hired to edit the *Wheelman*, a magazine published by Albert Pope, a bicycle manufacturer. The first issue was published in August 1882. McClure corresponded with Harriet, who now admitted that she did love him. They were married on September 4, 1883, much to the chagrin of her parents, especially her father.

McClure left the bicycle manufacturing company the following year to accept a position at the DeVinne printing company in New York City. He was dissatisfied with his position, however, and moved to the *Century* magazine, where he soon proposed specific changes, including a literary syndicate, to his superiors. McClure was politely informed that he should start his own business.

McClure left *Century* and started a literary syndicate in his apartment. His idea was simple: he would offer literature, including short stories and novels by well-known writers, to various newspapers at a very low cost. McClure visited writers and newspaper editors and then mailed announcements about his syndicate on October 4, 1884.

The enterprise nearly collapsed in the early months, but McClure persisted. By the end of the first year, he had secured enough newspapers to attract additional writers, who, in turn, attracted editors at other newspapers.

Within two years McClure's enterprise was too much for him to handle alone. He persuaded John Phillips, a friend from Knox College who had worked with him at the *Wheelman*, to help him. Phillips, unlike McClure, was extremely organized, and he applied a functional system to the office. This competency assured McClure that he could travel in search of new writers and newspapers. Indeed, he sailed to Europe and then journeyed across the United States. He procured work by various writers. As a result of selling literature to newspapers, McClure changed journalism in America.

McClure contemplated publishing a magazine. He discussed the idea with Phillips, who contributed a major investment of $4,500. McClure invested $2,800. The first issue of *McClure's* appeared in May 1893, during the panic in which banks had little cash. Of the 20,000 copies printed, 12,000 went unsold, and the magazine faced an uncertain future. In order to keep the magazine alive, McClure persuaded others to invest in the periodical or to purchase advertising space. Within a year *McClure's* had attracted thousands of subscribers and numerous advertisers. His magazine, which cost 15 cents, was less expensive than most periodicals.

When McClure persuaded Ida Tarbell, whom he had met in Paris, to write a biography of Napoleon, which began in the November 1894 issue, the magazine attracted additional readers and consequently advertisers. In fact, the circulation had doubled by the time the last article in the series was published. Tarbell joined the staff and wrote a series about Abraham Lincoln, which was also successful in helping the magazine attract new readers. McClure also published fiction by Robert Louis Stevenson, Anthony Hope, Rudyard Kipling, and other writers.

McClure approached Frank Doubleday about publishing books. This partnership published several works, including Tarbell's biography of Abraham Lincoln, before Doubleday grew tired of working with McClure and left to form another company.

The magazine, on the other hand, experienced increased circulation. McClure intuitively knew what Americans desired to read. By 1900 the circulation was almost 400,000.

Lincoln Steffens joined the staff a year later. Although he was hired as a managing editor, McClure immediately realized that Steffens was not suited for the position and suggested that he travel across the country and learn about society.

The course of magazine journalism was altered with the January 1903 issue, which contained "The Shame of Minneapolis" by Steffens, a chapter of the history of Standard Oil by Tarbell, and "The Right to Work" by Ray Stannard Baker, who had joined the staff in 1898. These articles, which exposed corrupt capitalists and politicians, represented what Theodore Roosevelt would call "muckraking" journalism in 1906. In an editorial, McClure claimed that all three articles might have been called "The American Contempt of Law."

Because of the issue's success, McClure continued to publish investigative articles by Tarbell, Baker, Steffens, and others. Unfortunately, McClure's grandiose schemes of expanding the magazine and starting a publishing company, life insurance company, and a bank caused Phillips to sell his interest in the magazine and leave. Steffens, Baker, Tarbell, and several other staff members left with him.

McClure hired George Kibbe Turner, C. P. Connolly, and Burton J. Hendrick as writers and Will Irwin as a managing editor. Turner wrote about vice and political corruption in 1907 and about Tammany Hall two years later. Connolly exposed the copper barons of Montana in 1906 and 1907. Hendrick explored the life insurance companies in 1906 and 1907 as well as the "Great American Fortunes" in 1907 and 1908. Will Irwin, who disagreed with McClure over editorial policy, left after a year. Although the magazine continued to expose corruption and graft, its circulation declined.

In 1911, Cameron Mackenzie and Frederick Lewis Collins purchased the magazine. Mackenzie departed in 1915, and Collins hired Charles Hanson Towne as managing editor. The magazine prospered under the Collins-Towne editorship, primarily because it catered to popular tastes. Muckraking articles were passé. Readers were not interested in learning about corruption.

The magazine's circulation increased to more than 500,000 in 1918 but declined a year later. Collins sold his interest in the magazine to Herbert Kaufman. Unfortunately, the circulation continued to decline, and the number of advertisers decreased. In 1921 bankruptcy was declared. Moody B. Gates, the publisher of *People's Home Journal*, purchased the magazine and hired McClure as editor. McClure, who had traveled to Europe during World War I, edited the magazine until 1926, when William Randolph Hearst purchased it. The magazine changed dramatically under Hearst and later was combined with the magazine *Smart Set*. The magazine ceased publication in 1930.

McClure's wife died the same year, but he lived another 19 years, residing primarily in New York City. He died in 1949.

First and foremost, McClure was interested in selling magazines. To do this he published muckraking articles that exposed corruption. These articles informed the citizenry, and as a result, some individuals called for legislation. In essence, he was indirectly responsible for the Progressive movement because his magazine illuminated the various crimes that had been committed by businesses, politicians, and private citizens.

REPRESENTATIVE WORK

McClure's (publisher and editor)

Dwight Macdonald
(1906–1982)

Dwight Macdonald, a critic who severely attacked Tom Wolfe's essay on the *New Yorker* in the mid–1960s, was born in New York City in 1906, and attended the Collegiate School, the Barnard School for Boys, the Phillips Exeter Academy, and Yale University, from which he graduated in 1928. Although he majored in history, he wrote extensively for several university publications, including two he edited.

A year after he graduated Macdonald was employed as a writer on the forthcoming Henry R. Luce publication *Fortune*, which appeared in 1930, and for seven years he wrote capitalistic articles concerning America's businesses and industries.

In 1937, Macdonald made an ironical move to the newly revamped *Partisan Review*. Founded by William Phillips and Philip Rahv in 1934, the original

Review was the foremost radical magazine for the creative Left. According to Frederick J. Hoftman, Charles Allen, and Carolyn F. Ubrich: "One of its chief aims was to provide a place for creative writing of leftist character, which was gradually being crowded out of *The New Masses* by the urgent demands of political and economic discussion. It began in New York City as a 'John Reed Club' publication — one of many established throughout the country to put the convictions of John Reed into practical action."*

The magazine combined with *The Anvil* in 1936 and became somewhat politically independent.

"The contents of the magazine changed. Disillusioned, the Party die-hards left, to concentrate their attention upon *The New Masses* and other orthodox journals. Contributions to *The Partisan Review* became ... more definitely literary and critical, less polemic, the political discussions confined to the editorial columns or incorporated into the points of view of certain critics and essayists. The magazine ... emphasized the "Trotskyist" position — world revolution, opposition to nationalism, and definite disapproval of Stalinist policies."†

While Macdonald was an editor and writer with the *Review,* he began writing for other publications, including the *New International, Nation, Harper's,* and *New Yorker.*

In 1943, Macdonald left the *Review* over a dispute concerning World War II. As he wrote in *Memoirs of a Revolutionist*: "After Pearl Harbor Rahv and Phillips had come to feel it was their war and their country, while I had remained disaffected. They wanted to reduce the magazine's political content and concentrate on literary criticism, while I wanted to continue the mixture as before."§

Macdonald published the first issue of *Politics* about six months later. This magazine, first a monthly then a quarterly, mirrored Macdonald's changing philosophy. From Marxism to empiricism, individualism, estheticism, and moralism, he wrote articles that questioned man's inability to progress without his need or desire to harm. The magazine published such writers as Bruno Bettelheim, Andrea Caffi, Albert Camus, Lewis Coser, Paul Goodman, Peter Gutman, Victor Serge, Simone Weil, and George Woodcock. Unfortunately, the magazine failed to earn a profit, and Macdonald ceased publishing it in 1949. He was also more interested in writing than in publishing. His book *Henry Wallace, the Man and the Myth* had appeared a year before.

In 1951, Macdonald became a staff writer for the *New Yorker,* where he remained until 1966. His book *The Ford Foundation: The Men and the Millions,*

**Frederick J. Hoftman, Charles Allen, and Carolyn F. Ubrich,* The Little Magazine: A History and a Bibliography *(Princeton, N.J.: Princeton University Press, 1947), pp. 166–67.*
†*Ibid., p. 168.*
§*Dwight Macdonald,* Memoirs of a Revolutionist: Essays in Political Criticism *(New York: Farrar, Straus and Cudahy, 1957), p. 25.*

which was published in 1956, was an expansion of several provocative articles he had written concerning the philanthropic organization. In addition to his articles for the *New Yorker*, which were ultimately collected and published in several volumes, he became the movie critic for *Esquire* in 1960, a position he held until 1966, when he became the magazine's political columnist.

Throughout much of the 1970s, Macdonald contributed to numerous magazines and taught in several universities. He died in 1982.

REPRESENTATIVE WORKS

Politics (1943–1949)
Henry Wallace, the Man and the Myth (1948)
The Ford Foundation: The Men and the Millions (1956)

David McReynolds
(1929–   )

David McReynolds was born on October 25, 1929, and was educated at the University of California, Los Angeles, from which he received his bachelor's degree in 1953.

A socialist as well as a pacifist, McReynolds held a number of jobs, including typist, ditch digger, shipping clerk, meter reader, and operator of a hot dog stand, before he became an editorial secretary at the offices of *Liberation* magazine. He served as an editorial board member from 1957 to 1967. In 1960 he became field secretary of the War Resisters League in New York City and wrote articles for the *WRL News*. From 1986 to 1988, he served as chair of the War Resisters International.

Involved in various organizations, particularly those that reflected his political views, McReynolds became an advocate of the Left and contributed to several periodicals, including *Fellowship*, *Mankind*, *New America*, *Village Voice*, *WIN*, and *Liberation*. In "Notes on Another Death — And Our Shadowed Future," for instance, which appeared in the *Village Voice* in 1968, McReynolds insisted that Robert F. Kennedy's death was merely part of a pattern that had surfaced in America.

In 1970, McReynold's book *We Have Been Invaded by the 21st Century: A Radical View of the Sixties* was published. In a compilation of articles that had appeared in the *Village Voice* and *Liberation*, McReynolds explored such issues as civil rights, Vietnam, homosexuality, and, of course, the New Left. Several articles concerned other countries. Unfortunately, these articles lacked a careful analysis of the countries' politics. Overall, however, the book was satisfying to most reviewers. Philip G. Altbach wrote, "Indeed, one of the remarkable things about this book is that McReynolds seems to have maintained a consistent moral and political position throughout a period of tremendous change."*

In describing McReynolds's style of writing in these advocating articles, Paul Goodman noted, "It is halfway between literature and politics, more 'committed' than partisan, more existentialist than analytic or programmatic, too honest to be propaganda, too personal and passional to be mere reportage, too journalistic to have much theoretical exploration or poetic depth."†

REPRESENTATIVE WORK

We Have Been Invaded by the 21st Century: A Radical View of the Sixties (1970)

Carey McWilliams
(1905–1980)

Carey McWilliams was born in 1905 in Colorado, where he attended public schools. He earned a law degree at the University of Southern California in 1927 and was admitted to the state bar the same year. From 1922 to 1938, he practiced law; during the same period he became engrossed in the problems of California's migratory workers, who were underfed, underpaid, and overworked by their employers. McWilliams, a staunch supporter of collective ownership, was denounced by the California's Associated Farmers. In 1939, Governor Culbert Olson appointed him commissioner of immigration and housing. That same year his exposé on labor conditions in California, particularly the conditions concerning migratory workers, appeared. Titled *Factories in the Field*, the book disturbed people from coast to coast, and the Associated Farmers organization decided to support Earl Warren's campaign for governor. Much to McWilliams surprise, Warren won the election, and McWilliams was immediately dismissed.

For the next several years, McWilliams devoted his time to writing. In 1942, for instance, *Ill Fares the Land: Migrants and Migratory Labor in the United States* appeared. Similar to *Factories in the Field*, the book explored the

---

*Philip G. Altbach, "Radical Pacifist," Progressive (December 1970):45.
†Paul Goodman, Introduction to We Have Been Invaded by the 21st Century: A Radical View of the Sixties, by David McReynolds (New York: Praeger, 1970), p. xv.

technological advancements in farming and the subsequent ruination of migratory laborers. In 1943, *Brothers Under the Skin*, a controversial book in which McWilliams explored and deplored racial discrimination in America, was published. A year later *Prejudice: Japanese-Americans, Symbol of Racial Intolerance* appeared.

In 1945, McWilliams became a contributing editor to the *Nation*, a position he held until 1951, when he was promoted to associate editor. Within a year he was promoted to editorial director. From 1955 to 1975, he served as the magazine's editor. He also wrote numerous exposé articles and books. His performance as editor, however, was extraordinary and the decisions he made had perhaps a greater effect on readers than any of his articles or books.

Like several editors before him, McWilliams published social criticism and controversial muckraking articles during the 1950s and 1960s, when other editors at other magazines often overlooked both forms of writing.

McWilliams introduced readers to such muckrakers as Ralph Nader, Fred J. Cook, Joseph Goulden, and Robert Sherrill. He was responsible for Hunter S. Thompson's article on the Hell's Angels, an article that earned Thompson a contract for a book about the outlaws of California.

McWilliams died in 1980.

REPRESENTATIVE WORKS

Factories in the Field (1939)
Ill Fares the Land: Migrants and Migratory Labor in the United States (1942)
Brothers Under the Skin (1943)
Prejudice: Japanese-Americans, Symbol of Racial Intolerance (1944)
Nation (editor)

Gene Marine
(1926–   )

Born in San Francisco in 1926, Gene Marine attended San Francisco State University in the late 1940s and worked intermittently from 1951 to 1962 in various positions, including news analyst, public affairs and program director, and news director at a radio station in Berkeley. From 1957 to 1959 he was an associate editor at *Frontier* magazine in Los Angeles, and from 1966 to 1969 he was a senior editor at *Ramparts* in San Francisco. From 1962 to 1964 he was involved in California politics, first as a campaign manager, then as a member of CBS's news staff. He also served as the *Nation's* West Coast correspondent for 10 years. These years of experience enabled him to become a freelance editor and writer in 1969. Although he contributed hundreds of articles to numerous periodicals, his best investigative exposés appeared in such books as *America the Raped*, *The Black Panthers*, and *Food Pollution*, which was co-authored by Judith Van Allen.

Marine, who was influenced by Carey McWilliams of the *Nation*, tried in his articles and books to dismiss stereotypes and replace them with facts. He wrote:

> I am most concerned about power that is wielded in the pursuit of private profit —
> even when, as is sometimes the case, those who wield the power don't under-
> stand what they're doing — and especially in the manipulation of popular think-
> ing that accompanies that pursuit. For example: Major networks, newspapers, and
> magazines often discuss serious issues, but most always confine their discussions
> within acceptable ideological boundaries — depriving Americans of the chance
> to hear other approaches. This doesn't make Walter Cronkite venal; he is merely
> conventional. I like books because they give me freedom to tell the truth, which
> I try to do in a language as clear as is within my command, avoiding political
> jargon that is as stereotyped as the ideas it would combat.*

Marine's first book *America the Raped*, which explored in-depth the ecological problems caused by technological progress, was timid in its approach. Seldom was forceful language used to get the author's message across. Whether this approach was appropriate for the topic could be debated. Like *The Black Panthers* and *Food Pollution*, however, it was an honest account of an often distorted subject and therefore an important thought-provoking study.

In 1972, Marine wrote *A Male Guide to Women's Liberation*.

REPRESENTATIVE WORKS

America the Raped (1969)
The Black Panthers (1969)
Food Pollution (1972)

John Marks
(1943–   )

John Marks was born to Doris and David Marks on February 21, 1943, in Orange, New Jersey, and attended Cornell University, from which he received his bachelor's degree in 1965.

*Jane A. Bowden, ed., Contemporary Authors, vol. 65–68 (Detroit: Gale Research, 1977), p. 387.

Marks was hired by the U.S. State Department in 1966 and served in the Foreign Service. "My first assignment was to have been London, but with my draft board pressing for my services, the State Department advised me that the best way to stay out of uniform was to go to Vietnam as a civilian advisor in the so-called pacification program," he wrote.*

Marks reluctantly agreed and served in Vietnam almost two years. When he returned he was assigned to the Bureau of Intelligence and Research, where he was introduced to the world of espionage. "Here I found the same kind of waste and inefficiency I had come to know in Vietnam and, even worse, the same sort of reasoning that had led the country into Vietnam in the first place," he wrote.†

In 1970, after the United States invaded Cambodia, thus escalating the war, Marks left the State Department. He was hired as an executive assistant to Senator Clifford Case of New Jersey, who opposed the war. Marks met Victor Marchetti, who had served in the U.S. Army in Germany during the early years of the cold war. When Marchetti left the service, he attended Pennsylvania State University, where he majored in history. He joined the Central Intelligence Agency (CIA) in 1955 and over the years became one of the agency's leading authorities on the Soviet Union. He served as a staff officer in the office of the director of the CIA, where he held several important positions, including executive assistant to the deputy director. Marchetti grew disillusioned with the agency when he realized what the agency's primary function was. He wrote: "The CIA did not ... function primarily as a central clearinghouse and producer of national intelligence for the government. Its basic mission was that of clandestine operations, particularly covert action — the secret intervention in the internal affairs of other nations."§

Marchetti attempted to expose the agency in a book, but before he wrote one word the agency and the federal government suppressed his efforts. Indeed, he was fighting both entities when he met Marks. He explained to Marks, who had a similar interest in intelligence, what had happened and in 1972 asked him to cowrite the book.

Although *The CIA and the Cult of Intelligence* was ultimately published in 1974, most, if not all, of the passages had to be screened by someone at the CIA. Few books had actually been written about the agency. Fewer still had revealed its internal mechanics. As one reviewer of the book noted: "For the increasing numbers of concerned citizens who vaguely feel they are being conned by government this book will be clarifying and infuriating. It destroys the CIA official cover story, that it has replaced its spies, adventurers, and assassins with rows of Princeton graduates reading foreign newspapers."**

---

*Victor Marchetti and John D. Marks, The CIA and the Cult of Intelligence (New York: Alfred A. Knopf, 1974), p. xiv.
†Ibid.
§Ibid., p. xii.
**Richard J. Barnet, "Killers and Jokers," New York Review of Books, October 3, 1974, p. 29.

Although Marks and Marchetti had hoped that the book would cause some members of Congress to write and pass legislation that would curtail the agency's apparent function, this did not happen. To this day, CIA operatives work in a climate based on paranoia.

From 1974 to 1978, Marks worked as an associate and then as project director at the Center for National Security Studies in Washington, D.C. While there, he wrote another exposé, *The CIA File*, which appeared in 1976.

From 1979 until 1981, Marks was at Harvard University, where he was first a fellow at the Institute of Politics of the John F. Kennedy School of Government and then a visiting scholar at the law school as well as a research associate of the Harvard Negotiation Project.

In 1979, Marks wrote *The Search for the "Manchurian Candidate,"* another lengthy exposé that examined CIA counterintelligence operations in the United States during the 1950s and 1960s. Marks detailed abuses, especially drug experiments and shock treatments that were part of the CIA's efforts to achieve mind control. He claimed that such activities threatened civil liberties. In 1980, Marks received an award from the organization Investigative Reporters and Editors.

Before Marks founded Search for Common Ground in Washington, D.C., in 1982, he worked as a consultant to the Union of Concerned Scientists.

Marks contributed articles to various publications, including *Playboy*, *Saturday Review*, *Rolling Stone*, and *Ramparts*.

REPRESENTATIVE WORKS

The CIA and the Cult of Intelligence (with Victor Marchetti, 1974)
The CIA File (1976)
The Search for the "Manchurian Candidate" (1979)

Karl Marx
(1818–1883)

Karl Heinrich Marx was born on May 5, 1818, in Trier, Prussia (now Germany), to parents who were Jewish and were descended from rabbis. His father, Heinrich, was baptized in the Evangelical Established Church, however, before his son was born.

Marx was encouraged by his father, a lawyer, to get a good education. When Marx completed high school in Trier, he attended the University of Bonn, where he studied history and Greek and Roman mythology for a year.

In October 1836 he enrolled at the University of Berlin, where he studied philosophy and law. Although he had been baptized when he was six, he grew disillusioned with Christianity when he enrolled in a course that concerned the prophet Isaiah. The course was taught by Bruno Bauer, who proclaimed that the Christian Gospels were mere fantasies and that Jesus had not lived. Before Bauer was dismissed from the university in 1839, he had influenced numerous impressionable students, including Marx. Marx continued his studies at the University of Jena, where he received his doctorate in 1841.

Marx contributed to the *Rheinische Zeitung*, a liberal democratic newspaper that had been founded in Cologne. Before 1843, Marx had become editor of the newspaper and was writing editorials about societal and economic issues, including communism. Under Marx's editorship, the newspaper was outspoken — so much so that the authorities suppressed it a year later.

In 1843, Marx married Jenny von Westphalen. The couple moved to Paris, where he studied socialism and communism and edited, with Arnold Ruge, the short-lived review, *Deutsch-Franzo-sische Jahrbucher* ("German-French Yearbooks"). Marx met Friedrich Engels, a contributor to the review, who was the son of a wealthy manufacturer. Although they would become collaborators, Marx offended the authorities by calling for an "uprising of the proletariat" and was subsequently expelled from France before they could contribute any collaborative articles to the review.

In 1845, Marx was living in Brussels. Engels, whose views were similar, also moved there. In 1845, they wrote *Die heilige Familie* (*The Holy Family*), which concerned Hegelian idealism and Bruno Bauer. They polemicized against Pierre-Joseph Proudhon, a French socialist, in *Misère de la Philosophie* (*The Poverty of Philosophy*), which was published in 1847.

One year later Marx and Engels wrote the *Manifesto of the Communist Party* for the Communist League, which was based in London. The *Manifesto* discussed from a historical perspective the differences between the classes and asserted that communism would put an end to classes forever.

Marx moved to Paris before the Belgian authorities could expel him. Then he moved to Cologne, where he edited the controversial communist newspaper *Neve Rheinische Zeitung* in the midst of a revolution that was sweeping several countries in Europe. He advocated a war with Russia as well as the nonpayment of taxes, for which he was indicted. Although he was acquitted, he was expelled from Prussia.

In 1849, Marx and his family moved to London, where he joined the Communist League. In addition to writing speeches and articles that advocated revolutionary associations, he and Engels wrote articles and essays on other topics for periodicals.

Marx and his family were extremely poor. Indeed, in 1850 they were evicted for not paying their rent, and several of his children died during the next few years. Of course, to Marx, his family's financial plight could be blamed on the "bourgeois."

In 1851, Charles A. Dana, the managing editor of the *New York Daily Tribune*, asked Marx to become a correspondent. Dana, who had been introduced to Marx in Cologne several years earlier and had learned about Marx's ideas, realized that Marx would be perfect for the position. At the time, Horace Greeley's newspaper was championing utopian socialist ideas based on Fourierism. Marx agreed and immediately, together with Engels, wrote articles about Germany, Turkey, England, and other countries in Europe. They also wrote about Russia, India, China, and the United States. He and Engels contributed articles that discussed military affairs, elections in England, and capitalpunishment. Occasionally, whenever the articles contained elements of personalized reporting, Dana would run the articles as editorials. Marx's articles were not necessarily biased, however; he researched well the topics he discussed.

Charles Blitzer wrote,

> Marx's American journalism owes its special character to what Engels described — perhaps immodestly, under the circumstances — as "that marvelous gift of apprehending clearly the character, the significance, and the necessary consequences of great historical events at a time when these events are actually in course of taking place, or are only just completed." More impressive than the breadth of his knowledge, the trenchancy of his wit, the felicity of his style — all of which were considerable — is the fact that in treating of current events Marx was able so consistently to distinguish the real from the illusory, the important from the trivial, the permanently significant from the momentarily impressive phenomena of his time.*

Marx and Engels contributed almost 500 articles to the newspaper. Marx wrote 350, while Engels wrote 125. They wrote more than 10 together. Although certain scholars believe Marx lowered his standards as a philosopher by contributing to a newspaper, it should be mentioned that no matter what he wrote, his philosophy was emphatically stated. His writing for the *New York Daily Tribune*, for instance, not only revealed his philosophical beliefs but advocated certain reforms. For instance, in "Parliamentary Debates — The Clergy Against Socialism — Starvation," Marx's attitude toward the philanthropists who supported the Ten Hours Bill of 1847 was vehemently cynical. He emphatically pointed out that the supporters were actually aristocratic landowners who were trying to get revenge for the abolition of the Corn Laws. Although Marx was writing about fact, his beliefs were revealed. Indeed, the reader immediately learned of his position toward the issue. Later in the article he informed the reader of an unholy alliance between the established church and the aristocracy and revealed that he disliked this alliance. In the next to the last paragraph of the article, Marx mentioned that in England there was a pair of invisible,

---

*Henry M. Christman, ed., The American Journalism of Marx and Engels, *with an Introduction by Charles Blitzer* (New York: New American Library, 1966), p. xxvii.

intangible, and silent despots that condemned individuals to their deaths or drove them from their land. According to Marx, the first was starvation; the second was forced emigration. Of course, Marx was acquainted with both. Perhaps this acquaintance not only enabled him to interpret information but enabled him to prophesy the numerous struggles that would occur between labor and industrialists and between industrialists and aristocrats.

Marx's earnings from his articles helped feed and clothe his family. When his articles were no longer needed 11 years later, however, his income was reduced substantially. If Engels as well as some relatives had not provided some financial assistance, Marx and his family would not have been able to live.

Marx, who had written a book on economic theory in 1859, became a major speaker for the International Working Men's Association in 1864. His efforts helped the organization increase its membership; by 1869 the organization had about 800,000 members.

In 1870, when the Franco-German War broke out, Marx disagreed with certain constituencies in Germany. When the French armies were defeated, an insurrection occurred in Paris. The Paris Commune, as it was called, was supported by Marx, who, after it was crushed, proclaimed its significance in the address *Civil War in France*. As a result, Marx's name became synonymous with revolution, but he was opposed by certain constituencies inside the International Working Men's Association. Although these constituencies were defeated at the congress of the International in 1872, the organization languished for several years and was disbanded in 1876.

Marx withdrew from various movements. He was consulted several times by several activists, but he refused to become a participant in their groups. His health deteriorated, especially when his wife died in 1881, and he died on March 14, 1883.

REPRESENTATIVE WORK

New York Daily Tribune (articles, 1851–1862)

Henry Mayhew
(1812–1887)

Henry Mayhew was a social investigating journalist who devoted his time to editing and publishing magazines. In addition to his investigative reporting, which resembled advocacy journalism, he wrote humor, drama, and novels.

The son of a London attorney, Mayhew was born in 1812. He attended Westminster School, but getting a formal education was not to his liking. He sailed to India, where he saw Calcutta. His stay was brief, and when he returned home his father demanded that he work with him to learn law.

Dissatisfied, Mayhew turned to literature and writing. In 1831 he and Gilbert à Beckett, an old friend from school, edited and published *Figaro in London*, which became a popular humorous illustrated weekly that had several imitators. The weekly ceased publication eight years later. In 1832, Mayhew edited a second magazine, *The Thief*. This periodical was the first magazine to use reprints and clippings from other publications. *Punch*, which Mayhew cofounded in 1841 and coedited until 1846, was immediately successful. Unfortunately, when the magazine changed financial control and consequently editorial policy, Mayhew severed his relationship with the publication. He realized he did not have to conform and instead became one of the best chroniclers of social conditions of his time. Like others of his day, he severely criticized laissez-faire philosophy and advocated social reform.

In 1849, Mayhew's voluminous survey of *London Labour and the London Poor* began in the *Morning Chronicle*. This detailed survey contained in-depth analyses of the lowest classes of London society. Although the work was incomplete, the articles were collected into two volumes and published in 1851. Other updated editions appeared later.

The Criminal Prisons of London, which Mayhew considered his most important contribution, was published in 1862. Again Mayhew's powers of reporting were unsurpassed. His eye for details, no matter how minute, his unsentimental sympathy, his humor, his appetite for odd facts, and his ability to get information contributed to one of the most important social documents of the time.*

In 1864, after having lived in Germany for most of 1862 and having visited the country on numerous occasions, Mayhew published *German Life and Manners*.

In 1870, Mayhew edited *Only Once a Year*, a magazine that almost lived up to its name; it failed after a few issues.

Mayhew died in 1887.

Mayhew advocated social reform. Like others of his day, he severely criticized laissez-faire philosophy; therefore, in that respect he could be classified as one of the advocacy journalists.

REPRESENTATIVE WORKS

London Labour and the London Poor (1851)
The Criminal Prisons of London (1862)
German Life and Manners (1864)

*David Daiches, ed., The Penguin Companion to English Literature *(New York: McGraw-Hill, 1971), p. 357.

H. L. Mencken
(1880–1956)

While Strunsky was writing during World War I in favor of American support for that conflict, H. L. Mencken was writing opposing arguments in his column "The Free Lance," which appeared in the *Baltimore Evening Sun*.

Mencken was born in 1880 in Baltimore to an affluent, bourgeois German-American family. He attended Professor Friedrich Knapp's Teutonic Institute and the Baltimore Polytechnic, where he excelled in chemistry and the natural sciences. He read voraciously both British and American literature and learned to play the piano. These continuing interests were later beneficial when he began writing essays and articles of criticism.

In 1899, Mencken obtained a job with the *Baltimore Morning Herald*, where he moved from one position to another, experiencing the responsibilities of the reporter as well as editor. In 1904 the *Morning Herald* was replaced by the *Evening Herald*, and Mencken rose to editor before the paper's demise two years later. He immediately moved to the *Baltimore Evening News* and then to the *Baltimore Sun*.

Mencken's writing was filled with agnosticism, elitism, and iconoclasm. These "isms" were reinforced by such thinkers and writers as Charles Darwin, Thomas Huxley, Friedrich Nietzsche, Herbert Spencer, William Sumner, and James Huneker. Mencken's literary efforts included not only news reports, editorials, reviews, features, and humor, but short stories, articles of criticism, and several researched studies such as the *Philosophy of Friedrich Nietzsche* and *The American Language*. Mencken was able to observe life around him and explain it vibrantly, as did the realistic novelists; indeed, color appeared in every sentence he composed.

In 1908, Mencken began reviewing books for the *Smart Set*, a magazine published in New York City. Mencken's reputation as a critic spread. In 1914 he and the magazine's drama critic, George Jean Nathan, became editors and together they produced much of the magazine's material. Mencken's contributions helped keep alive the spirit of the moral rebellion of the 1890s. According to Douglas C. Stevenson: "He defied the genteel assumption that American letters must be primarily Anglo-Saxon, optimistic, and morally uplifting. He ridiculed literary commercialism, dramatized the view that an essential function of art is to challenge accepted axioms, and conducted a boisterous onslaught against the 'snouters' who favored literary censorship."*

*Douglas C. Stevenson, "Mencken, Henry Louis," in Dictionary of American Biography: Supplement Six 1956–1960, ed. John A. Garraty (New York: Charles Scribner's Sons, 1980), p. 444.

When his column "The Free Lance" appeared in 1911, Mencken gave the readers of Baltimore something they had never seen. Indeed, he ridiculed municipal politics, public works, language, certain persons within the community, and national and international affairs. His *Smart Set* articles would be altered to suit the column and vice versa. Eventually these articles and columns were collected and published.

When World War I began, Mencken's column was filled with venom. He attacked the pro–English Americans who distastefully ridiculed Germans who had come to America. His sentiment was so strong that he eventually became a partisan of Germany and was severely criticized by other members of the press. In 1915, the *Baltimore Sun* dropped his column, and the *Sun* soon sent Mencken abroad as a correspondent in the hope that his absence would quiet his critics. When he returned in 1917, however, criticism still confronted him. The United States was in the war, and Mencken's un–American attitude seemed unforgivable to his critics. When he published *A Book of Prefaces* it was unduly and viciously attacked by reviewers. His book *The American Language* ultimately received critical acclaim and popularity, perhaps because the *Sun*'s editors did not assign any stories to him or because the book was published in a calmer period.

For the next several years, Mencken wrote furiously for the *Sun, Smart Set, Atlantic Monthly*, and the *Nation*, attacking big business, big government, suppression, the "Red Scare," the Ku Klux Klan, education, sexual morality, and other issues. Between 1919 and 1927, the six-volume *Prejudices* series was published. Although many of the articles had appeared in one or more of the publications mentioned, this series did include additional articles.

In 1923, because of financial and editorial problems, *Smart Set* ceased publication. One month later a new critical review backed by Alfred Knopf and edited by Mencken and Nathan appeared. Although the *American Mercury* was a better *Smart Set* in every respect, Nathan and Mencken's opposing personalities caused Nathan to leave before the magazine was a year old. Mencken's publication contained literary criticism, which the readers enjoyed and respected, and political criticism, which the readers questioned. Mencken's attitudes toward politics, for example, changed from one month to the next. His economics policy, which had been liberal to a certain extent, became conservative, and in the early 1930s he supported Franklin Roosevelt but attacked Roosevelt's New Deal policies. Finally, in 1933 he resigned from the magazine and devoted the rest of his life to writing for the *Sun* and collecting his essays and letters, which were published in several volumes.

Mencken was working for the *Sun* when he suffered a stroke in 1948; he died eight years later.

REPRESENTATIVE WORKS

The American Language (1919)
American Mercury (1923–1933)

Mary Adelaide Mendelson
(1917–   )

Although she did not major in journalism or work in the field, Mary Adelaide Mendelson became somewhat of a muckraker when she wrote *Tender Loving Greed: How the Incredibly Lucrative Nursing Home "Industry" Is Exploiting America's Old People and Defrauding Us All* in 1974.

Born in Grand Rapids, Michigan, in 1917, Mendelson received degrees from Radcliffe College in 1939 and from the University of Michigan in 1940. She earned a teaching certificate from Fenn College (Cleveland State University) in 1959. A former case worker for the Children's Aid Society and the American Red Cross, she also taught on the high school and community college level. She became a staff director of and consultant to various nursing homes and a director of and consultant to state and federal committees on nursing homes and gerontology. Mendelson saw firsthand the inhumane treatment of the elderly by nursing home personnel.

Mendelson's book was accepted by one publisher who was then frightened off by threats of legal action by the nursing-home industry. Fortunately, another company then published her work. Investigative reporters' curiosity was aroused by what Mendelson found, and others consequently conducted their own investigations and reported similar findings. Eventually, the federal as well as various state governments conducted investigations and as a result enacted legislation that policed the nursing-home industry.

REPRESENTATIVE WORK

Tender Loving Greed: How the Incredibly Lucrative Nursing Home "Industry" Is Exploiting America's Old People and Defrauding Us All (1974)

Morton Mintz
(1922–   )

Investigative muckraker Morton Mintz was born in 1922 in Ann Arbor, Michigan, and graduated from the University of Michigan in 1943. He began his newspaper career with the *St. Louis Star-Times* in 1946. A reporter who knew how to obtain controversial information, he remained at the *Star-Times* until 1950, when he was hired by the *St. Louis Globe-Democrat*. First as a reporter, then as an assistant city editor, Mintz learned various aspects of journalism. He moved to Washington, D.C., in 1958 and became a reporter of merit for the *Washington Post*. In addition to uncovering stories concerning baby-deforming drugs and the role of the United States Food and Drug Administration, Mintz wrote several book-length exposés such as *By Prescription Only* (1967), *The Pill: An Alarming Report* (1969), *America, Inc.: Who Owns and Operates the United States* (1971).

In 1986, Mintz wrote *At Any Cost: Corporate Greed, Women, and the Dalkon Shield*, the muckraking exposé of the A. H. Robins Company and the Dalkon Shield, an intrauterine device or IUD, which appeared on the market in 1971. Mintz examined the company's eagerness to promote and sell the device to generate profits before it proved the device's safety over time. Women who used it suffered from punctured uteri, pelvic infections, abortions, children with birth defects, and unwanted pregnancies. Even though officials of the company realized that the product had problems, they refused to take it off the market until it was revealed that the product was unfit for human use.

REPRESENTATIVE WORKS

By Prescription Only (1967)
The Pill: An Alarming Report (1969)
America, Inc.: Who Owns and Operates the United States (1971)
At Any Cost: Corporate Greed, Women, and the Dalkon Shield (1986)

Noel Mostert
(1929–   )

Noel Mostert was born on December 25, 1929, in Capetown, South Africa, to parents who farmed for a living.

Although Mostert started his journalistic career as a shipping correspondent for the *Cape Times* in Capetown in 1946, he became a foreign war correspondent for the United Press in 1947. This position lasted until 1953, the year he joined the staff of the *Montreal Star*, in Montreal, Quebec. Mostert served as a Broadway columnist and critic and a special foreign correspondent until 1962, the year he left to write full-time. He contributed articles to various periodicals, including *Harper's*, *Reader's Digest*, *Holiday*, and the *New Yorker*.

In 1975, Mostert wrote *Supership*, an exposé that provided evidence that suggested some large ships were not necessarily seaworthy.

Frontiers: The Epic of South Africa's Creation and the Tragedy of the Xhosa People was a large 1,300-plus-page book that was published in 1992. The book concerned the invasion of the Cape of Africa primarily by the Dutch and more specifically the ensuing battles between the Dutch and the Xhosa, the closest black tribe to the Cape. Nine wars occurred over the course of nearly a century, as Mostert pointed out, and thus the face of South Africa was changed forever. The resistance and final defeat of the Xhosa was the theme that dominated the book.

REPRESENTATIVE WORKS

Supership (1975)
Frontiers: The Epic of South Africa's Creation and the Tragedy of the Xhosa People (1992)

Ralph Nader
(1934–   )

Born to Rose and Nadra Nader on February 27, 1934, in Winsted, Connecticut, muckraking consumer advocate and lawyer Ralph Nader received his bachelor's degree from Princeton University in 1955 and his law degree from Harvard in 1958. Nader, unlike most students his age, sensed that something was amiss even as an undergraduate. Dwight David Eisenhower was president, and the youth were for the most part apathetic; Nader was appalled when he saw students' legal rights stripped by university administrators. Although he tried to interest them in defending their legal rights, he was not successful.*

When he left Harvard, Nader served briefly in the U.S. Army and then practiced law in Hartford, Connecticut. From 1961 to 1967, he taught history and government at the University of Hartford. Although he had written extensively about the failures by the automobile industry to improve its products, it was not until 1964, when he became a consultant to Daniel Patrick Moynihan, then assistant secretary of the U.S. Department of Labor, that his views concerning the federal government's role in implementing laws protecting consumers of automobiles were finally heard. Unfortunately, few politicians heeded what he said, except Moynihan. Consequently, he turned to writing an investigative report that exposed the ills of America's automobile industry, especially General Motors' Chevrolet Corvair. Titled *Unsafe at Any Speed: The Designed-in Dangers of the American Automobile*, the book was published in 1965 and became one of the most penetrating muckraking exposés of the decade.

Charles Moritz, ed., Current Biography Yearbook 1968 (New York: H. W. Wilson, 1968), p. 279.

The book influenced Congress to take an active role in regulating the automobile industry, particularly when Nader revealed to the media that he had been investigated and harassed by detectives hired by General Motors. The president of General Motors acknowledged that the company had indeed conducted an investigation and publicly apologized to Nader. Within six months the National Traffic and Motor Vehicle Safety Act was passed by the Senate and House and subsequently signed by President Johnson.

Nader, who had become a one-man lobby for the public, began to monitor the National Traffic Safety Agency. Eventually he turned his attention to health hazards, including mining, natural gas pipelines, and meat packing companies, to mention a few. In 1969 he founded the Center for Study of Responsive Law, which investigated various federal commissions such as the Federal Trade Commission, and in 1970 he initiated the Public Interest Research Group, which worked for consumer and political reform on community and college campuses. In addition to the numerous contributions to magazines and newspapers, Nader and his group of graduate students, law students, and journalists (Nader's Raiders) produced numerous investigative reports on such topics as air pollution, food additives, nursing homes, water pollution, pensions, corporate power, federal agencies, nuclear energy, and banking. He also wrote or cowrote *What to Do with Your Bad Car* (1970) and *Beware* (1971).

In 1971, Nader launched Public Citizen, Inc., a lobbying organization for consumers, primarily to counteract the power of corporate-sponsored lobbying organizations. He also founded the Center for Auto Safety, the National Insurance Consumer Organization, the Health Research Group, and the Project for Corporate Responsibility.

In 1973, Nader founded the Capitol Hill News Service, primarily to cover the unscrupulous activities of congressmen. A number of investigative reports appeared, including stories about questionable financing for campaigns and bribes in the guise of gifts, trips, and seminars offered to various congressmen by large lobbying organizations. Although the service was sometimes criticized for its handling of news, it nonetheless served a purpose.

Nader's organizations influenced the Nixon administration to establish several "watchdog" agencies, including the Occupational Safety and Health Administration, the Environmental Protection Agency, and the Consumer Products Safety Commission. At least eight consumer protection laws were enacted as a result of his organizations' efforts.

When Jimmy Carter became president, many of Nader's protégés were recruited for administration posts. As a result, Nader's activities were curtailed. Nonetheless, he was productive. Between 1973 and 1980, he wrote or cowrote numerous exposés including *You and Your Pension* (1973), *Corporate Power in America* (1973), *Action for a Change: A Student's Manual for Public Interest Organizing* (1973), *Working on the System: A Comprehensive Manual for Citizen Access to Federal Agencies* (1974), *The Commerce Committees* (1975),

The Environment Committees (1975), *The Judiciary Committees* (1975), *The Revenue Committees* (1975), *The Money Committees* (1975), *Ruling Congress* (1975), *The Ralph Nader Congress Project* (1975), *Government Regulation: What Kind of Reform?* (1976), *Taming the Giant Corporation* (1976), *The White House* (1977), *The Menace of Atomic Energy* (1977), and *The Lemon Book* (1980).

In 1980, Nader resigned as president of Public Citizen, Inc. He was determined to devote more time to organizing citizens in various communities. A year later he attacked the Reagan administration because of its probusiness leanings.

In 1983, Nader founded the U.S. Public Interest Research Group, which had support groups in at least 26 states. PIRG ultimately helped consumers in states like California to have laws enacted that saved them money on such items as automobile insurance.

Nader's criticism of big business was evident in 1986, when he coauthored the book *The Big Boys: Styles of Corporate Power*, which examined the leading executives of the U.S. Steel Corporation, General Motors, and other corporations. The subjects were thoroughly researched. Two years later he persuaded celebrities such as Dustin Hoffman and Paul Newman, among others, to demonstrate publicly the inflate-on-impact air bag for cars. He also wrote an article of advice to the next president of the United States, which was published in the *Harvard Business Review*.

In 1990, Nader coauthored *Winning the Insurance Game: The Complete Consumer's Guide to Saving Money*, which detailed the major types of insurance, including government programs such as Social Security and Medicare, and instructed consumers how to work with agents, policies, and forms. Three years later he coauthored *Collision Course: The Truth About Aviation Safety*, which used interviews, documented reports, and crash accounts, among other evidence, to illustrate the authors' concerns over the discrepancies in the information about airline safety, air traffic control, and the airline industry's equipment.

REPRESENTATIVE WORKS

Unsafe at Any Speed: The Designed-in Dangers of the American Automobile (1965)
Beware (1971)
You and Your Pension (with Kate Blackwell, 1973)
Corporate Power in America (with Mark Green, 1973)
The Commerce Committees (1975)
The Environment Committees (1975)
The Judiciary Committees (1975)
The Revenue Committees (1975)
The Money Committees (1975)
Ruling Congress (1975)
The Ralph Nader Congress Project (1975)
Government Regulation: What Kind of Reform? (1976)

Taming the Giant Corporation (1976)
The White House (1977)
The Menace of Atomic Energy (with John Abbotts, 1977)
The Lemon Book (1980)
The Big Boys: Styles of Corporate Power (with William Taylor, 1986)
Collision Course: The Truth About Aviation Safety (with Wesley J. Smith, 1993)

Jack Nelson
(1929-   )

Born in Alabama in 1929, investigative reporter Jack Nelson attended Georgia State University and Harvard University. His career as a hard-nosed, inquisitive reporter began in 1947, in Mississippi, with the *Biloxi Daily Herald*, for which he revealed illegal gambling payoffs and slot machine concessions. Even though his life was threatened more than once, he did not stop his investigations.

In 1952, Nelson joined the staff of the *Atlanta Constitution*, one of the better newspapers of the South, and he wrote investigative stories for more than 12 years. Several of the stories concerned vice and corruption in Liberty County, Georgia, and led to 22 indictments. Another series, for which Nelson won a Pulitzer Prize, uncovered the inhumane conditions in a state hospital.

Before Nelson joined the *Los Angeles Times* in 1965 as Atlanta's bureau chief, he wrote with Gene Roberts, Jr., the in-depth study *The Censors and the Schools*, which revealed how certain pressure groups tried to influence the selection and content of textbooks.

In 1970, Nelson moved to Washington, D.C., to work at the *Los Angeles Times'* Washington bureau. Within a few months, his curiosity had caused a tremor. When he wrote a revealing story about the FBI and its director, J. Edgar Hoover, the director immediately notified the management of the *Times* that Nelson should be fired. Hoover, who could have, in most cases, gotten his wish earlier in his career, failed to persuade the newspaper's management in this instance. Nelson, on the other hand, came across another interesting operation that had been performed by the FBI. According to John C. Behrens: "Nelson's sources put him onto a story that the FBI had paid criminal informants $36,500 to set up two Ku Klux Klan hitmen in Meridian, Mississippi. Police and FBI agents caught the two—one actually was a woman—attempting to plant a bomb in a Jewish businessman's home. The woman was killed in the shootout. The setup had become, in fact, an execution."*

*John C. Behrens, The Typewriter Guerrillas: Closeups of 20 Top Investigative Reporters *(Chicago: Nelson-Hall, 1966), pp. 171–72.*

Of course, none of those involved in the case — the FBI, the Meridian police, the Meridian Jewish community, or the Anti-Defamation League — wanted the story published, but the 6,000-word story appeared in the *Los Angeles Times*.

Nelson continued his investigations into the 1970s and 1980s. *The Orangeburg Massacre*, which was written with Jack Bass, another investigative reporter, uncovered the truth behind the whitewashed murders of three blacks on the campus of South Carolina State College. Several books, which displayed the same incisive prose, followed.

In 1975, Nelson became chief of the Washington bureau. Although his duties included administrative and reporting assignments, he performed exceptionally well in both. His preference was, of course, reporting.

In 1993, Nelson wrote the incisive *Terror in the Night: The Klan's Campaign Against the Jews*, which was based on information he had uncovered years earlier that resulted in the 6,000-word story mentioned above. The book described the Ku Klux Klan's anti–Semitic beliefs as well as the Klan's plan to bomb the home of Meyer Davidson, a community leader who had been outspoken about the synagogue bombings in Mississippi. Nelson explained that the Klan hated the Jews primarily because they believed the Jews had been responsible for inciting civil rights for blacks. Nelson described the setup as well as the ambush of Thomas Albert Tarrants III and Kathy Ainsworth. The FBI, which had informants inside the Klan, and officers of the local police department were at the scene when Tarrants and Ainsworth were about to plant the bomb. In the ensuing battle, Ainsworth was killed. Tarrants was arrested and ultimately sentenced to prison. The book, which was an example of muckraking journalism, was thoroughly researched and extremely well written.

REPRESENTATIVE WORKS

The Censors and the Schools (1963)
The Orangeburg Massacre (1970)
Terror in the Night: The Klan's Campaign Against the Jews (1993)

Jack Newfield
(1939–   )

Jack Newfield, a self-termed American New Leftist, was influenced by Murray Kempton and Albert Camus in terms of style and ideas. Newfield, who became a senior editor at the *Village Voice*, was born on February 18, 1939, in New York City, and he graduated from Hunter College in 1961. Although he contributed numerous articles to other publications, including *Playboy*, *Evergreen Review*, *Nation*, *New York*, and *Partisan Review*, his writing for the *Village Voice* concerned civil rights, lead poisoning, hippies, the 1968 Democratic Convention, Students for a Democratic Society, Vietnam, Nelson Rockefeller, John Lindsey, Theodore Sorensen, the media, poor whites, the legal system, Norman Mailer, Ralph Nader, Robert Kennedy, and any other politician, writer, or issue that affected him or his beliefs.

An advocate who believed in morality, laws, and equal justice, Newfield criticized the wrongs of American society but also praised what he found to be good in America.

Newfield's first book, *A Prophetic Minority*, which discussed the rise of the New Left, was published in 1966. His critically acclaimed analysis of Robert Kennedy, *Robert Kennedy: A Memoir*, appeared in 1969. The book was not a biography per se but rather a personal testament that criticized as well as praised. Newfield detailed the insurgencies of the 1960s that Robert Kennedy eventually grew to understand and confidently pronounced as societal necessities.

Newfield produced a collection of his articles in 1971. Titled *Bread and Roses Too: Reporting About America*, the articles were grouped according to the issues discussed or ideas advocated. One of the articles exemplified Newfield's ability to foster a certain mood and captured his attitudes toward President Nixon after a televised presidential address.

In 1972, Newfield wrote with Jeff Greenfield the popular *A Populist Manifesto: The Making of a New Majority*. The writers wrote in the Preface:

> This manifesto is a platform for a movement that does not yet exist. It is not a book about the 1972 campaign, or a blue-print for Utopia in 2001.
> It is instead an effort to return to American politics the economic passions jettisoned a generation ago. Its fundamental argument is wholly unoriginal: some institutions and people have too much money and power, most people have too little, and the first priority of politics must be to redress that imbalance.*

The authors then elaborated on issues such as banking, insurance, utilities, taxes, regulatory agencies, land reform, the media, crime, health, unions, and foreign policy, and they subsequently advocated reforms.

Newfield also wrote the arresting and controversial book *Cruel and Unusual Justice* in 1974, and with Paul Du Brul, he wrote *The Abuse of Power: The Permanent Government and the Fall of New York* in 1977. In 1984, he wrote the insightful book *The Education of Jack Newfield*. Newfield and Wayne Barrett criticized the men who surrounded Mayor Ed Koch in the penetrating,

---

*Jack Newfield and Jeff Greenfield, A Populist Manifesto: The Making of a New Majority *(New York:* Praeger, 1972), p. ix.

muckraking journalistic study *City for Sale: Ed Koch and the Betrayal of New York*, which was published in 1989. The authors claimed that these men were as crooked as a dog's hind legs. Newfield and Barrett disclosed that Koch had turned over parts of City Hall to those he said he opposed. The book was not necessarily a balanced report, but the authors' claims were accurate.

REPRESENTATIVE WORKS

A Prophetic Minority (1966)
Robert Kennedy: A Memoir (1969)
Bread and Roses Too: Reporting About America (1971)
A Populist Manifesto: The Making of a New Majority (with Jeff Greenfield, 1972)
Cruel and Unusual Justice (1974)
The Abuse of Power: The Permanent Government and the Fall of New York (with Paul Du Brul, 1977)
The Education of Jack Newfield (1984)
City for Sale: Ed Koch and the Betrayal of New York (with Wayne Barrett, 1989)

Bernard Nossiter
(1926–1992)

Born on April 10, 1926, to Rose and Murray Nossiter in New York City, economics journalist and muckraker Bernard Nossiter received his bachelor's degree from Dartmouth in 1947 and his master's degree from Harvard a year later. In 1952 he worked as a reporter for the *New York World Telegram and Sun* and wrote articles for Carey McWilliams and the *Nation*. These articles were, he believed, too controversial for any newspaper.

In 1955, Nossiter became the national economics reporter for the *Washington Post*, a position he held until 1964. From 1964 to 1979, he served as an economics correspondent for the newspaper, first in Paris, then Asia, then London. He moved to the *New York Times* in 1979, primarily to head the newspaper's bureau at the United Nations.

In addition to the numerous articles for the *Nation* and other periodicals, Nossiter wrote the critical but analytical book *The Mythmakers: An Essay on Power and Wealth* in 1964. He explained the economic policies of President John F. Kennedy and argued that the United States should emulate Japan and France in planning its economic future. *Soft State: A Newspaperman's Chronicle of India* followed in 1970.

Britain — A Future That Works was published in 1978 and argued that England's growth would rely on its varied cultural skills rather than on its manufacturing firms. Nossiter's arguments regarding England differed greatly from those of most political and economic observers of the time.

In 1987, Nossiter wrote *The Global Struggle for More: Third World Conflicts with Rich Nations*, which examined the progression of the Third World after World War II. Nossiter attacked foreign aid and argued that tough policy conditions should be attached to World Bank loans to poor countries.

Nossiter's last book, *Fat Years and Lean: The American Economy Since Roosevelt*, which was published in 1990, was a chatty account of American economic policy making from the depression to the present. Nossiter discussed the people who were responsible for the decisions, including their intellectual and class perspectives as well as the positions they took on whether and how to fight unemployment. He criticized supply-side economics as well as the conservatives who supported the theory. He also criticized big labor and President Ronald Reagan.

Nossiter died of cancer in 1992.

REPRESENTATIVE WORKS

The Mythmakers: An Essay on Power and Wealth (1964)
Soft State: A Newspaperman's Chronicle of India (1970)
Britain — A Future That Works (1978)
The Global Struggle for More: Third World Conflicts with Rich Nations (1987)
Fat Years and Lean: The American Economy Since Roosevelt (1990)

Thomas Paine
(1737–1809)

Born in 1737 to a lower-class Quaker family in Thetford, Norfolk, England, Thomas Paine attended Thetford Grammar School. When he was 16, he left home by ship and sailed as far as London, where he became an apprentice to a staymaker. London at this time was, according to Howard Fast, "as close an approximation of hell as is possible to create on this earth."* Fast described the city in these terms:

> The enclosure laws of the previous two centuries had created a huge landless population that gravitated ... mostly toward London, to form a half-human mob, not peasants, not craftsmen — the first tragic beginnings of a real working class.

*Howard Fast, ed., The Selected Work of Tom Paine: Set in the Framework of His Life (New York: Duell, Sloan and Pearce, 1945), p. ix.

... Starvation, thievery, murder, and drunkenness were the order of the day. The section where these people lived was known as the Gin Mill; gin was their only escape. No doubt, when Paine went into the Gin Mill, when he sought to escape staymaking through that valley of hopelessness, gin was his surcease too. He went as low as the people, suffered with them, attempted their avenues of escape, and thereby came to understand them.†

Paine learned of Newtonianism from attending philosophical lectures given by Benjamin Martin, James Ferguson, and others. He was also influenced by classical antiquity, which was commonly used by deists when confronted by churchmen. For instance, if Paine were questioned whether men could live morally without Christianity, he would mention that Aristotle, Plato, and Socrates had lived before Christ, and yet they had signs of nobility. Another influence was freemasonry's relationship to the religions of ancient Egypt, the Persians, and the Druids. These four influences — Quakerism, Newtonianism, classicism, and the early Eastern religions and freemasonry — formed four major religious premises: (1) nature is divine, (2) nature is law, (3) man must be a part of this divine revelation; and (4) an attempt must be made to re-establish man's relations with this natural law in politics and religion.§ From these premises Paine's political philosophy grew.

After numerous jobs in numerous places, Paine got a job as a tax collector. He disliked the position, however, and returned to staymaking. He tried other trades such as cabinetmaking and cobbling, but despair followed him.

From 1768 to 1774, Paine was an excise officer at Lewes, Sussex. He was dismissed for addressing Parliament on behalf of the excisemen who had requested higher wages. Since he had lost his business and was in debt, he borrowed enough money to sail to America.

Benjamin Franklin, whom Paine had met in London, helped him find employment. Paine worked as an editor for Robert Aitken, the publisher of the *Pennsylvania Magazine*. Almost immediately, Paine's advocacy journalism earned him a reputation as one of the foremost writers of his day. In addition to writing antislavery essays, he wrote for the revolutionary cause. Within the revolutionary climate, Paine was at ease; he knew that his hour had arrived and that his political and religious philosophies would ignite the fuse of perhaps the greatest power ever witnessed.

Paine served as editor of the *Pennsylvania Magazine* for approximately 18 months. In 1776 he published *Common Sense*, which influenced the makers of the "Declaration of Independence," and the first number of *The Crisis*, which encouraged the soldiers of the Revolutionary War. In 1780 he published *Public Good*, in which he urged the nation to become the owner of western lands

---

†Ibid., *pp. ix–x.*
§*Harry Hayden Clark*, Thomas Paine: Representative Selections, with Introduction, Bibliography, and Notes *(New York: American Book Co., 1944), pp. xv–xvi.*

claimed by Virginia. During 1782 and 1783, he wrote six letters for the *Providence Gazette*, in which he defended taxation of Rhode Island by the federal government. In 1791, after having returned to England, he published the first and second parts of *The Rights of Man*, which was a reply to Edmund Burke's critical *Reflections on the French Revolution*. *The Rights of Man* advocated that England needed a revolution similar to that which had occurred in France. Paine was charged with sedition; before his trial, however, he escaped to France, where he wrote the third part of *The Rights of Man*. In 1793 he wrote the first part of *Age of Reason*; the second part appeared three years later.

Although *Common Sense, The Crisis, The Rights of Man*, and the *Age of Reason* were perhaps his most important writings, Paine also wrote *Dissertation on the First Principles of Government, Dissertations on Government, the Bank, and Paper Money, Decline and Fall of the English System of Finance, Letter to Washington, Agrarian Justice, Discourse to the Theophilanthropists, Letters to the Citizens of the United States*, and *Reply to the Bishop of Llandoff*.

According to Harry Hayden Clark, Paine assumed that men were by nature altruistic. He was convinced that every man was endowed by the creator with certain natural rights. He believed in rational principles to promote progress. He was convinced that these principles had to be in the form of a constitution. He assumed that in order to promote the good for all there had to be a governmental body to which the people had access.** Paine, of course, was not the first political philosopher. Indeed, Voltaire, Locke, Milton, to name a few, preceded him. Paine's writing was different, however, As Fast mentioned:

"They wrote abstractly of the pattern of change; Paine wrote realistically of the method of change. They were philosophers who created political philosophy; Paine was a revolutionist who created a method for revolution. They moved men to thought; Paine moved men to thought and action. They dealt with theory and ideals; Paine dealt with the dynamics of one force playing against another."††

In *Common Sense* Paine tried to persuade the reader that America had the capabilities to break with England. Although his points were abrupt, they had an impact.

Excerpts of *Common Sense* were printed in newspapers and, as a result, Paine's beliefs about "independence" united Americans throughout the colonies. Without question, the popular pamphlet helped initiate the Revolutionary War and served as a model for the Declaration of Independence, which was written several months later.

**Ibid., *pp. xxxiv–li.*
††*Fast, ed.,* Selected Work of Tom Paine. *p. xii.*

REPRESENTATIVE WORKS

The Pennsylvania Magazine (editor)
Common Sense (1776)
The Crisis (1776)
Public Good (1780)
The Rights of Man (1791–1792)
Age of Reason (1793–1796)

Andrew (Drew) R. Pearson
(1897–1969)

Drew Pearson was born on December 13, 1897, in Evanston, Illinois, to Edna and Paul Martin Pearson. His father, a Quaker, taught at Northwestern University and then Swarthmore College, where he founded Chautauqua, an educational service. Later he became governor of the Virgin Islands.

Pearson attended Phillips Exeter Academy, a prestigious preparatory school and Swarthmore College, from which he graduated in 1919. Pearson served as editor of the college newspaper and founded the Intercollegiate Press Association.

Like his two brothers and sister, Pearson worked for his father in Chautauqua. Then he worked in the Balkans for the British Red Cross. Pearson, who desired to learn as much as he possibly could about other countries, then worked for the American Friends Service Committee in Serbia, Montenegro, and Albania.

In 1921, Pearson returned to the United States and taught industrial geography for a year at the University of Pennsylvania. He could not escape the desire to travel, however. He found employment as a seaman aboard a ship that was bound for the Orient. He toured numerous countries, including Japan, China, the Philippines, Australia, New Zealand, India, South Africa, and England. He contributed stories based on his exploits to numerous newspapers.

Although Pearson enjoyed traveling and writing about his observations, he returned to the United States in 1924 and taught commercial geography for a year at Columbia University.

In 1925, Pearson returned to the Far East, where he explored other countries. He contributed stories to newspapers. The same year he married the Countess Felicia Gizyeka, the daughter of Eleanor "Cissy" Patterson. Patterson was the publisher of the *Washington Times-Herald*.

One year later Pearson became foreign editor of the *United States Daily*. This position allowed him to travel to Geneva to report on a naval conference, to Paris and Dublin to report on the secretary of state, who was meeting with dignitaries, and to Havana to report on President Coolidge's meeting with dignitaries. Pearson's marriage, which had produced one daughter, ended in divorce in 1928.

Pearson joined the staff of the *Baltimore Sun* in 1929 and reported on the London Naval Conference and the Cuban Revolution, among other major events abroad. He was made chief of the newspaper's Washington bureau and eventually met Robert S. Allen, who headed the *Christian Science Monitor*'s Washington bureau. Both had similar interests; indeed, both had attempted to have similar muckraking stories accepted by their respective editors. Neither had had any success, however. Their editors were not interested in candid and penetrating pieces that explored, and sometimes exposed, certain lives in Washington. Pearson and Allen collaborated on *The Washington Merry-Go-Round*, which was published anonymously in 1931 and revealed the lives of the most influential power brokers who lived in the nation's capital. The book became a best seller, and Pearson and Allen wrote a sequel, *More Merry-Go-Round*, in 1932. Eventually readers learned the identities of the authors, and Allen and Pearson lost their jobs. They persevered, however, and created the column "The Washington Merry-Go-Round" in 1932, which was syndicated to newspapers across the country by United Features.

The column, which was similar to the books, required a lot of work. Pearson and Allen worked about 18 hours a day, investigating the House, the Senate, the presidency, and practically every major department of the federal government. They also collaborated on *The Nine Old Men* and *Nine Old Men at the Crossroads*, published in 1936 and 1937, respectively, which concerned the aging members of the United States Supreme Court.

Before Allen left Pearson and the column in 1942 to serve in the U.S. Army, they had created a news program for the National Broadcasting Company and had created the comic strip "Hap Hazard," which satirized Washington.

Pearson, who had married Luvie Abell in 1936, was now responsible for the column. He penetrated the Washington elite and exposed corruption; he revealed in skillful fashion the unusual, if not eccentric, characteristics of certain officials. Pearson, who claimed that Secretary of State Cordell Hull had hoped World War II would bleed the Soviet Union white, was called "a chronic liar" by Franklin D. Roosevelt. He belittled Secretary of War Patrick J. Hurley when he claimed that Hurley had rehearsed ballroom entrances before a mirror. Pearson revealed that some elected officials had taken bribes, while other officials had leaked evidence to members of certain committees.

Pearson, who had hired Jack Anderson years earlier, made him an associate and gave him a byline in the late 1950s. Anderson helped Pearson with the column and helped him write the books *U.S.A.: Second-Class Power?* and *The Case Against Congress*, which were published in 1958 and 1968, respectively.

In the 1960s Pearson revealed that Attorney General Robert F. Kennedy had authorized electronic surveillance of the telephones of Dr. Martin Luther King, Jr. He also disclosed that Thomas J. Dodd, Democratic senator from Connecticut, had diverted monies from dinners and campaign contributions to his personal account. Dodd was eventually censured by the Senate.

Pearson was sued numerous times for his muckraking revelations and allegations, but he seldom lost.

Before he died in 1969, Pearson admitted that he was proud of his column; after all, it had caused certain governmental bodies to draft and enact ethical policies. He was also proud of the Friendship Train, which he had organized after World War II. The train had brought American food to people living in Greece, Italy, Austria, Germany, and France.

The column, which was appearing in almost 600 newspapers at the time of Pearson's death, continued under Jack Anderson.

REPRESENTATIVE WORKS

The Washington Merry-Go-Round (with Robert S. Allen, 1931)
More Merry-Go-Round (with Robert S. Allen, 1932)
"The Washington Merry-Go-Round" (column with Robert S. Allen, 1932)
The Nine Old Men (with Robert S. Allen, 1936)
Nine Old Men at the Crossroads (with Robert S. Allen, 1937)
U.S.A.: Second-Class Power? (with Jack Anderson, 1958)
The Case Against Congress (with Jack Anderson, 1968)

David Graham Phillips
(1867–1911)

David Graham Phillips was born in Madison, Indiana, in 1867. Son of a Republican banker, he attended Asbury College and later Princeton, from which he graduated. Determined to be a journalist and novelist, he became a staff member of the *Cincinnati Commercial Gazette,* then a staff member of its rival newspaper, the *Times-Star.* Within three years he moved to New York City.

First Phillips worked on Charles A. Dana's *Sun,* to which he contributed numerous articles; then he moved to Pulitzer's *World,* for which he wrote a series of articles on large businesses and trusts. He also traveled as a foreign correspondent for the *World* to England, where he reported on a disastrous collision of two British ships.

Upon Phillips' return, Pulitzer, who recognized his talent for writing articles with punch, offered him an editor's position; Phillips accepted. In addition to working for the *World*, he wrote for magazines, which he believed had a greater power than newspapers.

Thus Phillips turned his attention to such periodicals as the *Saturday Evening Post, Cosmopolitan, Appleton's Booklover's Magazine, McClure's, Pearson's, Success, Book News Monthly, Arena*, and *Everybody's*. Article after article criticized various political figures, but there was occasional praise for some politicians. Nelson W. Aldrich was one of Phillips' subjects.

When his first novel *The Great God Success* was published in 1901, Phillips' devotion to writing articles weakened. A year later he resigned from the *World* and completed another novel, *A Woman Ventures*. Although these novels were thought to be based on people Phillips knew, it was merely the ideas, circumstances, and problems of the characters that caused this illusion. For instance, *The Cost*, which was published in 1904, and *The Plum Tree* and *The Deluge*, which were published a year later, mirrored reality, and in each book Phillips presented his progressive campaigns. These novels were followed by the *Light-Fingered Gentry* in 1907, in which he examined the insurance scandals, *The Fashionable Adventures of Joshua Craig* in 1909, *The Husband's Story* in 1910, *The Conflict* in 1911, *George Helm* and *The Price She Paid* in 1912, and *Susan Lenox: Her Fall and Rise* in 1917. These novels concerned municipal, state, and national corruption; women in society; and even women's independence. In most of these novels, Phillips included political or industrial corruption. Although his novels were not critically successful, they were popular among buyers and readers, and they provided an accurate historical account of what was occurring in American society.

As mentioned, Phillips' contributions to magazines decreased as he devoted more time to writing fiction, but in 1906 the first article of "The Treason of the Senate" series appeared in *Cosmopolitan*. According to Irving Dilliard:

> The nine installments opened with an exposé of the numerous corporate connections of Senator Chauncey M. Depew of New York....
> Senator Depew and his New York colleague, Thomas C. Platt, were described by Phillips as having been chosen by the state legislature at Albany "by and for the interests" to join "the sensational rank and file of diligent, faithful enemies of their country." Nelson W. Aldrich of Rhode Island, Henry Cabot Lodge of Massachusetts, William B. Allison of Iowa, Joseph B. Foraker of Ohio, Arthur P. Gorman of Maryland and many other Senators of the day came off little better at Phillips' hands.*

Phillips' articles and novels created controversy but initiated interest in three amendments, which were ultimately submitted and ratified. These

Irving Dilliard, "Six Decades Later," in Muckraking: Past, Present and Future, *ed. John M. Harrison and Harry H. Stein (University Park, Penn.: Pennsylvania State University Press, 1973), p. 7.*

included the Sixteenth, Seventeenth, and Nineteenth amendments, which allowed the government to collect income taxes, voters to elect United States senators, and women to vote.

Unfortunately, Phillips did not live to see these amendments enacted. In 1911, Fitzhugh Goldsborough, who had persuaded himself that Phillips had written critically of his family in *The Fashionable Adventures of Joshua Craig*, confronted Phillips and fired several bullets into his body. Phillips died the next day.

REPRESENTATIVE WORKS

The Great God Success (1901)
A Woman Ventures (1902)
The Cost (1904)
The Plum Tree (1905)
The Deluge (1905)
"The Treason of the Senate" (1906)
Light-Fingered Gentry (1907)
The Fashionable Adventures of Joshua Craig (1909)
The Husband's Story (1910)
The Conflict (1911)
George Helm (1912)
The Price She Paid (1912)
Susan Lenox: Her Fall and Rise (1917)

Thomas Powers
(1940–   )

Thomas Powers, an investigative, muckraking reporter who won a Pulitzer Prize in 1971 for his story on Diana Oughton, a radical youth who was killed in Greenwich Village, was reared in New York City. Born on December 12, 1940, he graduated from Yale University in 1964. He worked for two years as a reporter in Rome, Italy, for the *Rome Daily American* before he returned to New York City to work for the United Press International.

Powers' first book *Diana: The Making of a Terrorist*, which was an expanded version of his award-winning story, was published in 1971. Powers explored the numerous unpredictable causes for Oughton's tragic ending. Two years later, in *The War at Home: Vietnam and the American People, 1964–68*, he examined in depth the societal and attitudinal changes of America and its people toward the Vietnam War.

The book that was perhaps Powers' most important exposé appeared in 1979. Titled *The Man Who Kept the Secrets: Richard Helms and the CIA*, the book revealed the questionable subversive operations of the CIA that occurred while Helms was associated with the agency. Powers, who questioned the agency's role in the world, a role he believed had become a problem, discussed in the introduction four aspects of the problem:

> (1) American intervention in foreign countries always matters more to the nation in question than it does to the United States. Yet the decision to proceed is often reached in a manner which is shockingly casual....
> (2) Just as American power has more sway in other countries than it can claim by right, local CIA officers exert a disproportionate influence on local events, especially after a decision to intervene has been reached....
> (3) The CIA has been too quick to surrender responsibility for what allies undertake with its aid, and other high officials in Washington have been too ready to let it do so....
> (4) Perhaps the most troubling aspect of the CIA is the hardest to explain, because it represents at once both the field of its greatest success and its passive acceptance of fatal dangers about which there is very likely nothing to be done....[*]

Throughout the book, attention was focused on Helms and the various clandestine operations performed by members of the agency, but Powers considered the actions in reference to the four aspects. Thus the candid revelations substantiated the problem Powers had proposed. The writing, on the other hand, was descriptive. Powers' insight into the American political structure enabled the reader to comprehend what would ordinarily be a complex subject.

Although Powers was somewhat poetic in his descriptions of the various relationships between the executive branch of the federal government and the CIA, the facts he disclosed were undeniably true.

Powers, who became a contributing editor at the *Atlantic Monthly*, compiled a series of essays that had appeared in *Commonweal* and published them in 1982 under the title *Thinking About the Next War*. In this book, Powers suggested that a limited nuclear war was inevitable, especially between the United States and the Soviet Union. As in his previous books, Powers revealed the details of this particular issue through its impact on individuals and disclosed the various forces that drove societies toward nuclear obliteration as well as the effects of this prospect on the minds of parents and their children.

In 1993, Powers examined the German physicist Werner Heisenberg as well as Nazi Germany's failure to produce an atomic bomb in *Heisenberg's War*. According to Powers, the Nazi leaders paid scant attention to what other nations were doing in nuclear physics. The program that had been started in

---

[*]*Thomas Powers,* The Man Who Kept the Secrets: Richard Helms and the CIA *(New York: Alfred A. Knopf, 1979), pp. viii–x.*

Nazi Germany in 1939 was abruptly halted in 1942, however, when Heisenberg informed Albert Speer that an atomic bomb could not be produced fast enough to alter the course of the war. Powers recounted America's unceasing attempts to learn what was occurring inside Heisenberg's laboratories in Berlin and Leipzig. The book was thoroughly researched and well written.

REPRESENTATIVE WORKS

Diana: The Making of a Terrorist (1971)
The War at Home: Vietnam and the American People, 1964–68 (1973)
The Man Who Kept the Secrets: Richard Helms and the CIA (1979)
Thinking About the Next War (1982)
Heisenberg's War (1993)

Robin Reisig
(1944–   )

Robin Reisig was born in 1944 and was reared in a comfortable suburb of Detroit. Attending private schools in Bloomfield Hills, she matriculated at Wellesley, a New England Ivy League college, where she worked for the school newspaper. During the summers she worked for several newspapers, including the *Free Press* in Detroit and the *Patriot Ledger* in Boston.

Upon graduation, Reisig moved to the South, where she encountered numerous individuals who were less fortunate in life than she. She was hired as a reporter by the *Southern Courier* and covered local events, including murder trials. Although Reisig matured as a reporter, she grew tired of the South.

Reisig applied to the Columbia Journalism School and was accepted. By the time she graduated, she was determined not to work on a newspaper. As a result of a friend's encouragement, however, she was invited to contribute several articles to the *Village Voice*, which she gladly accepted. Her first article, which concerned the telephone company, was published in 1969. Her second article concerned women who defied bars restricted to men. Reisig contributed other articles, but most took several weeks to research and write. Her income was strained as a result. After a year, she was assigned stories that required even more time to investigate and write. One of these articles, "The Vets and Mayday," which was published in the *Village Voice* in 1971, described the People's Lobby Week, specifically the staged operation called Dewey Canyon III, in which veterans carried out a simulated search and destroy mission among the citizens of Washington, D.C. Reisig acknowledged that the veterans' demonstration greatly affected members of the Senate Foreign Relations Committee. This article, like others she wrote, was an example of advocacy journalism that appeared in the *Village Voice* and other periodicals during this period.

Reisig contributed lengthy articles to the paper, but she was not paid nearly enough. After all, she had invested a considerable amount of time on each story. Nonetheless, she contributed to the *Village Voice* with the hope that she would be offered a staff position. She wrote about prostitution as well as what it was like to go back to Wellesley. Finally, after five years of contributing to the paper, she asked about a full-time staff position. The editors informed her that such a position was not available.

Reisig stopped writing for the *Village Voice* before she turned 30. She moved to Boston, where she found a job as a reporter for the underground newspaper *The Real Paper*.

Concerning her experience at the *Village Voice*, Reisig said: "I felt that most of my experience ... was a very positive one. I loved writing for the *Voice*. I was able to write about subjects I cared about in the way I chose, and that was what mattered to me. It may mean I didn't earn much, but I knew that and made that choice consciously."*

James Ridgeway
(1936–   )

James Ridgeway was born on November 1, 1936, in Auburn, New York. He was educated at Princeton University, from which he received his bachelor's degree in 1959. He began his career as a journalist with the *Wall Street Journal*, where he learned to write concise, accurate stories on the economic conditions of the United States. From 1962 to 1968, he worked as an investigative reporter for the *New Republic*; he gathered information from industrial, educational, and governmental reports and then wrote exposés on such subjects as water pollution, auto safety, unethical business practices, and the energy crisis. In 1968, together with Andrew Kopkind, he founded and edited *Mayday*, which ultimately became *Hard Times*, a Washington-based journal that exposed industrial and governmental corruption.

The same year Ridgeway's controversial study *The Closed Corporation: American Universities in Crisis* was published. Ridgeway claimed that American universities, especially the research universities, had changed into military and industrial rather than educational institutions because of the research performed by professors for the government and industry.

*Ellen Frankfort, The Voice: Life at the Village Voice (New York: William Morrow, 1976), p. 99.

Ridgeway's study, which appeared when students were calling for more power on campuses, revealed that certain institutions such as the Massachusetts Institute of Technology and Johns Hopkins University were involved in developing military weapons, including missiles. Other major universities were involved in other forms of military research.

From 1970 to 1974, Ridgeway worked as an associate editor of *Ramparts*, which published investigative exposés. In his second book-length study, *The Politics of Ecology*, which appeared in 1970, Ridgeway first exposed the environmental pollution by industries, particularly the petroleum industry, and then claimed that the laws failed to prosecute or even fine the companies responsible. Indeed, the laws favored the polluters, according to Ridgeway, by allowing the companies to exploit natural resources and by providing tax breaks for their efforts.

Ridgeway, who became a staff writer as well as a political columnist for the *Village Voice* in 1974, became the paper's Washington correspondent several years later. Ridgeway also contributed articles to such periodicals as *Parade* and *Rolling Stone*. In addition to several books or guides on energy-efficient living, he wrote in 1973 the muckraking exposé *The Last Play: The Struggle to Monopolize the World's Energy Resources*, which concerned pork barreling in the oil industry by such oil cartels as Mobil, Gulf, Texaco, and Shell. In 1980 he wrote *Who Owns the Earth?* which discussed the development of energy from renewable sources.

In 1991, Ridgeway edited *The March to War*, an anthology of articles, transcripts of press briefings, congressional hearings, and outpourings from such luminaries as Henry Kissinger and Pat Buchanan about the Gulf War. The same year he wrote *Blood in the Face: The Ku Klux Klan, Aryan Nations, Nazi Skinheads, and the Rise of a New White Culture*, which explored racist organizations and the ugly atrocities that were perpetrated upon innocent individuals in society.

One year later Ridgeway and Jean Casella edited the book *Cast a Cold Eye: The Best in American Opinion Writing, 1990–1991*. The essays, which were from the nation's newspapers and magazines, discussed Clarence Thomas, the U.S. invasion of Panama, and child care, among other topics.

REPRESENTATIVE WORKS

Mayday (cofounder and editor)
Hard Times (founder and editor)
The Closed Corporation: American Universities in Crisis (1968)
The Politics of Ecology (1970)
The Last Play: The Struggle to Monopolize the World's Energy Resources (1973)
Who Owns the Earth? (1980)
Blood in the Face: The Ku Klux Klan, Aryan Nations, Nazi Skinheads, and the Rise of a New White Culture (1991)

Jacob Riis
(1849–1914)

Jacob Riis exposed the ruthless and greedy landlords of New York's lower East Side.

Born in Ribe, Denmark, in 1849, Riis was exposed to journalism when he helped his father publish a weekly paper. After he spent four years in Copenhagen apprenticing to a carpenter, however, he hoped to make carpentry his career when he set sail to the United States. Unfortunately, the economy of the United States was shaky, and Riis at 21 was unemployed and homesick. In order to survive, he held odd jobs and slept in alleys, barns, and police stations. He even tramped from New York City to Philadelphia to work for a family from Denmark. Finally, after three miserable years, he obtained employment with one of the New York news associations.

Three years later, in 1877, Riis was working for the *New York Tribune* as a police reporter. According to Charles A. Madison:

> Police headquarters was then on Mulberry Street, in the very heart of the East Side slum district. Haunting the place day and night, he soon made firsthand acquaintance with thousands of poor and depraved local denizens caught in police roundups. What he saw made him both compassionate and indignant. He frequently visited the benighted neighborhood, alone or in the company of a policeman, during the hours of two to four in the morning in order to see it "off its guard." Poking about the "foul alleys and fouler tenements," he studied their wretched inhabitants asleep in their filth and foulness.*

Riis empathized with the misfortunate, for he had experienced ill conditions too, and as he learned the reasons for these medieval conditions he realized that the public had to know. Through numerous investigations and interviews, he learned that the lower East Side "was developed by builders who herded the incoming immigrants — Irish followed by German, Jewish, and Italian — into their dark, airless, and unsanitary tenements."† The landlords neglected the property and turned their backs when tenants allowed others to live with them, which created impossible living conditions. The politicians cared little about the criminals, pimps, prostitutes, beggars, drunks, tramps, and homeless children who wandered the streets and alleys.

Riis wrote numerous stories depicting the inhumane conditions. He exposed the cruelty involved and the pain of these victims, and he advocated for improvements. Finally, in 1884, his efforts caused the creation of the Tenement House Commission, which investigated Riis' claims.

---

*Charles A. Madison, How the Other Half Lives — Jacob A. Riis *(New York: Dover, 1971), p. v.*
†Ibid., *p. vi.*

In 1888, Riis was hired by the *Evening Sun* and wrote his monumental book *How the Other Half Lives*, which presented to the public the horrors he had witnessed. Theodore Roosevelt, the police commissioner at the time, read the book and immediately instituted measures of reform.

Riis' popularity grew; he addressed church audiences and contributed articles to magazines. He even associated with Dr. Charles Parkhurst, the popular minister, in his social reform efforts. In 1892 he wrote *The Children of the Poor*, which was followed by *Out of Mulberry Street* in 1898, *The Making of an American* in 1901, and *Children of the Tenements* in 1903.

Riis died from heart disease in 1914.

REPRESENTATIVE WORKS

How the Other Half Lives (1888)
The Children of the Poor (1892)
Out of Mulberry Street (1898)
The Making of an American (1901)
Children of the Tenements (1903)

Thomas B. Ross
(1929–   )

Thomas B. Ross was born in New York City in 1929 and attended Yale University, from which he received his bachelor's degree in 1951. Later he attended Harvard University. He served in the U.S. Navy in the early 1950s. In 1958 he joined the *Chicago Sun-Times* as a reporter. He worked in Europe and later in Washington, D.C., where he eventually became chief of the Washington bureau.

While working in Washington, D.C., Ross met David Wise, who served as chief of the *New York Herald Tribune*'s Washington bureau from 1951 to 1966. They wrote *The U-2 Affair* in 1962, which concerned the U-2's spy mission into the Soviet Union. In 1964 in the book *The Invisible Government*, the authors examined several political machinations, including Richard Nixon's desire to have the invasion of Cuba planned by the Eisenhower administration take place before the 1960 presidential election. Three years later they wrote another intriguing book entitled *The Espionage Establishment*. The authors presented two controversial theories regarding the CIA. They claimed that (1) the CIA was not responsible to or controllable by any political body except itself and (2) the CIA engaged in domestic operations. Needless to say, the book was an eye-opener and captured the attention of the House and the Senate.

REPRESENTATIVE WORKS

The U-2 Affair (1962)
The Invisible Government (1964)
The Espionage Establishment (1967)

Charles Edward Russell
(1860–1941)

Perhaps the most persistent of the muckrakers was Charles Edward Russell, who was born in Davenport, Iowa, in 1860. His parents, especially his father, were abolitionists who were accustomed to criticism for their antislavery beliefs. Russell attended St. Johnsbury Academy in Vermont.

When Russell returned to Davenport, he worked for his father, who was the editor of the *Davenport Gazette*. Learning the basics of journalism, Russell obtained a position with the Minneapolis *Journal*. For the next 20 years, he worked as a reporter or editor for the *Detroit Tribune, New York Commercial Advertiser, New York Herald*, and *Chicago Examiner*. From 1894 to 1897 he was city editor of the *New York World*. From 1897 to 1900, he was managing editor of the *New York American*. In 1900 he became publisher of William Randolph Hearst's *Chicago American*, a position he held for two years.

When Russell's wife died in 1901, he battled depression, and his health deteriorated. For the next three years, he devoted his time to writing a book on American music. He stopped the project in 1905 when Erman Ridgway, the editor of *Everybody's*, asked him to write several articles on the meat-packing industry. According to C. C. Regier:

> Russell called his series ... "The Greatest Trust in the World," and he began with these words: "In the free republic of the United States of America is a power greater than the government, greater than the courts or judges, greater than legislatures, superior to and independent of all authority of state or nation." He showed how the packers had acquired this power through their relations with the railroads, and he described with care the evolution of monopoly control. In the course of his articles he pointed out that the men who wielded this incredible power were personally kindhearted, well-intentioned individuals, themselves victims of a vicious economic order.*

Russell's articles catapulted him into muckraking fame. In addition to writing articles about child labor, corruption in the railroading industry,

---

*C. C. Regier, The Era of the Muckrakers *(Chapel Hill: University of North Carolina Press, 1932), pp. 132–33.*

electoral fraud, and people who had made fortunes under questionable circumstances for *Everybody's*, he also contributed similar exposés to *Hampton's*, which was edited by Benjamin B. Hampton.

Russell revised his articles and produced several books such as *The Greatest Trust in the World*, *The Uprising of the Many*, and *Lawless Wealth*. When the latter book was published, Russell's political ideas were not dissimilar to socialism, which was becoming popular, and he joined the Socialist party. In 1909 his book *Why I Am a Socialist* was published. For several years, in several political campaigns, he ran as the Socialist candidate but lost. His muckraking articles under the heading "Where Did You Get It, Gentlemen?" which had been published in *Everybody's* in 1907, had severely criticized men of wealth, specifically Thomas Fortune Ryan, who had made a fortune through his association with the New York Metropolitan Street-Railway Company. These articles caused Russell to be blacklisted by most New York magazines.†

In 1917, Russell's enthusiastic support for President Wilson's obligations to World War I forced him to leave the Socialist party. That year he was appointed to the Root Mission to Russia, and two years later he served as a member of President Wilson's Industrial Commission.

For the rest of his life, Russell served the unfortunate of society. In 1909, for instance, he had helped implement the National Association for the Advancement of Colored People. In 1914 he had written a series of articles for *Pearson's* on how advertisers had stopped the most important form of journalism, muckraking. Russell argued for civil liberties, penal reform, and a government that represented everyone, not just a select few.

Russell wrote several biographies, one of which won a Pulitzer Prize, before he died in 1941.

REPRESENTATIVE WORKS

The Greatest Trust in the World (1905)
The Uprising of the Many (1907)
Lawless Wealth (1908)
Why I Am a Socialist (1909)

Rachel Scott
(1947–   )

Former investigative reporter Rachel Scott was born in 1947 in Iowa. She graduated from Kansas State University in 1969. Immediately upon her

†*Ibid., p. 143.*

graduation, she entered journalism as a reporter for the *Winston-Salem Journal* of North Carolina.

After a year, Scott became a freelance writer who contributed investigative articles to various magazines. In 1972 she wrote *A Wedding Man Is Nicer Than Cats, Miss: A Teacher at Work with Immigrant Children*, which was a delightful account of the meeting of two cultures — the inhabitants of an English manufacturing town and the immigrant children of Runjabi (Indian Sikhs and Pakistani Muslims). Her book related the problems of the English school where the children were introduced to their new language and customs.

Scott returned to newspaper journalism in 1974, when she became a reporter for the *Baltimore Sun*. Scott, who specialized in environmental problems as well as industrial safety, resigned from the newspaper to investigate occupational diseases caused by various safety problems in industry. Her investigation, which exposed safety hazards in such industries as mining, printing, auto manufacturing, and foam rubber, among others, was published in 1974 under the title *Muscle and Blood*. As a result of her incisive and critical exposé, she served as the director of health and safety of the Illinois Industrial Commission in the mid–1970s.

In 1977 she worked as an investigative reporter and editor for *Environmental Action*. Before she became a spokesperson for the Environmental Protection Agency in 1979, she worked as a writer and editor for the U.S. Department of Labor.

Scott's book, like Paul Brodeur's *Expendable Americans*, was not only publicized in magazines and on television, but initiated similar action by other investigative reporters.

REPRESENTATIVE WORKS

Muscle and Blood (1974)
Environmental Action (editor)

George Seldes
(1890–1995)

One of the last muckraking journalists to be born before the turn of the century, George Seldes was born on November 16, 1890, in Alliance, New Jersey. He attended high school in nearby Vineland and the East Liberty Academy in Pittsburgh.

Having an idealistic view of the press, which was contrary to reality, Seldes obtained a position as a reporter with the *Pittsburgh Leader*; then he worked as an editor with the *Pittsburgh Post*. After three years, he furthered his formal education at Harvard, where he remained for a year. Penniless, he returned to the *Post*. He was offered the managing editor's position of *Pulitzer's Review* three years later. Although he did not dislike New York City or the Bohemian lifestyle of Greenwich Village, he sailed to England to cover World War I. To Seldes, Europe was another world. Until the United States entered the war in 1917, he worked for the United Press, rewriting wire copy. When he learned that his homeland had declared war, however, he immediately enlisted and eventually became a member of the American Expeditionary Force's press section. Dispatches were published in such newspapers as the *Los Angeles Times*, *Detroit Free Press*, *Philadelphia Press*, *St. Louis Globe-Democrat*, and the *Atlanta Constitution*.

When the war ended, Seldes remained in Europe as a correspondent for the *Chicago Tribune*. He investigated the Irish disturbances during the postwar period. In 1920 he was in Italy, where he witnessed the so-called Red uprising. The same year he was in Germany, where he observed the Kapp *Putsch*. During the famine of 1922 and 1923, he smuggled news out of Moscow. In 1925 he was expelled from Italy for being the first to report that Mussolini was a military puppet who was supported and controlled by the chambers of commerce and the manufacturing associations of that country and that Mussolini had been responsible for the assassination of his political rival.

Seldes reported on the French army in Syria in 1926 and "was accused by the French of starting a mutiny in the Foreign Legion when he interceded to save the life of a deserter."* He was threatened by the Arabs because they believed that his dispatches were anti–Arab. In 1927 he investigated Mexico and the Avila documents.

What Seldes had witnessed undeniably distressed him. When he resigned from the *Tribune* in 1928, he returned to the United States, contributed anti-Fascist articles to various magazines, and wrote numerous volumes that exposed manipulation of the press by big business. In 1929 *You Can't Print That*, a book filled with European stories that had been suppressed, was published. *Freedom of the Press* appeared six years later, while *Lords of the Press* was published in 1938. Other volumes of press criticism followed.

Seldes wrote about international problems too. In 1931, for example, *Can These Things Be!* was published. In it, Seldes predicted accurately what was to occur 10 years later. In 1934, *Iron, Blood and Profits*, a book concerned with the corrupt munitions industry, appeared; one year later his book exposing Mussolini's fascist rise to power was published.

Although Seldes became a correspondent to cover the war in Spain for the *New York Post* in 1936, he returned a few months later and wrote *You Can't Do That*, which analyzed the rights of labor rather than the war.

*Maxine Block, ed., Current Biography: 1941 (New York: H. W. Wilson, 1941), pp. 767–68.

In 1940, after writing two additional books, Seldes founded *In Fact*, a four-page weekly newspaper devoted to controversial stories that other newspapers would not print. Although he received financial support from Bruce Minton, a member of the American Communist party, his paper was not, as Minton and the party realized later, devoted to any party's philosophy. According to Derek Shearer:

> *In Fact*'s circulation skyrocketed — due entirely to Seldes' popularity — and the Party's position became untenable. It was clear that Seldes could not be pushed out without wrecking *In Fact*. The Party decided instead to write off the venture as a failure. By the fall of 1940 Minton's name had vanished from the masthead, and by early 1941 he had stopped contributing altogether.†

Seldes' newspaper printed exposés that linked members of the National Association of Manufacturers (NAM) to Nazi Germany and Fascist Italy. Through pre–World War II support by such NAM members as General Electric, American Telephone and Telegraph, and Ford Motor Company, Nazi Germany rose to be a world power. His newspaper's circulation eventually increased to 176,000 before its demise in 1950. During McCarthy era certain groups canceled their subscriptions. Since Seldes refused advertising, funds to publish the newspaper dwindled when subscriptions were canceled.

When *In Fact* stopped publication, Seldes continued his investigative exposés in book form such as *Tell the Truth and Run*, which was published in 1952.

Seldes edited the popular book *The Great Quotations* in 1961. This book emphasized the history of ideas more than literary value and contained a helpful topical index.

For the next two decades, Seldes lived in relative obscurity in rural Vermont with his wife, Helen Wiesman, who died in 1979. He wrote *Never Tire of Protesting* in 1968 and *Even the Gods Cannot Change History* in 1976.

In 1985, Seldes edited the popular book *The Great Thoughts*, which contained utterances of pure nonsense as well as great thoughts. Two years later he wrote the insightful autobiography *Witness to a Century: Encounters with the Noted, the Notorious, and the Three SOBs*. Seldes was in his 90s when he penned this book, so he recounted more than 70 years of his life in and out of journalism. Although he seemed to suffer at times when he presented accurate information, his opinions of certain individuals, including political leaders, were critical but honest.

Seldes died in 1995.

REPRESENTATIVE WORKS

You Can't Print That (1929)
Iron, Blood and Profits (1934)

†Derek Shearer, "George Seldes: Muckraker Emeritus," Ramparts 12, no. 2 (August–September, 1973): 20.

Lords of the Press (1938)
Facts and Fascism (1943)
In Fact (founder and editor)

Robert Sherrill
(1925–   )

Born in Frogtown, Georgia, on December 24, 1925, Robert Sherrill received a bachelor's degree from what is now Pepperdine University in 1949 and a master's degree from the University of Texas at Austin in 1956. Sherrill, a newspaperman turned muckraking journalist, worked on newspapers until 1954 and taught at Texas A & M University and the University of Missouri. In 1960 he joined the *Texas Observer,* where he, together with such journalists as Ronnie Dugger, Willie Morris, and Larry L. King, enabled readers to understand not only the in-depth details of state politics but entertained them with articles that explored quite candidly the mechanics of the political process at the national level.

After three years, Sherrill moved to the *Miami Herald,* where he was made chief of the capital bureau in Tallahassee. Two years later he became Washington editor of the *Nation.*

Sherrill's experiences in the nation's capital enabled him to write such exposés as *The Accidental President* (1967), which was a critical biography of President Lyndon Johnson; *Military Justice Is to Justice as Military Music Is to Music* (1970), which provided a vivid account of how the military dispensed justice; *Why They Call It Politics: A Guide to America's Government* (1972), which featured a disturbing portrait of those elected to serve their country; and *The Saturday Night Special, and Other Guns with Which Americans Won the West, Protected Bootleg Franchises, Slew Wildlife, Robbed Countless Banks, Shot Husbands Purposely and by Mistake, and Killed Presidents* (1973), which criticized the lobbying organization of the National Rifle Association as well as the gun-control advocates who believed that legislation could actually solve an age-old problem.

Sherrill contributed shocking articles to such periodicals as *Harper's, Playboy,* and *Esquire.* In 1974, in an article that appeared in the *New York Times* magazine, Sherrill revealed to readers that the existing evidence of the 1969 Chappaquiddick drowning of Mary Jo Kopechne contradicted Senator Edward Kennedy's account. Sherrill criticized journalists for failing to conduct a thorough investigation. In 1976 he wrote *The Last Kennedy: Edward M. Kennedy of Massachusetts, Before and After Chappaquiddick,* which concerned Ted Kennedy's life.

Sherrill eventually devoted more time to writing articles and books and less time to the *Nation*. In addition to writing about politics, he examined other subjects such as the petroleum industry. For instance, in 1983 he wrote *The Oil Follies of 1970–1980: How the Petroleum Industry Stole the Show (And Much More Besides)*.

Perhaps Sherrill's most insightful exposé concerned politics in the South. First published in 1968, *Gothic Politics in the Deep South: Stars of the New Confederacy* was revised in 1969 and again in 1991. In his review of the book, Patrick Goldstein noted:

> A savvy reporter with a masterly writer's touch, Sherrill offers incisive, barbed portraits of the scoundrels who emerged as the stars of the so-called New Confederacy, racist demagogues [*sic*] like Georgia's Talmadge and Lester Maddox, Louisiana's Leander Perez, Mississippi's Ross Barnett and James Eastland, Arkansas' Orval Faubus and, of course, Alabama's George Wallace.*

REPRESENTATIVE WORKS

The Accidental President (1967)
Gothic Politics in the Deep South: Stars of the New Confederacy (1968)
Military Justice Is to Justice as Military Music Is to Music (1970)
Why They Call It Politics: A Guide to America's Government (1972)
The Saturday Night Special, and Other Guns with Which Americans Won the West, Protected Bootleg Franchises, Slew Wildlife, Robbed Countless Banks, Shot Husbands Purposely and by Mistake, and Killed Presidents (1973)
The Last Kennedy: Edward M. Kennedy of Massachusetts, Before and After Chappaquiddick (1976)

Upton Sinclair
(1878–1968)

In 1904, Upton Sinclair was asked by Fred D. Warren, editor of the magazine *Appeal to Reason*, to write about the slaves of industry. Warren had apparently read Sinclair's novel *Manassas*, which concerned the slave problem in the South and the abolitionist movement, and had been intrigued by Sinclair's radical ideas. Sinclair immediately responded to Warren's offer and went to Chicago, where, for seven weeks, he investigated the meat-packing industry. *The Jungle*, a novel which was more fact than fiction, was the result. The book was first serialized in Warren's magazine. Then, after several rejections because

---

*Patrick Goldstein, "Steal Magnolias," Los Angeles Times Book Review, *November 24, 1991, p. 2*.

of its controversial subject matter, it was accepted by Doubleday, Page and Company in 1906, when the company learned from investigations that what Sinclair had written was basically true. The book, published during the muckraking years, became an instant best seller.

Sinclair, who was born in 1878 in Baltimore, had learned of privation at an early age. His father was from an aristocratic Southern family that had been ruined by the Civil War. A traveling salesman who turned to alcohol to forget his problems, he seldom earned enough for his family. Sinclair's mother came from a wealthy Baltimore family. Although she could have used financial help from her parents to raise Sinclair, she refused to ask them for money. The contrast between wealth and poverty not only molded Sinclair's philosophy and writing but disturbed him so much that he eventually joined the socialist movement.

When Sinclair was 14, he attended City College of the City University of New York, where he started writing for magazines. He had started writing novels, mostly pulp fiction, by the time he graduated in 1897. From 1897 to 1901, he attended graduate school at Columbia University, where he learned that serious fiction, not adventure fiction, could have an impact on society. He soon realized that readers were not receptive to novels perpetrating ideas of reform. After three efforts, he turned to his romantic Civil War novel *Manassas*, in which his socialistic ideas were disguised. Published in 1904, it was perhaps the best of his early novels.

When *The Jungle* was published, *Manassas* was forgotten, and justifiably so. *The Jungle* presented the story of a Lithuanian family who had moved to Chicago to find the American dream, only to have that dream turn into a nightmare of death, brutality, and exploitation. Sinclair declared that improvements in working and living conditions could only be gotten from a new economic structure: socialism. *The Jungle*, although it had flaws, was a powerful story. Because it was based on fact, it ultimately led to investigations of the meatpacking industry by the government, which eventually applied pressure and instituted regulations.

Sinclair wrote several muckraking novels, including *The Metropolis* (1908), *The Moneychangers* (1908), *King Coal* (1917), *Oil* (1927), and *The Flivver King* (1937), the Lanny Budd series, and nonfiction. He died in 1968.

The Jungle contained the elements found in literary new journalism, including scene-by-scene construction, the third-person point of view, abundant description, and realistic, if not actual, dialogue. Because Sinclair was exposing the corruption that occurred within the meat-packing industry, he can also be considered a muckraker.

The Jungle, merely one example of the many muckraking books and articles that appeared during this period, depicted so graphically the unsanitary conditions as well as the unequal treatment of immigrants in meat-packing plants that readers became outraged. The federal government enacted the Pure

Food and Drug Act and the Meat Inspection Act in an attempt to counter the grim picture Sinclair had painted.

REPRESENTATIVE WORKS

Manassas (1904)
The Jungle (1906)

W. T. Stead
(1849–1912)

Born in 1849 in England, Stead learned from his mother and his father, a Congregational minister, the puritanical convictions that ultimately ruled his life.

During his teenage years, Stead contributed to the *Northern Echo*, which had been founded in Darlington in 1870 and was the first halfpenny morning newspaper to be published. The owner, J. Hyslop Bell, was so impressed with Stead, as well as with his writing, that he appointed him editor. At once Stead made improvements. In addition to borrowing revolutionary design mechanics from American newspaper publishers, he borrowed American reporting methods such as the in-depth interview, which Horace Greeley had perfected. Soon his ideas of social reform were published, and those people he opposed such as the Tories were never the same. The *Northern Echo* had a new, much stronger voice then, and the readers read with vigor. Under Stead the paper became a national voice as its circulation increased.

Under the editorship of John Morley, the *Pall Mall Gazette*, which had been founded in 1865 by George Smith and Frederick Greenwood for the purpose of providing political and literary articles to the upper English classes, was an eight-page evening newspaper that cost two cents. In 1880, Stead became Morley's assistant editor. Although they were extremely opposite in every respect, including dress, their relationship lasted until Morley entered Parliament. Stead was made editor and began his crusades. It is interesting to note that Stead termed his muckraking journalism "new journalism," a term which Matthew Arnold borrowed when he criticized the sensationalism of Stead's *Pall Mall Gazette*.*

Stead's causes were many. He denounced the slums in London. He spoke to General Gordon when the Mahdi rebelled in the Sudan; Stead claimed that General Gordon should be sent to confront the Mahdi. He advocated for a

*Piers Brendon, The Life and Death of the Press Barons *(New York: Atheneum, 1983), p. 75.*

stronger navy. In 1885 he revealed juvenile prostitution in a series of articles called "The Maiden Tribute of Modern Babylon." In addition to conducting an investigation into London's prostitution, Stead purchased Eliza Armstrong, a 13-year-old girl, from her mother and took her to a brothel. Posing as a rake, Stead drank alcohol and smoked tobacco. Although he did not have sexual intercourse with Eliza, he knew he could have done so if he had desired. Stead reported the event.†

While Stead was reveling from all the attention he was given, Eliza Armstrong's father accused him of abduction. When the case was tried, Stead was found guilty. He had not, according to the court, obtained the father's permission. As a result, he was sentenced to three months' imprisonment. Stead's articles and his trial increased the *Gazette*'s circulation by almost 33 percent.

Upon his release Stead began another crusade; this time he preached that England was ready for a government controlled by journalists. To him the press was the "engine of social reform," the "Chamber of Initiations," the "voice of democracy," the "apostle of fraternity," and the "phonograph of the world."§ Therefore he believed that the press should be represented in Parliament and should have access to every governmental body or department. As he carried out this crusade, the *Gazette* suffered, and the newspaper's publisher, Henry Yates Thompson, regrettably tried to curb the editor. Consequently, Stead turned his attention to the sexual behavior of certain members of Parliament as well as affluent businessmen such as Sir Charles Dilke, who had committed adultery with a Parliament member's wife, and Edward Langworthy, who had deserted his wife.

Once again Stead was cautioned by the publisher. In 1890, Stead resigned and began the *Review of Reviews*, a magazine that, in addition to publishing original muckraking articles, digested information from other periodicals. Instantly successful, the *Review of Reviews* had American and Australian editions within two years. Stead's magazine grew, and he continued his crusades for the good of mankind.

In 1897, Stead wrote *Satan's Invisible World Displayed; or Despairing Democracy*, which concerned the Lexow Commission's investigation into New York City's corrupt police department and the department's apparent tie to Tammany Hall. Stead revealed the corruption and exposed the method by which an officer achieved a higher position: payoffs. He exposed the corruption that occurred when certain police officers were paid by representatives of illegal businesses for "protection." He closely examined the evidence and critically analyzed the corrupt ties between the police department and certain members of Tammany Hall. He exposed the undeniable graft that linked the two together and offered some explanation as to why and how such corruptible practices grew.

†Ibid., *pp. 76–77.*
§Ibid., *pp. 78–79.*

Stead was perhaps England's most prolific muckraker. He exposed the ills of society: prostitution, police corruption, poor housing, and the sexual behavior of certain politicians, among other issues. More importantly, in addition to presenting the facts, he interpreted those facts for the reader — even to the extent of explaining the possible consequences. In some of his exposés he recorded accurately the conversations that occurred between the participants, whether they were police officers speaking in reference to favors or payoffs to prostitutes or whether they were politicians speaking in reference to the same police officers. Such conversations served as additional evidence for his exposés; concurrently, they enlightened the reader as to the kinds of characters who engaged in illegal activities.

Stead's muckraking journalism forced the government to implement commissions and measures that not only improved living conditions for the poor and increased the size of the navy, but raised the age of consent of adolescent prostitutes. His attacks on the unscrupulous behavior of certain politicians prevented them from seeking reelection. His investigative, sensational articles caused some members of Parliament to think before they acted.

In 1912, Stead perished along with 1,500 others aboard the *Titanic* when it struck an iceberg and sank.

REPRESENTATIVE WORKS

Pall Mall Gazette (1880–1890)
Review of Reviews (1890–1912)
Satan's Invisible World Displayed; or Despairing Democracy (1897)

Lincoln Steffens
(1866–1936)

Born in San Francisco in 1866, Lincoln Steffens attended a military academy in San Mateo and the University of California, from which he graduated in 1889. He then traveled abroad and attended the universities of Berlin, Heidelberg, and Liepzig, and the Sorbonne in Paris. When he returned to the United States in 1892, he settled in New York City, where he obtained a reporting position on the *New York Evening Post*. For five years he worked at the *Post*, advancing from reporting general news to covering Wall Street and later the police when Theodore Roosevelt was the commissioner. Steffens' reporting for the *Post*, which included the Reverend Charles H. Parkhurst's accusations and revelations of a corrupt police force, helped earn for him an excellent reputation.

Thus when he was offered the position of city editor of the *Commercial Advertiser* in 1897, he immediately accepted.

Four years later, at the invitation of John S. Phillips, Steffens joined *McClure's*, whose staff included such revolutionary figures as Ida Tarbell and Ray Stannard Baker. Steffens, although he had accepted the managing editor's position, believed that he could better serve *McClure's* by traveling and reporting; S. S. McClure, the publisher, agreed.

Steffens traveled to St. Paul to write an article about Frederick Weyerhauser, who had become a millionaire from the lumber business. From St. Paul he traveled to St. Louis to investigate political corruption, which Joseph Folk, the circuit attorney, was fighting. "With a local journalist, Claude H. Wetmore, Steffens published...'Tweed Days in St. Louis.'"* "The Shame of Minneapolis" followed. This article concerned a politician named Ames who had been elected mayor by the Republicans and by the Democrats. After serving several terms, Ames hired people who had criminal records to run city hall; he also dismissed about half of the police officers. Steffens informed the reader how Minneapolis had been saved from Ames and his criminals.†

Steffens revisited St. Louis and claimed that the conditions were worse than what he had witnessed in Minneapolis. Next, he visited Pittsburgh and learned that it, too, had similar conditions. Steffens then visited Philadelphia, Chicago, Cleveland, and Cincinnati. It seemed every major city had problems — from police corruption to city bosses who hired common criminals.

As each article appeared, Steffens' popularity increased. In 1904, *The Shame of the Cities*, a collection of his city articles, was published. The same year he turned his attention to state governments and wrote several articles in which he described how Tom L. Johnson of Ohio and Robert M. La Follette of Wisconsin were challenging corruption within their states.

Two years later Steffens and several other muckraking journalists of *McClure's* purchased *Frank Leslie's Popular Monthly* and changed its name to the *American Magazine*. The same year his second book *The Struggle for Self-Government* appeared.

In 1907, Steffens resigned from the *American* and worked as an editor at *Everybody's*, contributing background articles on the new reformers, who included Theodore Roosevelt and Eugene Debs. Two years later he published the *Upbuilders*, which contained positive portraits of various reformers throughout the country.

For the next several years, Steffens traveled to Boston and to Los Angeles to report on the conditions and on the trial of two labor leaders, the McNamara brothers, who had been accused of exploding dynamite in the offices of

*Louis Filler, "Steffens, Lincoln," in Dictionary of American Biography, vol. 22, ed. Robert Livingston Schuyler (New York: Charles Scribner's Sons, 1958), pp. 625–26.
†C. C. Reigier, The Era of the Muckrakers (Chapel Hill: University of North Carolina Press, 1932), pp. 60–61.

the *Los Angeles Times*. The dynamite devastated the building and killed 21 people. Instead of merely reporting the trial, Steffens tried to intervene; indeed, he attempted to negotiate a settlement between the newspaper's proprietor and the McNamaras. When the negotiation failed to materialize, Steffens was severely criticized and ostracized by the antireformist press and by his friends.

By 1911 muckraking was becoming a thing of the past, and Steffens realized it. Before World War I, he traveled to Europe to observe and gather information on municipal conditions; much of what he learned was similar to what he had gathered on American cities.

Steffens traveled to Mexico to observe the Mexican Revolution. He admired Venustiano Carranza's courage and leadership.

Three years later Steffens returned to Europe with Charles R. Crane to observe the war and study the February Revolution in Russia. He covered the armistice negotiations and in 1919 interviewed Lenin, whom he greatly respected. For the next eight years, he spent most of his time in Europe. Reformation was occurring there, and he was determined to witness the progress.

In 1927, Steffens made his home in Carmel, California. His *Autobiography*, which was published in 1931, became a best-seller. Because of the book's popularity, he was asked to lecture throughout the country and to write for newspapers. He performed these functions until he suffered a heart attack in 1933. He died three years later. Steffens' muckraking journalism undeniably influenced certain politicians to make reforms, to "clean house." His attacks on various city bosses and their illegal activities stirred readers from coast to coast. Indeed, readers became so irate that city and state legislators realized that they had to manage problems or the readers would vote for someone else in the next election. Eventually, Steffens' articles, like those of other muckrakers, were taken seriously by political bosses.

REPRESENTATIVE WORKS

The Shame of the Cities (1904)
The Struggle for Self-Government (1906)
Upbuilders (1909)
Autobiography (1931)

Gloria Steinem
(1934–   )

Feminist, activist, columnist, writer, editor Gloria Steinem was born on March 25, 1934, in Toledo, Ohio. Her father and mother divorced before she reached adolescence, but her mother, who had formerly worked as a reporter before she married, obtained a similar position in Toledo and was able to support her daughter and herself in a modest fashion.

Steinem moved to Washington, D.C., to live with her older sister. When she completed her secondary education, her mother made the financial arrangements so she could attend Smith College. Of course, Steinem proved to be an excellent student and soon received scholarships. When she graduated in 1956, she received a fellowship to travel and study at the University of Delhi and the University of Calcutta. Upon her return to the United States, she first worked as the director of the Independent Research Service in Cambridge, Massachusetts, and then as a writer for *Esquire* in New York City, to which she contributed "The Moral Disarmament of Betty Coed" and "Student Prince." Although she remained with *Esquire* for several years, she moved to *Show* in 1963. Perhaps her most important contribution to *Show* was "A Bunny Tale," which was based on her experience as a bunny in a Playboy Club. Articles about her humorous exposé of Hugh Hefner's dream turned reality appeared in news magazines, and Steinem's career as a journalist was secure. Her byline was seen in such publications as *Life, Vogue, McCall's, Cosmopolitan,* and *Glamour,* and she wrote for the NBC series "That Was the Week That Was."

Steinem, who became a celebrity for what she wrote and for what she advocated for women, wrote features on James Baldwin, Julie Andrews, Jackie Kennedy, Barbra Streisand, Truman Capote, Michael Caine, Dame Margot Fonteyn, and Lee Bouvier, and on topics such as women and power, Englishmen and their opinions of American women, fashion, popular culture, Lefrak City, and women's liberation, to mention a few.

In each interview she conducted, Steinem captured intelligently the scene, the personality, especially the mannerisms and the moods. Some of her profiles included colorful descriptive passages about the person interviewed. Some of these passages allowed the personalities to present themselves in their own words. For most of the interviews, she included background information, information that she deemed beneficial to the reader. Her advocating articles logically explored issues that concerned her as a woman. Usually she presented the facts and then her beliefs as to what should be done to correct the problems. If she believed that the problems could be better illustrated with description or anecdotes, she would use either or both.

In 1968, Steinem was hired by Clay Felker to write for his newly resurrected *New York* magazine. Steinem wrote numerous advocacy articles about women, marriages, and politics. She attacked Eugene McCarthy and Richard Nixon, she supported Norman Mailer's and Jimmy Breslin's political aspirations, and she wrote and spoke with vengeance for numerous minority groups. Her *New York* column "The City Politic" was never subtle as long as there was a cause of some kind.

In the late 1960s, Steinem became involved in the feminist movement, and in 1972 she became editor of *Ms.*, a magazine founded for the liberated woman. *Ms.* promoted the ideas of Steinem and other feminists. By the mid–1970s the magazine had attracted 500,000 readers.

Steinem was one of the commissioners appointed by President Jimmy Carter to the National Committee on the Observance of International Women's Year in 1977. She was awarded a Woodrow Wilson Scholarship to study feminism at the Woodrow Wilson International Center for Scholars the same year.

During the 1980s, Steinhem continued editing *Ms.*, as well as supporting various women's organizations. A collection of her essays, articles, and diary entries was published in 1983 under the title *Outrageous Acts and Everyday Rebellions*. The collection included "I Was a Playboy Bunny," "Ruth's Song," which concerned her mother, and articles on several famous women. The collection was an example of literary journalism as well as advocacy journalism.

In 1986, Steinem's insightful biography of Marilyn Monroe was published. Titled *Marilyn: Norma Jean*, the book was more realistic than other biographies of Monroe in the sense that it focused on her personality and entire life, not just the years in Hollywood. Indeed, Steinem revealed a warm human being who had childlike qualities. Unfortunately, the child was trapped in a woman's body.

One year later *Ms.* was sold to a large Australian communications conglomerate. Steinem was retained as a consultant to the publication. Even though the magazine was sold again, Steinem remained as editor. In 1988 she became an editorial consultant to Random House, a publishing firm.

In 1992, Steinham wrote *Revolution from Within: A Book of Self-Esteem*, which was a self-help book that attempted to inform readers how to boost their self-esteem. Steinem used other sources, including Margaret Mead and Chief Seattle, as well as her own life, for inspiration. She offered literature, nature, art, meditation, and connectedness as means of finding and exploring the self.

In her review of the book for *Newsweek*, Laura Shapiro wrote:

> Self-help books sell like crazy, especially among women, and Steinem's has everything: goddesses, guided meditation, directions on how to find the child within, dream diaries and droplets of wisdom from a range of sources including the Gnostic Gospels and Koko, the talking gorilla. If anything distinguishes "Revolution from Within" from dozens of other contributions to the genre, it's Steinem's feminist politics, which are prominent or at least discernible throughout.[*]

Moving Beyond Words, a book of six essays, three of which had appeared in magazines, was published in 1994. The essays included "What If *Freud* Were *Phyllis?*" in which Steinem claimed that Freud's theories had been based on

---

[*]*Laura Shapiro, "Little Gloria, Happy at Last," Newsweek, January 13, 1992, p. 64.*

the assumption of male superiority. In "Sex, Lies and Advertising," she examined the advertising business as it applied to magazines. In "The Strongest Woman in the World," Steinem described the female bodybuilder Bev Francis. She wrote about wealthy women who had lost control of their trust funds in "The Masculinization of Wealth." In "Revolving Economics," she detailed how worldwide census and accounting practices undervalued women's labor and in "Doing Sixty," Steinem explored her life at age 60.

REPRESENTATIVE WORKS

Ms. (co-founder and editor)
Outrageous Acts and Everyday Rebellions (1983)
Revolution from Within: A Book of Self-Esteem (1992)
Moving Beyond Words (1994)

Philip Stern
(1926–1992)

Born in New York City in 1926, Philip Stern received his bachelor's degree from Harvard University in 1947. Then he moved to New Orleans, where he worked as a reporter and editorial writer for the *New Orleans Item*. After a year, however, he resigned, and for the next several years he worked as a legislative assistant to Representative Henry M. Jackson and then as an assistant to Senator Paul Douglas and as an assistant to Wilson W. Wyatt. From 1953 to 1956 he served as the director of research and as the senior editor of the *Democratic Digest* for the Democratic National Committee. From 1957 to 1961, he worked as an editor and later publisher of the *Northern Virginia Sun*. After another year of public service, he turned what he had learned from politics and journalism into several best-selling exposés, including *The Great Treasury Raid* and *The Rape of the Taxpayer*.

In 1974, Stern became a special assignment reporter for the *Washington Post*, a position he held for more than a year. Stern, who was devoted to investigative journalism, founded the Fund for Investigative Journalism for the sole purpose of enabling journalists to learn what functions the institutions in American society were performing.

Stern died in 1992.

The Rape of the Taxpayer exemplified Stern's form of investigative muckraking. Instead of belaboring a point to the extent that it irritated the reader, he used simple words and sentences to say what would ordinarily be discussed in complex jargon. Stern, like Goulden and other muckraking journalists, revealed what he had learned by providing examples or incidents.

REPRESENTATIVE WORKS

The Great Treasury Raid (1964)
The Rape of the Taxpayer (1972)

I. F. Stone
(1907–1991)

One of the major alternative radical forces in the 1950s and 1960s was *I.F. Stone's Weekly*, named after its founder and publisher.

Stone, who was born Isidor Feinstein in Philadelphia in 1907, was reared by his Russian-Jewish immigrant parents in Haddonfield, New Jersey. His crusading journalistic career began at age 14, when he published the *Progressive*, a monthly in which he strongly attacked William Randolph Hearst's "Yellow Peril" campaign, supported Mahatma Gandhi, and backed Woodrow Wilson's ideas concerning the League of Nations. Because Stone was devoting most of his time to the paper and very little to his high school studies, his father forced him to abandon the enterprise. Stone's journalistic ability enabled him to become a reporter for the *Haddonfield Press* and a correspondent for the *Camden Courier-Post* before he graduated from high school in 1924.

Stone attended the University of Pennsylvania and worked concurrently for the *Philadelphia Inquirer*. After three years of college and working, he became a reporter and editor for the *Camden Courier-Post*, and later he became a reporter and editorial writer for the *Philadelphia Record*. In 1933, when the publisher of the *Courier-Post* and *Record* acquired the *New York Post*, he moved to New York City and wrote editorials for the latter paper. Stone, who had grown extremely interested in American politics, believed in an ideal world, a moral world. He did not believe in Western religions, however, primarily because of the evil that existed in the world. He believed that if God as envisaged in such religions existed, then evil could not exist. Ultimately, he rejected socialism and Marxism, too, because of the injustices that persisted in socialist and communist states.

In 1938, Stone became an associate editor of the *Nation*, a post he held for two years. When he moved to Washington, D.C., in 1940, he served as the magazine's Washington editor. For six years he covered the capital, reporting the truths, half-truths, and lies spoken and published by members and officers of the federal government. In addition to his duties for the *Nation*, Stone joined the staff of *PM*, a New York City liberal daily that had been founded and financed by Marshall Field in 1940. Primarily a newspaper of opinion interspersed with quality photography and interpretative articles, the newspaper was eventually sold in 1948 to Bartley Crum, who changed the name to the *New York Star*. The *Star* died a year later. Nonetheless, Stone had written several stories of importance, including ones about the 1946 exodus of World War II Jewish survivors who were determined to establish a nation and the Israeli-Arab war in 1948 that "culminated in the creation of the independent Jewish state."*

When *PM* was sold, Stone moved to the *Star*. When it folded, he moved to the newly launched *New York Daily Compass*, a liberal newspaper similar to *PM*. For three years he was a reporter and columnist who wrote according to his beliefs, but the paper ceased publication in 1952. Although Stone tried to get jobs with other newspapers and magazines, including the *Nation*, he was not successful. In January 1953, the first issue of his *I.F. Stone's Weekly*, a four-page miniature of fact and opinion, appeared. According to *Current Biography*: "Doing his own research, reporting, writing, editing, and proofreading, Stone achieved a high quality publication. Accurate, well-written, and interesting, it was graced by an attractive format and typeface and enlivened by Stone's idiosyncratic wit and humor."†

Stone analyzed every major issue in Washington, determining whether it needed further investigation. He uncovered facts that other journalists had overlooked. Oftentimes, he included quotations from officials that contradicted other sources. To say that some in Washington had misspoke themselves would be an understatement. Stone revealed numerous inconsistencies as well as apparent lies. He realized early on that politicians or anyone, for that matter, who held a powerful office had a tendency to lie. He also realized that answers could be found if one took the time.

The weekly prospered. Indeed, within the first decade its circulation increased from 5,000 to 20,000. In 1968, after he suffered a heart attack, Stone changed to bi-weekly publication. When the publication ceased in 1972, it had more than 70,000 subscribers and was known to readers from coast to coast.

Stone, who had written articles and reviews for the *New York Review of Books*, became a contributing editor in 1972. Several book-length exposés as well as compilations of his articles and columns were published.

Stone died in 1991.

REPRESENTATIVE WORK

I. F. Stone's Weekly

Charles Moritz, ed., Current Biography Yearbook 1972 (New York: H. W. Wilson, 1972), p. 415.
†*Ibid., p. 416.*

Simeon Strunsky
(1879–1948)

Simeon Strunsky was born in 1879 in Vitebsk, Russia, and was brought to New York City when he was seven. He received several Pulitzer scholarships to Columbia's Horace Mann School and to Columbia College (Columbia University); he graduated from the latter in 1900.

Strunsky worked for the *New International Encyclopedia* from 1900 to 1906 and then joined the staff of Oswald Garrison Villard's *New York Evening Post*, where he wrote numerous editorials and humorous essays on current events. In 1912 his essays concerning Theodore Roosevelt's efforts to regain the White House received considerable recognition. Strunsky's perceptiveness was evident, for even Roosevelt enjoyed reading them. His style, which was evidently influenced by such writers as William Hazlitt and G. K. Chesterton, was extremely witty.

In addition to writing for the *Post*, Strunsky contributed to Villard's *Nation* and the *Atlantic Monthly*. His essays were collected and published under the titles *The Patient Observer and His Friends* and *Belshazzar Court*. In 1918 he published his first novel *Prof. Latimer's Progress*, which concerned New York City, but his essays, although mild compared to the muckraking exposés, became his dominant form of expression. For example, when World War I began, Strunsky advocated Allied support and laissez-faire economics, satirized the Germans, and opposed Bolshevism.

In 1920, Strunsky became chief editorial writer of the *Post*, but four years later, when Thomas W. Lamont, the owner, sold the paper to Cyrus H. K. Curtis, Strunsky joined the *New York Times*, for which he wrote editorials and the weekly column "About Books — More or Less." Cyrus H. K. Curtis was, Strunsky believed, too conservative about editorial policies.

In 1932, Strunsky was given the responsibility of writing "Topics of the Times," a daily column on the editorial page, which he wrote until his death in 1948. Immediately, Strunsky incorporated his liberal political beliefs; he learned, however, that a column contained little space for his ideas. Consequently, *The Living Tradition* was published in 1939, followed by *No Mean City* five years later. His last book, *Two Came to Town*, was published a year before his death.

Strunsky, an advocate for the American way of life, held onto his liberal beliefs until the end. His writing, much of it informal, less vehement perhaps than that of the earlier advocating journalists, awakened the public and the politicians to his way of thinking.

REPRESENTATIVE WORKS

The Patient Observer and His Friends (1911)
Belshazzar Court (1914)

The Living Tradition (1939)
No Mean City (1944)
Two Came to Town (1947)

Mark Sullivan
(1874–1952)

Mark Sullivan was born on September 10, 1874, in Avondale, Pennsylvania, to Julia Gleason and Cornelius Sullivan, who had emigrated from Ireland. Sullivan lived on a farm that his parents owned and attended the West Chester Normal School. He wrote insightful news stories about academics for the *West Chester Village Record*.

In 1892, after graduation, Sullivan worked as a reporter for the *West Chester Morning Republican* until 1893, when he, together with John Miller, purchased the *Phoenixville Republican*. Sullivan gained additional experience in journalism as an editor and publisher.

Although Sullivan enjoyed working on the *Republican*, he realized that a college education would help him procure a more productive position. In 1896 he was admitted to Harvard. Upon graduation he sold his share of the *Republican* and then worked as a reporter for E. A. Van Valkenberg's *Philadelphia North American* before he returned to Harvard to study law. Sullivan contributed articles concerning the environment, politics, and travel to the *Boston Transcript* primarily because he needed the money to finance his education. In 1901 his investigative article "The Ills of Pennsylvania" was published in the October issue of the *Atlantic Monthly*. Sullivan revealed that local and state officials had accepted bribes from hospitals and other institutions for political favors. One of the first muckraking articles about politics, this article also presented Sullivan's patriotic views of America.

After Sullivan received his degree in law in 1903, Edward W. Bok, editor of the *Ladies' Home Journal*, hired him to investigate the patent medicine business. Sullivan learned, among other things, that Lydia E. Pinkham, whose name appeared in advertisements for a popular remedy, had actually died in 1883. Sullivan explained how manufacturers of patent medicine used their advertising contracts to persuade magazine and newspaper publishers not to investigate the patent medicine industry in the article "The Patent Medicine Conspiracy Against Freedom of the Press," which appeared in *Collier's Weekly* in 1904.

Sullivan's work for Bok was impressive, and he was hired as a journalist by the editor of *McClure's* in 1905. One year later he moved to *Collier's*. Sullivan's relationship with the magazine lasted until 1919, so he must have produced what Robert J. Collier, the publisher, desired.

Sullivan, who married Marie McMechen Buchanan in 1907, not only started a family, but, in addition to contributing articles to *Collier's* that promoted progressivism, he began the biting column "Comment on Congress" in 1908. This column, which was widely read, initiated the fight by Republicans against Speaker of the House Joseph G. Cannon. Sullivan also supported Chief Forester Gifford Pinchot, who had criticized Secretary of the Interior Richard Ballinger for his unethical behavior in administering policy. Sullivan believed in the puritan work ethic and consequently supported those who exhibited the same. Concurrently, he realized that this ethic was the basis for one's pursuit of happiness and individuality. Thus he opposed conformity.

As Otis L. Graham, Jr., wrote, however:

> A time came ... when Sullivan, like so many progressives whose social philosophy was composed of a mixture of Jefferson, Sumner, and Alger, realized that he was rubbing elbows inside the movement with men who had no love for individualism and the competitive race and who dreamed of a more collective life. When he realized this he denounced them as false liberals, and when in the postwar years they gradually purloined the word for a philosophy he hated, Sullivan with remarkable consistency followed his brand of progressivism into the camp of Roosevelt's enemies.*

When the Progressive party formed in 1912, Sullivan became an ardent supporter of Theodore Roosevelt, much to the chagrin of Norman Hapgood, the editor of *Collier's*, who supported Woodrow Wilson. The two disagreed for months, even though Hapgood realized that Collier, the publisher, sided with Sullivan. Eventually, Hapgood resigned, and Sullivan was promoted to editor in 1914. The magazine, like other muckraking publications of the time, had changed. Indeed, its everyday operations depended on advertising revenues. Consequently, advertisers, which were primarily businesses, were seldom criticized in print. Concurrently, candidates of the Progressive party had been defeated in 1912, and the party had disintegrated. When the United States entered World War I, readers' concerns were not necessarily focused on domestic issues. Thus *Collier's* under Sullivan gave up muckraking journalism. Instead, the magazine criticized Wilson and his policies toward the war.

In 1917, Sullivan resigned as editor, but he continued to write articles for the magazine until 1919, when he became the Washington correspondent of the *New York Evening Post*. In 1923 he was hired to write a column, which was syndicated, for the *New York Herald Tribune*. He contributed the column until his death. The same year he started *Our Times: The United States, 1900–1925*, a six-volume descriptive history of the United States from 1900 to 1925.

---

*Otis L. Graham, Jr., An Encore for Reform: The Old Progressives and the New Deal *(New York: Oxford University Press, 1967), pp. 87–88.*

During the 1920s, Sullivan strongly opposed the progressive ideas of Robert La Follette and promoted prohibition and lower taxes. He opposed labor unions and special-interest legislation. He supported his friend Herbert Hoover during the 1930s. In 1938 his autobiography *The Education of an American*, which described his life and political beliefs, was published.

Sullivan criticized Franklin Roosevelt and his socialistic policies during the late 1930s and early 1940s primarily because he believed that such measures would threaten individualism.

Sullivan died on August 13, 1952.

Although Sullivan spent most of his journalistic career writing a column for a newspaper, he was highly respected for his muckraking journalism, which promoted progressive reform.

REPRESENTATIVE WORKS

Phoenixville Republican (editor and publisher)
"The Ills of Pennsylvania" (1901)
"Comment on Congress" (1908–1919)
Collier's Weekly (editor)
Our Times: The United States, 1900–1925 (1926–1935)
The Education of an American (1938)

Harvey Swados
(1920–1972)

Harvey Swados was better known as a novelist perhaps than as a critical essayist who promoted socialism for the working man, especially the blue-collar worker, but he was undoubtedly an advocate for the faceless citizen.

Born in Buffalo, Swados received his bachelor's degree from the University of Michigan in 1940. Upon graduation he worked for a few years in several factories while he tried to establish himself as a writer. From 1942 to 1945 he served as a radio officer in the U.S. Merchant Marine.

Swados wrote short stories and essays for various periodicals, including *Esquire, Partisan Review, Saturday Evening Post*, and *Nation*. In 1955 his first novel *Out Went the Candle* was published; it was followed a year later by a collection of short stories, *On the Line*. The short stories concerned the problems of factory employees, as Charles Shapiro wrote:

> Swados ... has shown his understanding for the problems of the industrial laborers; and in *On the Line* he extends this compassion....

Swados has chosen to dramatize a steady tension between the dehumanizing effect of the line and the dreams of the workers who try, at first, to preserve their private enthusiasms — one man plans to be a professional singer, another worker wishes for a new car, a third wants his son's love — as the assembly belt rolls on. The factory must destroy the individuality of each man, and as this cruel process is exposed, we come to accept the line as well as despair of it. The little tragedies, placed together, become a damning indictment.*

Swados taught at several universities, including the University of Iowa, Sarah Lawrence College, San Francisco State University, and the University of Massachusetts at Amherst. He continued, however, to write novels such as *False Coin*, *The Will*, *Standing Fast*, and *Celebration*, which was published posthumously in 1975. He also wrote short stories, essays, and a biography of Estes Kefauver. His essays and short stories were collected and published as separate volumes.

Swados died in 1972.

The essay "The Jungle Revisited" informed the reader that although times had changed since Upton Sinclair wrote his book *The Jungle*, the basic problem was the same; that is, a job in a meat plant was not attractive, challenging, or lucrative for most workers. An employee did basically what was done in Sinclair's day.

REPRESENTATIVE WORKS

On the Line (1956)
A Radical's America (1962)

Jonathan Swift
(1667–1745)

Jonathan Swift was born in Ireland on November 30, 1667. His father, Jonathan, a solicitor, had immigrated to Ireland from England around 1660. He died before Swift was born. Swift's mother, Abigail Errick, was born in Ireland to parents who had immigrated from England.

Although Irish, Swift referred to himself as English. When he was one, his nurse brought him to England, where he remained until he was four. His mother, who feared the sea, stayed in Ireland. When Swift was returned to Ireland, his mother left him with relatives and eventually moved to England.

---

*Charles Shapiro, "Harvey Swados: Private Stories and Public Fiction," in Contemporary American Novelists, ed. Harry T. Moore (Carbondale: Southern Illinois University Press, 1964), pp. 188–89.

Swift started attending the Kilkenny School when he was six and received an excellent education. When he was 14, he enrolled at Trinity College, the University of Dublin, where he excelled in several languages. He earned the bachelor's degree in 1686 and then started work toward the master's degree. Three years later he left Ireland with other Protestants primarily to escape a questionable political climate, as Richard Talbot, earl of Tyrconnel, promoted Catholicism.

Swift became an administrative secretary to Sir William Temple, a respected English diplomat who had retired to Moor Park, his country estate. Swift helped Temple immensely; he wrote his letters and edited his writings for publication. He also delivered messages from Temple to the king. In his spare time, he read numerous books in Temple's personal library and wrote very poor eulogistic poems that imitated the style of Abraham Cowley. Swift enjoyed working for Temple, but his health deteriorated because of the damp climate.

In 1690, Swift returned to Ireland, but his health did not improve. In less than a year he was back at Moor Park. While he worked for Temple, he completed his master's degree at Oxford University. In 1693 one of his first essays was published. Titled *An Answer to a Scurrilous Pamphlet, Lately Printed, Intituled, A Letter from Monsieur De Cros*, the essay defended Temple against attacks that had been made about him when he was a diplomat for Charles II. The anonymous essay appeared in pamphlet form and was filled with sarcasm.

In 1694, Swift was ordained into the Church of Ireland and was assigned to northern Ireland, one of the poorest areas, which he disliked. Indeed, within two years he was back at Moor Park, where he remained until 1699, the year Temple died.

While he was living and working at Moor Park, Swift wrote *A Tale of a Tub. Written for the Universal Improvement of Mankind. Diu multumque desideratum. To which is added, An Account of a Battel Between the Antient and Modern Books in St. James's Library*. In this work he defended Temple and his assumption that the learning of the ancients was superior to that of the moderns against Richard Bentley, who had attacked Temple and his literary notion. The essay was published anonymously in 1704. Swift did not necessarily agree with Temple; he was merely offended by Bentley's tone, which had sounded too personal. Swift redefined "ancient" and "modern" and had a battle between books in a library, which represented each term. Through allegories, Swift satirized values as well as religion, preferring the Church of England and Church of Ireland over Catholicism and Protestantism.

Swift became chaplain to Charles, earl of Berkeley, in Ireland. He also became vicar of Laracor and was given the prebend of Dunlavin in St. Patrick's Cathedral in Dublin. This position encouraged him to become involved in religious and political affairs in England. In 1701, for instance, he returned to England and learned that four Whig ministers might be impeached because they had been charged with arranging treaties without consulting or informing Parliament. Swift, who considered himself a Whig, criticized the impeachment of the four Whig ministers in *A Discourse of the Contests and Dissensions Between the Nobles and the Commons in Athens and Rome, with the Consequences they had upon both those States*, which was published the same year.

Swift returned to Ireland in 1702 and earned the doctor of divinity degree from Trinity College later that year. He devoted most of his time to his parish and to St. Patrick's Cathedral.

In 1707, Swift returned to England as a representative of the Church of Ireland, but he was more productive as a writer than as a negotiator for funds. His poetry and essays appeared in *The Tatler*, which was published by Richard Steele.

At this time, Swift realized that he differed with the Whigs. The Whigs supported Protestant dissenters who did not support the Test Act; Swift was loyal to the Church of England and consequently supported the Test Act. His writing therefore attacked the dissenters and their views toward the Test Act. He also called for the queen to appoint virtuous men to positions of power.

Swift returned to Ireland in 1709. The Whigs, who had taken control of Parliament in 1708, were ousted in 1710, and the political climate in England changed drastically when Robert Harley's ministry came to power. Swift returned to England, and Harley paid the "First Fruits and Twentieth Parts"—fees that had been paid by the clergy in Ireland to the British Crown—to Swift. Harley, who favored a coalition government, persuaded Swift to write on behalf of the new Tory government. Swift, who now referred to himself as an "Old Whig," was like Defoe in that he supported Harley's "initially moderate but eventually extremist Tory ministry."*

The Tory ministry published the *Examiner*, a weekly paper, in 1710. Harley asked Swift to serve as writer and editor. Swift captured the public's attention almost immediately and was invited to cabinet meetings, formal dinners, and gala affairs at Windsor. Yet his essays were conservative, for the most part, in that he defended certain actions of the ministry and advocated peace. He attacked John Churchill, duke of Marlborough, among others, claiming that he was corrupt and an enemy of England. Like the *Tatler* and later the *Spectator*, the *Examiner* published letters addressed to the editor, responses from the editor, and essays that contained fables and other literary devices to enhance the topic being discussed. Swift's writing was straightforward, yet filled with sarcasm. He stopped editing the paper in 1711 and returned to writing political propaganda in pamphlet form, such as the best-selling *The Conduct of the Allies, And of the Late Ministry, In Beginning and Carrying on the Present War*. This pamphlet summarized the ministry's perspective toward the war with France and then presented strong arguments for peace. Swift also charged that

*Laura Ann Curtis, ed., The Versatile Defoe (Totowa, N.J.: Rowman and Littlefield, 1979), p. 10.

the Whigs had prolonged the War of the Spanish Succession primarily for selfish reasons. The writing was terse and clear, and the arguments were sound. The reader easily understood the author's points and subsequently reacted to those points.

Swift observed the feuding between Harley and Henry St. John, who was made Viscount Bolingbroke in 1712 and called for a unilateral treaty with France. Harley desired that the Dutch be included; eventually, his desires were fulfilled when the Treaty of Utrecht was signed in 1713.

The same year Swift was made dean of St. Patrick's Cathedral in Dublin. He returned to England, however, where he attempted to ease the tension between Harley and St. John. Unfortunately, it was too late. Swift wrote the controversial *The Publick Spirit of the Whigs: Set Forth in their Generous Encouragement of the Author of the Crisis: With Some Observations on the Seasonableness, Candor, Erudition, and Style of that Treatise* and faced possible prosecution because the Tories no longer reigned. The queen had died in 1714; George I and the Whig ministry had assumed power. Swift immediately left England for Ireland, where he served as dean of St. Patrick's Cathedral. He eventually wrote about the exploitation and enslavement of Ireland by England as well as the friction between the various political and religious factions that made up Irish society.

Swift favored restrictions on Catholics and dissenters, but he opposed economic restrictions on Ireland by England. He expressed these views in *A Proposal for the Universal Use of Irish Manufacture, In Cloaths and Furniture of Houses, etc., Uterly Rejecting and Renouncing Every Thing wearable that comes from England*, which was published in 1720. In a series of letters, he argued against using coins manufactured by William Wood, who had been authorized by England to coin a hundred thousand pounds worth of Irish coins. Swift claimed that the coins contained too little copper and would glut the market, thus reducing the value of money. Wood's authorization was withdrawn in 1725.

Although Swift's satiric *Travels into Several Remote Nations of the World. In Four Parts. By Lemuel Gulliver, First a Surgeon, and then a Captain of several Ships* was published in 1726, he continued to write political essays. In 1729, for instance, his *A Modest Proposal for Preventing the Children of Poor People from being a Burthen to their Parents, or the Country, and for making them Beneficial to the Publick* was published. In this attack on England's treatment of the Irish people, Swift proposed that children of the poor inhabitants of Ireland should be sold to the wealthy for food. He compared the poor to cattle and provided images of slaughtering and cooking the children. Swift used analogies, metaphors, and other literary devices to strengthen his arguments. The pamphlet, which was easily understood, was controversial because of its subject matter.

Swift wrote an occasional political essay and numerous poems during the next several years. After 1734, however, his interest in writing declined. Ill health and a forgetful memory bothered him until his death in 1745. He was 77.

Swift's political essays were early examples of advocacy journalism. As an advocate of political and religious thought, he persuaded multitudes of people, including clergy and representatives of governments, to accept his particular positions.

REPRESENTATIVE WORKS

An Answer to a Scurrilous Pamphlet, Lately Printed, Intituled, A Letter from Monsieur De Cros (1693)

A Discourse of the Contests and Dissensions Between the Nobles and the Commons in Athens and Rome, with the Consequences they had upon both those States (1701)

A Tale of a Tub. Written for the Universal Improvement of Mankind. Diu multumque desideratum. To which is added, An Account of a Battel Between the Antient and Modern Books in St. James's Library (1704)

The Conduct of the Allies, And of the Late Ministry, In Beginning and Carrying on the Present War (1712)

The Publick Spirit of the Whigs: Set Forth in Their Generous Encouragement of the Author of the Crisis: With Some Observations on the Seasonableness, Candor, Erudition, and Style of That Treatise (1714)

A Proposal for the Universal Use of Irish Manufacture, In Cloaths and Furniture of Houses etc., Uterly Rejecting and Renouncing Every Thing wearable that comes from England (1720)

A Modest Proposal for Preventing the Children of Poor People from being a Burthen to their Parents, or the Country, and for making them Beneficial to the Publick (1729)

Tad Szulc
(1926-   )

Born in Warsaw, Poland, on July 25, 1926, Tad Szulc attended the University of Brazil before he began a twenty-year career as a foreign and diplomatic correspondent for the *New York Times*. Szulc, an investigative muckraking reporter who covered several coups in South America, including the overthrow of Juan Peron in Argentina, uncovered President Kennedy's Bay of Pigs invasion as well as the support of the United States for Pakistan.

As a correspondent, Szulc served not only in Latin America, but in Southeast Asia, Eastern Europe, and the Middle East. His critical but incisive coverage of the "Prague Spring" in Czechoslovakia caused him to be expelled from the country. During the Nixon administration, Szulc was assigned to the Washington bureau. As a result of his frank exposés on political issues, his telephone was tapped. This did not intimidate Szulc, who had written such controversial books as *Twilight of the Tyrants* (1959), *The Cuban Invasion: The Chronicle of a*

Disaster (cowritten by Karl E. Meyer, 1962), *The Winds of Revolution: Latin America Today and Tomorrow* (1963), *Dominican Diary* (1965), *The Bombs of Palomares* (1967), *Compulsive Spy: The Strange Case of E. Howard Hunt* (1973), and *Innocents at Home: America in the 1970s* (1974). Henry Kissinger's wiretapping efforts were of little use. Szulc's unpopularity with certain officials as well as his unorthodox reporting techniques became an issue, however, which forced him to argue with his editors over his stories.

Szulc resigned in 1972 and devoted his time to writing exposés for such periodicals as the *New Republic, New York, Forbes, Saturday Review, Foreign Policy Quarterly, Penthouse, Rolling Stone, Columbia Journalism Review,* and the *New Yorker.* He wrote *The Energy Crisis* in 1974 and *The Illusion of Peace: Foreign Policy in the Nixon Years* in 1978, which critically analyzed foreign policy decisions made by the Nixon administration.

In 1986, Szulc wrote *Fidel: A Critical Portrait*, which was about Fidel Castro. Szulc had met the Cuban leader in 1959 and then again in 1984, when he spent several days with him, discussing his life. The biography was unofficial, but Szulc had access to Castro, his people, and his materials. Approximately 5,000 pages were then transcribed from the tapes. The book, which was the first full-length biography of Castro, was critically acclaimed for its candid, indepth treatment of the military leader and his rise to power. Szulc examined Castro's philosophy, his life, and his strained relations with the United States.

In 1990, Szulc covered some five decades in the book *Then and Now: How the World Has Changed Since World War II*, in which he examined political parties, various leaders, and numerous regimes throughout the world. One year later he explored the issue of illegal and semilegal immigration of Jews into Israel arranged by such organizations as the Palestinian Jewish underground, the Haganah, Israel's foreign intelligence service, and two of the American Jewish community's philanthropic organizations — the Joint Distribution Committee and the Hebrew Sheltering and Immigrant Aid Society. The title of this work was *The Secret Alliance: The Extraordinary Story of the Rescue of the Jews Since World War II.*

REPRESENTATIVE WORKS

Twilight of the Tyrants (1959)
The Cuban Invasion: The Chronicle of a Disaster (1962)
The Winds of Revolution: Latin America Today and Tomorrow (1963)
Dominican Diary (1965)
The Bombs of Palomares (1967)
Innocents at Home: America in the 1970s (1974)
The Energy Crisis (1974)
The Illusion of Peace: Foreign Policy in the Nixon Years (1978)
Fidel: A Critical Portrait (1986)
Then and Now: How the World Has Changed Since World War II (1990)
The Secret Alliance: The Extraordinary Story of the Rescue of the Jews Since World War II (1991)

Ida Tarbell
(1857–1944)

A large number of the muckraking exposés were published in *McClure's*, which Samuel Sidney McClure founded in 1893. McClure had a stable of writers who contributed dozens of articles. One of these writers was Ida Tarbell, who was born in 1857 in Pennsylvania. Her father was a carpenter who later built wooden oil tanks, and her mother was a teacher. In high school, Tarbell developed an interest in science, particularly biology. After she graduated, she attended Allegheny College. Upon graduation she accepted a teaching position at Poland Union Seminary in Poland, Ohio. Within two years, she had enough of teaching. She returned to Allegheny College, where she received a master's degree. She was hired by the editor of the *Chautauquan*, a monthly magazine that was conservative in its editorial policy. After one year, she had become the managing editor, but she desired to visit Paris and study there.

After eight years of writing and editing, Tarbell traveled to Paris, where she remained for two years living with friends, writing articles about Paris and France for American newspapers, writing a short story for *Scribner's*, attending lectures at the Sorbonne, and doing research on the French Revolution, especially on Madame Roland.

In 1892, S. S. McClure met Tarbell and persuaded her to write a biography of Louis Pasteur. This work was published a year later. When she returned to the United States in 1894, McClure hired her to write more biographies, including a series on Napoleon Bonaparte and a series on Abraham Lincoln.

Tarbell's biographies were so successful that she was made an associate editor of the magazine. McClure realized her potential and valued her past work; it was no surprise when he assigned to her what eventually became the most ambitious assignment of her career, *The History of the Standard Oil Company*. For five years she researched and investigated the company, producing 19 articles for *McClure's*, which appeared collectively in 1904 in a two-volume set. According to James Playsted Wood:

> The articles showed that Standard Oil was magnificently organized, that it functioned superbly, but that the methods by which the corporation had been built included bribery, fraud, violence, the corruption of public officials and railroads, and the wrecking of competitors by fair means and foul. What had started out to be a study of a great business became, by virtue of the facts uncovered, an exposé of big business as sometimes practiced.*

The articles glorified Tarbell's name in the public's eye, but certain businessmen and politicians had little respect for her. They believed she had unjustly

---

*James Playsted Wood, Magazines in the United States (New York: Ronald, 1971), p. 132.

given the Standard Oil Company a bad name. For fear of being exposed, they tolerated her, however.

In 1905, Tarbell traveled through Kansas and Oklahoma and reported on the oil strikes and the controversies that resulted. Two years later the federal government filed antitrust suits against the Standard Oil Company.

Tarbell, together with other frustrated editors and writers at *McClure's*, including John S. Phillips, Ray Stannard Baker, Lincoln Steffens, and Albert Boyden, purchased *Frank Leslie's Popular Monthly in 1906.* They immediately changed the periodical's name to the *American Magazine* and recruited Finley Peter Dunne and William Allen White.

For the new magazine, Tarbell wrote articles on the tariff and women. An independent woman, Tarbell could not sympathize with the suffrage movement. Through observation and investigation, she had grown to distrust politicians and other group leaders who claimed they could achieve human progress through politics and group activity.

When Henry Ford implemented his assembly line system, Tarbell traveled extensively from one factory to another. What she observed and learned, she reported, thinking that progress was perhaps on the way. In 1915 she resigned from the *American Magazine,* but she wrote and lectured for the next 20 years. For instance, four years after she had resigned she traveled abroad to report on the Paris Peace Conference. In 1926 she traveled to Italy to report on Mussolini's industrial ideas, which she respected.

In addition to articles and short stories, Tarbell wrote several biographies. She died in 1944.

REPRESENTATIVE WORK

The History of the Standard Oil Company (1904)

George Kibbe Turner
(1869–1952)

George Kibbe Turner was born on March 23, 1869, to Sarah Ella Kibbe and Rhodolphus Turner, in Quincy, Illinois. When his father died several years later, his mother married James Dayton.

Turner attended public schools and then matriculated at Williams College, from which he graduated in 1890. He was hired as a reporter by Samuel Bowles, who edited the *Springfield Republican* of Massachusetts. Turner enjoyed journalism, but he began to write short stories and novels after his marriage to Julia Hawks Parker in 1892. *McClure's* published several of his short stories and, in 1902, his first novel, *The Taskmaster*, which depicted realistically and accurately the abusive relationship between employers and employees.

When Lincoln Steffens, Ray Stannard Baker, Finley Peter Dunne, Ida Tarbell, and others left *McClure's* to publish the *American Magazine*, S. S. McClure hired Turner in 1906 to investigate various topics and write muckraking articles. Soon Turner had replaced Steffens as the magazine's expert on urban affairs. One of his first assignments was to investigate the revolutionary commission form of municipal government that had been successfully tried in Galveston, Texas. As Turner explained in the article "Galveston: A Business Corporation," the new system was the result of a natural disaster. On September 8, 1900, a hurricane came ashore and literally destroyed the city. The government needed money for public works, but taxpayers needed money to rebuild homes or businesses that had been lost. Turner explained that the "Deepwater Committee," which had been "formed to secure national appropriations for deepening the city's harbor," took matters into its hands:

> It planned ways and means of raising money, of satisfying creditors, of building public works, and it especially considered the formation of some agency to take over the management of the ruined city—a strong, responsible, centralized city government which would really govern. Now there were two systems which the city would certainly not adopt. She had tried them and found them wretched failures. The first was government by a mayor and ward alderman; the second was government by a mayor and a board of aldermen elected at large.*

Turner explained each system and provided reasons for failure. Then he explained the new system and provided reasons for its success. The article's impact was dramatic. Politicians in cities across the country requested copies of the article, while certain newspapers published it in its entirety. The system's popularity was so great that numerous states amended statutes to permit its adoption.

McClure, who had been working on an article about Chicago, directed Turner to go to Chicago to investigate possible criminal activity. Turner uncovered a corrupt police department that not only allowed but protected certain criminal activity, including gambling and prostitution. The article "The City of Chicago: A Study of the Great Immoralities" appeared in *McClure's* in 1907. When it was published, it caused a stir among readers, and certain politicians in Chicago reacted appropriately by creating a commission in 1910 to investigate criminal activity, especially vice. The commission's report "The Social Evil in Chicago" was the result, and this report and the *McClure's* article influenced other municipalities to conduct similar investigations and enact appropriate legislation that would stop or at least curtail such activity.

*George Kibbe Turner, "Galveston: A Business Corporation," McClure's Magazine (October 1906):610.

The same year Turner was sent to Boise, Idaho, to interview Harry Orchard, who had assassinated Frank Steunenberg, the former governor of the state, in 1905. Orchard, who had been an officer of the Bourne Miners' Union, had acted under the direct instructions of "Big" Bill Haywood and others who disliked Steunenberg's militant attitude toward miners while he was serving as governor. Orchard, who was found guilty, informed Turner about his life and evil deeds, and the story resulted in *The Confessions and Autobiography of Harry Orchard*, which *McClure's* published in 1907.

In "Our Navy on Land," which was published in 1907, Turner criticized the military's ability to defend the nation. As a result, President Theodore Roosevelt ordered the navy to literally circle the globe.

Two years later Turner investigated possible criminal activity in New York City and wrote the insightful exposé "Tammany's Control of New York by Professional Criminals," which charged that prostitution had become almost legalized. Five months later he continued his investigation of vice in New York City in the disturbing article "The Daughters of the Poor." Turner claimed that New York City had become the leading city in the world for recruiting young girls, particularly poor immigrants, for prostitution. His articles were indirectly responsible for congressional action; indeed, the bill that became the Mann-Elkins Act of 1910, which banned white slave traffic from interstate commerce, was introduced one month after the publication of "The Daughters of the Poor."

In 1910, with the assistance of John E. Lathrop, Turner wrote "Billions of Treasure" for *McClure's*. Turner accused the secretary of the interior of neglecting his public responsibility when he gave certain lands in Alaska to the Guggenheim trust. The same year Turner and trust expert John Moody wrote the series "The Masters of Capital in America," which argued that business could stabilize the economy. As David Mark Chalmers wrote:

> While the explicit theme of "The Masters of Capital in America" was the power that wealth was placing in the hands of a few, the implicit argument was much more in keeping with Turner's previously expressed ideas. As if to counterbalance the traditional objections, he eulogized the sense of responsibility of the great magnates. Huge combinations were inevitable and necessary to prevent the wastefulness of competition and to rationalize business.†

In essence, Turner, like Burton Hendrick, Alfred Henry Lewis, and Will Irwin, believed that many problems could be solved by the industrial system or by a person's individualistic nature.

When muckraking declined in popularity, Turner left *McClure's* and devoted his time to writing fiction and scripts for films. Although he wrote

---

†*David Mark Chalmers,* The Social and Political Ideas of the Muckrakers *(New York: Citadel, 1964), p. 24.*

several popular novels, he did not describe his exploits in an autobiography as did some muckraking journalists.

Turner died in 1952.

REPRESENTATIVE WORKS

"Galveston: A Business Corporation" (1906)
"The City of Chicago: A Study of the Great Immoralities" (1907)
The Confession and Autobiography of Harry Orchard (1907)
"Our Navy on Land" (1907)
"Tammany's Control of New York by Professional Criminals" (1909)
"The Daughters of the Poor" (1909)
"Billions of Treasure" (1910)
"The Masters of Capital in America" (1910–1911)

Gore Vidal
(1925–   )

Eugene Luther Vidal, or Gore Vidal, was born on October 3, 1925, at the United States Military Academy in West Point, New York, where his father was an instructor in aeronautics. Vidal's grandfather, Thomas Pryor Gore, was Oklahoma's first senator. Vidal stayed with his grandfather in Washington, D.C., primarily to assist him, until his parents divorced in 1935. He learned about history and politics from reading books on the subjects to his grandfather, who was blind, as well as from leading his grandfather around the nation's capital. He attended St. Alban's School and then the Los Alamos School in New Mexico for a year. He completed his high school education at the prestigious Phillips Exeter Academy, where, in addition to writing for the academy's *Review*, he organized a student group that opposed America's involvement in World War II. His political philosophy had been molded by his grandfather's isolationist beliefs.

When Vidal graduated in 1943, he intended to enroll at Harvard. He enlisted, however, in the U.S. Army Reserve Corps and served on a transport ship in the Aleutians. Vidal read during his off-duty hours and wrote the novel *Williwaw*, which was published in 1946. The novel concerned the conflicts between crew members on board a military craft.

Vidal was released from service in 1946 and obtained a position editing books at E. P. Dutton, a New York publishing company. Within six months he left Dutton and moved to Antigua, Guatemala, believing he could earn his living from writing novels. *In a Yellow Wood*, which he had completed before he left New York City, appeared in 1947, to mostly favorable reviews. The novel depicts a veteran of World War II who has to adjust to civilian life. *The City and the Pillar* explores one character's realization that he is a homosexual. To say the least, the book was attacked by certain critics for its unusual subject matter when it was published in 1948.

Vidal, who contracted hepatitis in 1947, returned to the United States for a while and then toured Europe, traveling through North Africa as well as Italy. After about two years, he returned to the United States. In 1950 he purchased "Edgewater," a mansion in New York. Over the next several years, he wrote *The Season of Comfort* (1949), a slightly disguised autobiography of his early years; *A Search for the King* (1950), which described the search of Blondel de Neel for Richard the Lion-Hearted; *Dark Green, Bright Red* (1950), which depicted the various exploits of an American mercenary soldier; *The Judgment of Paris* (1952), which concerned an American who wandered through Europe; and *Messiah* (1954), which focused on a new religion. These novels were dismissed by most critics, and Vidal's financial resources dwindled. His estate required maintenance, and it was evident that his novels were not going to sell.

Vidal wrote teleplays for several television programs. Later, he moved to Hollywood and wrote screenplays for Metro-Goldwyn-Mayer. Vidal's intention was to earn enough money in a relatively brief period so he could return to writing novels. Toward the end of the decade, however, he wrote for the stage. His first success was an adaptation of his *Visit to a Small Planet*, which had appeared on television in 1955. *The Best Man*, a satire about American politics, followed in 1960. He wrote other plays, but none were as successful as these.

By the early 1960s, Vidal had returned to the novel. *Julian* was published in 1964 and concerned Flavius Claudius Julianus, the Roman emperor who attempted to restore paganism. *Washington, D.C.*, the first novel in his series about American history and politics, was published in 1967. *Burr* followed in 1973 and was enjoyed by critics. The last book, *1876*, which was published in 1976, was criticized by some reviewers for not having a major character to carry the plot.

Vidal also wrote the controversial satire *Myra Breckinridge*, which focused on transsexuality and American culture. The novel, published in 1968, was followed by *Myron* in 1974, which concerned the further exploits of Myra. The critics panned the latter because the novel's situations were too repetitive.

Although Vidal penned other historical and political novels, including *Creation* (1981), *Lincoln* (1984), *Empire* (1987), *Hollywood* (1990), and *Live from Golgotha* (1992), he also wrote numerous advocating essays for several periodicals throughout the 1950s, 1960s, 1970s, and 1980s. These essays, which concerned politics, Broadway, literature, public television, writers, pornography, sex, flying, and himself, were collected in several books, including *Rocking the Boat, Sex, Death, and Money, Reflections Upon a Sinking Ship, Matters of Fact and Fiction (Essays 1973–1976), The Second American Revolution and Other*

Essays (1976–1982), At Home: Essays 1982–1988, A View from the Diner's Club: Essays 1987–1991, The Decline and Fall of the American Empire, and *United States: Essays, 1952–1992.* Regarding Vidal's essays, Robert Graalman noted:

> Vidal argues just as emphatically for his beliefs as he does to reject a political tag. He can be an articulate and vigorous commentator against, for example, such a topic as the horrors of television advertising, for something as grand as governmental responsibility, and most forcibly for a more humane, realistic, and finally liberating attitude on the subject of sexuality in Western civilization.[*]

Vidal's essays contained personal references to others as well as allusions to historical events and figures. Many contained clips from his past. In several essays about politics, one theme was ever present — that the United States was controlled by a few power brokers and corporations such as the Chase Manhattan Bank and CBS. As Robert E. Kiernan pointed out, "Vidal is ... a vocal critic of the American establishment."[†] In summarizing his assessment of Vidal's essays, Kiernan wrote: "The essays, like the novels, are a banquet of canapés. They may leave one hungry for logical fair play, as the novels leave one hungry for plot, but the canapés are so tasty withal that more conventional fare seems unflavored."[§]

In his review of *Reflections Upon a Sinking Ship,* Edgard Z. Friedenberg wrote:

> For Americans who are devoted to freedom remain by and large committed to the belief that freedom should be enjoyed by all the people; that democracy is the proper source of liberty and dignity, which all would come to share and prize if democracy were functioning properly. Vidal's book is both haunted and held together by the implication that this belief is false. But he himself never concludes that it is.[**]

In 1992, Vidal wrote *The Screening of History,* which contained reminiscences of his childhood and early manhood. These reminiscences were mixed with the films that he saw when he was young. An unusual autobiography because of this technique, it nonetheless provided another side to Vidal.

REPRESENTATIVE WORKS

Rocking the Boat (1962)
Sex, Death, and Money (1968)
Reflections Upon a Sinking Ship (1968)

---

[*]*Robert Graalman, "Gore Vidal (3 October 1925–)," in* American Novelists Since World War II: Second Series, *ed. James E. Kibler, Jr. (Detroit: Gale Research, 1980), p. 346.*
[†]*Robert F. Kiernan,* Gore Vidal *(New York: Frederick Ungar, 1982), p. 111.*
[§]*Ibid., p. 117.*
[**]*Edgar Z. Friedenberg, "Patriotic Gore," in* New York Review of Books, *June 19, 1969, p. 35.*

Homage to Daniel Shays: Collected Essays, 1952–1972 (1972)
Matters of Fact and Fiction (Essays 1973–1976) (1977)
The Second American Revolution and Other Essays (1976–1982) (1982)
Armageddon? Essays, 1983–1987 (1987)
At Home: Essays 1982–1988 (1988)
A View from the Diner's Club: Essays 1987–1991 (1991)
The Decline and Fall of the American Empire (1992)
United States: Essays, 1952–1992 (1993)

Nicholas von Hoffman
(1929–   )

Advocating and literary journalist Nicholas von Hoffman was born in New York City on October 16, 1929, and educated at the Fordham Prep School. Von Hoffman entered journalism in the 1960s, after he had served as an associate director of the Industrial Areas Foundation and as Saul Alinsky's chief organizer of the Woodlawn Organization, which was founded to serve the needs of Chicago's southside black community.

In 1963, von Hoffman became a staff member of the *Chicago Daily News*, for which he covered the civil rights movement, including the movement called "Freedom Summer" in Mississippi. His revelations were ultimately collected in the diarylike *Mississippi Notebook*, which appeared in 1964. He also wrote interpretative stories on American universities and the students who attended the various campuses. His book *The Multiversity: A Personal Report on What Happens to Today's Students at American Universities*, which was published in 1966, explored the same issues.

In 1966, von Hoffman joined the staff of the *Washington Post*, where, in addition to writing a column several times a week, he wrote stories on student riots, hippies, the Chicago Democratic convention, and Watergate. According to Benjamin Bradlee, former editor of the *Washington Post*, "von Hoffman's dispatches as written were landmarks in the early, timid years of the new journalism: personal, pertinent, articulate, vital glimpses of man trying to make it in a more and more complicated world."*

Von Hoffman's book *We Are the People Our Parents Warned Us Against*, which told through the characters' own words what life in the San Francisco's Haight-Ashbury district was like, was published in 1968.

A collection of von Hoffman's columns for the *Washington Post* appeared under the title *Left at the Post* in 1970. His columns were powerful. Indeed,

---

*Nicholas von Hoffman, Left at the Post (Chicago: Quadrangle Books, 1970), p. 8.

what von Hoffman wrote "produced more angry letters to the editor than the work of any other single reporter" in the newspaper's history, according to Chalmers M. Roberts.†

Von Hoffman broadened his interests in the 1970s, when he debated James J. Kirkpatrick on CBS's "Sixty Minutes" and contributed numerous articles to such periodicals as the *Progressive, Harper's Bazaar, New Times,* and *Esquire.* Although he left the *Washington Post* in 1976, he became the Washington correspondent for the London-based *Spectator* magazine the same year. He also continued to write articles as well as books. For instance, his critical examination of politics in America, *Make-Believe Presidents; Illusions of Power from McKinley to Carter,* appeared in 1978.

In 1984, von Hoffman wrote the critically acclaimed novel *Organized Crimes,* which concerned the Chicago underworld of the 1930s. He had not written a novel since the 1960s.

Four years later von Hoffman returned to nonfiction with a biography titled *Citizen Cohn* that penetrated the controversial lawyer's social environment. Von Hoffman began with Roy Cohn's death from AIDS and then presented in chronological order almost every villainous deed that he had committed. Von Hoffman examined Cohn's possessive mother, who had despised her husband and had had a commanding effect on her son. Cohn, according to von Hoffman, was a closet homosexual until his mother died; then his affairs became well-known. Von Hoffman also discussed Cohn's ongoing battles with the IRS and the New York State Bar Association. The book, which contained numerous quotes from Cohn's friends and enemies, revealed that Cohn was merely interested in law because it had provided the means to a particular end. The book was praised by critics for its coverage but not necessarily for its depth.

In 1992, von Hoffman wrote *Capitalist Fools: Tales of American Business, from Carnegie to Forbes to the Milken Gang,* which was part biography and part history. Von Hoffman critically examined Malcolm Forbes and the men he profiled in his magazine, claiming that the executives had profited from buyouts and stock-option plans while their businesses declined. Although sarcasm appeared throughout the narrative, von Hoffman honored certain heroes such as B. C. Forbes, Malcolm's father who had founded *Forbes* magazine; Daniel McCallum, who had operated the railroads during the Civil War; and John Patterson, the maverick tyrant who had been responsible for building the National Cash Register company. According to von Hoffman, the number of executives who can be classified as heroes has decreased:

> These sorts of people are far more infrequent now. There are some marvelous people who have done wonderful things — I mention a few in the book — but the culture has changed enormously. One of the themes of this book is that in the

† *Chalmers M. Roberts, "Hoffman, Nicholas von," in* Contemporary Authors, *vol. 81–84, ed. Francis Carol Locher (Detroit: Gale Research, 1979), p. 586.*

process of creating itself, business changed the culture that made it — it ate its young. The commercial parts of our society use pleasure ubiquitously to sell merchandise and teach people to become obsessive pleasure lovers: "I won't do it unless it's fun; I don't like that teacher because he or she is not entertaining." Well, some things are arduous and they do hurt.§

One of von Hoffman's columns illustrated his advocating journalistic style. Opinionated, stereotypical, the column seemed to be against fat black women who received welfare — that is, until the last three sentences. In these sentences, von Hoffman presented the women's arguments and then, through the use of a metaphor, illustrated their predicament. The metaphor suggested that immediate measures should be implemented to correct the problem discussed.

REPRESENTATIVE WORKS

Mississippi Notebook (1964)
We Are the People Our Parents Warned Us Against (1968)
Left at the Post (1970)
Make-Believe Presidents: Illusions of Power from McKinley to Carter (1978)
Citizen Cohn (1988)
Capitalist Fools: Tales of American Business, from Carnegie to Forbes to the Milken Gang (1992)

Alice Walker
(1944–   )

Alice Walker was born on February 9, 1944, in Eatonton, Georgia. She was the youngest of eight children — five boys and three girls. Her parents, Willie Lee and Minnie Walker, were sharecroppers who earned a meager living toiling in fields. Walker respected her parents, especially the behavior of her mother, who told Walker and the other children numerous stories.

When Walker was eight years old, she was wounded in one eye by a BB that one of her brothers had fired from a gun. Her parents could not get her to a hospital because they did not own a car. A week later they brought her to a physician who pronounced that the eye was permanently injured. Scar tissue formed over the eye, causing Walker to become self-conscious. Instead of playing with other children, she read and wrote.

The scar tissue was removed when Walker was 14 years of age. Walker excelled in school and became valedictorian as well as queen of her senior class.

§*Wendy Smith, "PW Interviews: Nicholas von Hoffman," in* Publishers Weekly, *September 21, 1992, p. 72.*

She applied for a scholarship for handicapped students to attend Spelman College in Atlanta. Walker received the scholarship and began her studies in 1961. Atlanta was experiencing civil rights demonstrations at this time, and some faculty members at Spelman encouraged students to participate. Influenced by Staughton Lynd and Howard Zinn, two historians, Walker participated in demonstrations in Atlanta. Having experienced racial discrimination, Walker realized that demonstrations were necessary to achieve equal rights.

After two years at Spelman, Walker received a scholarship to attend Sarah Lawrence, a prestigious college for women in New York. Before she received her bachelor's degree there in 1965, she traveled throughout Africa, became pregnant, contemplated suicide, and had an abortion. Walker wrote numerous poems immediately following the abortion, poems about the civil rights movement, Africa, love, and suicide. She gave the poems to one of her instructors, Muriel Rukeyser, who was so impressed by Walker's ability that she gave the poems to her literary agent. Walker's first book of poetry was *Once: Poems* (1968).

Walker's first taste of literary success came in 1967, however, when "The Civil Rights Movement: How Good Was It?" won the *American Scholar* essay contest. The same year she married Melvyn Leventhal, a white civil rights lawyer, whom she had met while working in Mississippi during the summer of 1966. They moved to Mississippi, where Leventhal filed discriminatory suits and Walker engaged in voter registration drives and welfare reform. Later she worked as the writer-in-residence at Jackson State College. She received a fellowship from the MacDowell Colony in New Hampshire in 1967 and wrote her first novel, *The Third Life of Grange Copeland* (1970), which revealed racial bigotry and its effects on a black family in the South. Reviews of the novel were mixed.

In 1971, Walker received a Radcliffe Institute fellowship that allowed her to escape the South. She lectured at several universities in the early 1970s. In 1973, while she was living in Massachusetts and her husband was still in Jackson, Walker published three books: *Revolutionary Petunias and Other Poems* (1973), which was nominated for a National Book Award and won the Lillian Smith Award; *In Love and Trouble: Stories of Black Women* (1973), which received the Richard and Hinda Rosenthal Award from the American Institute of Arts and Letters; and *Langston Hughes: American Poet* (1973), a biography that she had written for children.

In 1974, Leventhal and Walker moved to New York City, where she accepted a position as contributing editor for *Ms.* magazine. In addition to contributing to *Ms.*, Walker wrote her second novel, *Meridian* (1976), which concerned the civil rights movement and its effect on three young people — a black woman, a black male activist, and a Jewish civil rights worker. Her third book of poems, *Goodnight, Willie Lee, I'll See You in the Morning*, was published in 1979.

Although Leventhal's and Walker's marriage had produced a daughter, they agreed to a divorce in 1976. Walker moved to San Francisco. Her second collection of short stories, titled *You Can't Keep a Good Woman Down*, appeared in 1981. The stories concerned characters from a wider social spectrum than those in her previous collection. Some reviewers found the stories too partisan.

In 1982, Walker's epistolary novel *The Color Purple* was published to critical acclaim. The novel focused on the oppression black women experienced in their relationship with black men. Concurrently, it focused on sisterhood, specifically the relationship between Celie and Nettie. The novel was nominated for a National Book Critics Circle Award and received a Pulitzer Prize and an American Book Award.

A year later appeared *In Search of Our Mothers' Gardens: Womanist Prose*. Walker had written these essays between 1966 and 1982. In the title essay, she wrote about three types of black women, as Barbara T. Christian notes, "the physically and psychologically abused black woman; the exceptional black woman torn by 'contrary instincts,' who, in order to try to fulfill her creativity, is forced to repress the sources from which it comes; and the new black woman who can freely recreate herself out of the legacy of her maternal ancestors."[*]

In the essay "One Child of One's Own," Walker questioned the idea that motherhood was in and of itself an evil for women. To Walker and other feminists, women have thought they had to choose between being mothers and being creative in the arts. Unlike certain feminists, however, Walker acknowledged that this perception was the result of the social system in which people lived.

The book, which was an example of advocacy as well as literary journalism, was divided into four parts, in which Walker looked at the civil rights movement, sexist and racial attitudes, children, and the future. Most of the essays contained biographical information. As Ben Okri wrote, "*In Search of Our Mothers' Garden* is unique in its blending of the facts of a life and the solutions that must emerge from (not be superimposed on) an understanding of the facts."[†] The essays had appeared in several publications, including *Ms.*, *Mother Jones*, *Black Scholar*, *Conditions*, and *New York Times*.

Horses Make a Landscape More Beautiful, Walker's fourth collection of poetry, was published in 1984. Another collection of essays appeared in 1988. Titled *Living by the Word: Selected Writings, 1973–1987*, the collection contained 27 entries that covered a broader range of topics than had her previous collection of essays. Walker reported on China, Jamaica, and Milledgeville, Georgia. She wrote about a horse named "Blue"; nature; an antiwar demonstration at the Concord Naval Weapons Station at Port Chicago, California; Dennis Banks, an Indian Movement leader; and Dessie Woods, a prisoner in Georgia, among other topics. This collection was slighted by some critics for its short length. As Noel Perrin wrote:

Barbara T. Christian, "Alice Walker (9 February 1944–)," in Afro-American Fiction Writers After 1955, *ed. M. Davis and Trudier Harris (Detroit: Gale Research, 1984), p. 265.*
†Ben Okri, "Colouring Book," New Statesman, June 22, 1984, p. 24.

Living by the Word is subtitled *Selected Writings, 1973–1987*. It's a short book for a collection that gathers material from a 15-year period — less than half as long as her first book of nonfiction, *In Search of Our Mothers' Gardens*. One possible reason is that most of the early material has already been picked over. In her preface to the earlier book Ms. Walker says that the pieces in it were written between 1966 and 1982. That's a huge overlap. It may be that this new child was born a year or two prematurely.§

Walker's next major novel was *The Temple of My Familiar*, which was published in 1989 and covered several hundred years — from precolonial Africa to postslavery North Carolina to modern-day San Francisco. The characters, including Miss Lissie, an old woman who had fascinating former lives, and Mr. Hal, her gentle companion, changed and evolved as their stories were told.

In 1991, Walker published another volume of poetry, titled *Her Blue Body Everything We Know: Earthling Poems, 1965–1990*. In this collection, Walker spoke with a voice of despair mixed with anger and occasional humor. A year later she wrote *Possessing the Secret of Joy*, a novel about an African woman who suffered physical and emotional anguish after she demonstrated loyalty to her beleaguered people by undergoing an unusual operation.

REPRESENTATIVE WORKS

In Search of Our Mothers' Gardens: Womanist Prose (1983)
Living by the Word: Selected Writings, 1973–1987 (1988)

Josiah Flynt Willard
(1869–1907)

Josiah Flynt, who dropped the name Willard, was born on January 23, 1869, to Mary Bannister and Oliver Willard in Appleton, Wisconsin. He was reared, however, in Evanston, Illinois. His father, a retired minister and former editor of the *Chicago Post*, taught at the Biblical Institute until he died when Flynt was eight.

Flynt wandered away from home numerous times. He also wandered away from the boarding school he attended. His mother and his two sisters traveled to Germany when he was 15. Flynt, who eventually finished school, lived with a friend of the family and attended a small college in Illinois. Formal education was not to his liking, however. He preferred tramping throughout the

§*Noel Perrin, "Another Sojourner,"* New York Times Book Review, *June 5, 1988, p. 43.*

countryside to sitting in a classroom listening to someone lecture. He left college and worked briefly on a farm in Pennsylvania and then worked briefly for a railroad in Buffalo, New York. Flynt stole a horse and buggy, sold it, and then stole another and was apprehended. He was sent to a reform school, from which he eventually escaped. He then tramped through the countryside for several months. Finally, he was arrested and incarcerated for a month.

After Flynt's release, he worked briefly on a farm in New York and then sailed to Germany to join his family. His mother, who operated a school for girls in Berlin, enrolled Flynt in the University of Berlin. Flynt tried to study and even started a major in economics, but the desire to be somewhere else instead of sitting in a classroom was overwhelming and he left the university without earning a degree.

Flynt tramped throughout Europe and became known as "Cigarette," primarily because of his slight stature. In 1890, while he was in England, he met Oscar Wilde, Arthur Symons, and Aubrey Beardsley, among other notable literary and artistic figures.

Although Flynt had much to write about, including literature and art, one of his first articles concerned his experiences as a hobo. "The American Tramp" was published in the *Contemporary Review* in August 1891. Flynt returned to Berlin, where he continued his studies and found employment. The urge to wander struck him, however, and he left Berlin and tramped to Russia. He met Ibsen and Tolstoy, and worked briefly on the latter's farm. Flynt continued to write about his numerous exploits for various magazines. These articles depicted with incredible accuracy the dismal life of a hobo. For instance, in 1897 he wrote "The Criminal in the Open," which recounted the act of stealing that resulted in his incarceration.

Flynt returned to America in 1898 primarily to work as a writer. He was immediately asked by a manager of the Pennsylvania Railroad to inspect the company's policies concerning tramps who frequently jumped freight trains to travel to other cities. Flynt accepted the assignment, which lasted several months.

In 1899, Flynt's first book, *Tramping with Tramps,* was published and made him famous almost immediately. Indeed, no writer before Flynt had depicted with such authority and uncanny realism an existence that most readers had never known.

The following year Flynt met Alfred Hodder, who had been an academician, and together they wrote a series of articles for *McClure's.* "True Stories from the Under-World," which concerned criminal behavior, especially those criminals who comprised the community called the underworld, began in the August 1900 issue and was one of the first series that could be labeled muckraking journalism. The editor introduced the series with the following note:

> The following story is the first of a series by Josiah Flynt and Francis Walton,
> men who have spent many years studying the criminal classes. Their methods

are original. They live among the criminals and are known amongst the "profession" as men of their own class. It is needless to say that their life amongst them is not to break the laws, but to understand as thoroughly as possible the motives and methods of that great part of the community which they describe as "The Under-World." These stories are not fiction in the ordinary sense; they are entertaining stories, but more than this they are philosophical studies, about a class concerning which the great mass of people knows nothing, except that they are law-breakers. All the names in these stories are fictitious, but the characters are real and the incidents have all occurred at various times and places. The stories are intended to point a moral as well as adorn a tale.*

"Francis Walton" was, of course, Hodder's pseudonym. The series, which was extremely popular among readers, revealed that the police and certain criminals were not necessarily enemies; it was published in book form under the title *The Powers That Prey* the same year.

Flynt continued with his exploration of this topic in the book *Notes of an Itinerant Policeman*, which was published later the same year. According to Flynt, the police had to have ties with certain criminals in order to serve society. After all, certain criminals knew the streets, the shady characters, and the identity of those who had committed certain crimes.

Flynt's series "In the World of Graft," which was an excellent example of muckraking journalism and brought him additional acclaim because of its popularity, began in the February 1901 issue of *McClure's*. The editor introduced the series with this note:

> Just one year ago, through an arrangement made with *McClure's*, Mr. Josiah Flynt undertook an investigation of the criminal classes in several of the leading cities of the United States. These studies were made, not to gratify an idle curiosity, but in the hope that they will aid the movement now in progress to better the government of our cities. For fifteen years Mr. Flynt has spent much of his time among the vagrant and criminal classes of this country and Europe, living with them under their own conditions. It is a mere coincidence that these articles are published just as Chicago and New York are arousing to the need of reform. It should be remembered that Mr. Flynt writes of what he saw in the spring of 1900, but practically the same conditions exist today.†

Flynt had interviewed certain criminals and reported their opinions about criminal activity. He included explanations for certain terms and phrases so readers could easily understand the criminals' language. For instance, he introduced such terms as "joint" (for an illegal liquor store), "fix" (for bribe), "mob" (for organized crime), "pinch" (for arrest), "pull" (for influence), "one who had squared it" (for becoming honest), among others.

*Josiah Flynt and Francis Walton, "True Stories from the Under-World," McClure's Magazine *(August 1900):356.*
†Josiah Flynt, "In the World of Graft," McClure's Magazine *(February 1901):327.*

According to the criminals, police departments were corrupt and consequently police officers were responsible for as much criminal activity as the criminals. Harold S. Wilson wrote, "The magazine had published many articles on criminals and their apprehension, but nothing had equaled Flynt's conversation with 'guns,' the full-time thieves, who seem to have been better informed about the 'system' than many in public office."§

Flynt's interviews had occurred in New York, Chicago, Boston, Philadelphia, Pittsburgh, and other cities, and he reported that Chicago was the only honest city (frankly corrupt) while New York was a dishonest city. The series was published in book form under the title *The World of Graft* the same year.

Flynt then turned to fiction, completing a novel that was published in 1902. He was drinking almost every day, however. In order to stop drinking, he accepted a position with a railroad in the Indian Territory, where alcohol was prohibited. Within a few weeks, he missed the taste of alcohol so badly that he returned East.

By 1905, Flynt's health was poor; alcohol had taken its toll. Nonetheless, he accepted a magazine assignment to visit Russia and report about what he observed. Flynt contributed several articles before he became seriously ill in Germany. Eventually, after spending several weeks in bed, he returned to the United States.

In 1906, Flynt accepted an assignment from a magazine to investigate poolroom racketeering in Chicago. Flynt, unable to conduct all of the necessary investigations because of his health, sought help from friends. The articles discussed the various gambling activities and the unusual criminals who were responsible. The articles contained the same fluid style but lacked the punch of the moralistic muckraking journalist.

In 1907, soon after these articles were published, Flynt died of pneumonia. His autobiography *My Life*, which was filled with sketches, was published posthumously a year later.

Although Flynt abused his body by living like a tramp and drinking, he wrote two of the earliest and most insightful series of muckraking journalism about topics that other muckraking journalists subsequently investigated. In essence, he laid the groundwork and, to a certain extent, established the tone for other muckraking journalists.

REPRESENTATIVE WORKS

Tramping with Tramps (1899)
"True Stories from the Under-World" (1900)
The Powers That Prey (1900)
Notes of an Itinerant Policeman (1900)
"In the World of Graft" (1901)
The World of Graft (1901)
My Life (1908)

§*Harold S. Wilson*, McClure's Magazine and the Muckrakers *(Princeton, N.J.: Princeton University Press, 1970), pp. 123–24.*

David Wise
(1930–   )

David Wise was born in New York City on May 10, 1930, and was educated at Columbia University. He worked for the *New York Herald Tribune* in various capacities, including as a reporter, White House correspondent, and chief of the Washington bureau from 1951 to 1966. Principally a political reporter and investigator, he wrote, with Thomas B. Ross, *The U-2 Affair* in 1962, when interest in the Francis Gary Powers' spy mission was at its zenith. Two years later the authors brought out another document appropriately entitled *The Invisible Government*, a book which included several important revelations about the political machinations in Washington, D.C. For example, Wise and Ross disclosed that Richard Nixon had wanted the Cuban invasion to take place before the 1960 election. More important, the authors examined the special group "54/12," which, at the discretion of the president, had the power to rule on certain clandestine operations without the approval of Congress.

In 1967, Wise and Ross wrote another intriguing book entitled *The Espionage Establishment*. The authors attempted to prove the validity of two controversial theories regarding the CIA — the organization was not responsible to or controllable by any political body except itself and the organization engaged in domestic operations.

Six years later, without the aid of Ross, Wise wrote another disturbing document titled *The Politics of Lying: Government Deception, Secrecy and Power*. Wise not only recapitulated what he and Ross had mentioned in previous books but attacked the Wartime Information Security Program, the government's dubious role in the Dominican Republic and South Vietnam, and the press's failure to investigate and report the lies perpetrated by political leaders and agencies.

Wise, who contributed articles of a similar nature to magazines, wrote another in-depth political exposé in 1976. *The American Police State: The Government Against the People* discussed the manipulations of the Nixon administration. The book was indicative of Wise's direct approach.

In 1988, Wise wrote the penetrating book *The Spy Who Got Away: The Inside Story of Edward Lee Howard, the CIA Agent Who Betrayed His Country's Secrets and Escaped to Moscow,* which told the story of the first CIA defector to the Soviet Union. Wise interviewed ex–CIA agent Edward Lee Howard in 1987, two years after his defection to the East, and combined the information he obtained from Howard with other information he had collected over the years and revealed what had been a confusing chain of events. Indeed, Wise told how Howard destroyed the United States' espionage network in the Soviet Union, how he was fired from the CIA, how he was placed under surveillance by the FBI, how he managed to escape to Moscow, and how he betrayed the

CIA by exposing certain secrets to the Soviet KGB. The book was riveting, to say the least, primarily because it contained the elements usually found in a suspense novel.

Four years later Wise wrote *Molehunt: The Secret Search for Traitors That Shattered the CIA*, which revealed that the search for spies inside the CIA actually destroyed the careers of some loyal officers as well as the lives of certain members of their families. The agency was also paralyzed by the search. Indeed, the agency halted its operations against the Soviet Union during the height of the Cold War. Wise's narrative was as absorbing as it was carefully researched. The book was based on more than 600 interviews with more than 200 individuals.

Wise explored similar espionage topics in at least three novels: *Spectrum* (1981), *The Children's Game* (1983), and *The Samarkand Dimension* (1987).

REPRESENTATIVE WORKS

The U-2 Affair (1962)
The Invisible Government (1964)
The Espionage Establishment (1967)
The Politics of Lying (1973)
The American Police State: The Government Against the People (1976)
The Spy Who Got Away: The Inside Story of Edward Lee Howard, the CIA Agent Who Betrayed His Country's Secrets and Escaped to Moscow (1988)
Molehunt: The Secret Search for Traitors That Shattered the CIA (1992)

SELECTED BIBLIOGRAPHY

BOOKS

Arlen, Michael J. *Living Room War.* New York: Viking, 1969.

Behrens, John C. *The Typewriter Guerrillas: Closeups of 20 Top Investigative Reporters.* Chicago: Nelson-Hall, 1977.

Block, Maxine, ed. *Current Biography: 1941.* New York: H. W. Wilson, 1941.

Bowden, Jane A., ed. *Contemporary Authors.* vol. 65–68. Detroit: Gale Research, 1977.

Brendon, Piers. *The Life and Death of the Press Barons.* New York: Atheneum, 1983.

Chalmers, David Mark. *The Social and Political Ideas of the Muckrakers.* New York: Citadel, 1964.

Christgau, Robert. *Christgau's Record Guide: Rock Albums of the Seventies.* New York: Ticknor and Fields, 1981.

Christman, Henry M., ed. *The American Journalism of Marx and Engels*, with an Introduction by Charles Blitzer. New York: New American Library, 1966.

Clark, Harry Hayden. *Thomas Paine: Representative Selections, with Introduction, Bibliography, and Notes.* New York: American Book Co., 1944.

Cleaver, Eldridge. *Soul on Ice.* New York: McGraw-Hill, 1968.

Curtis, Laura Ann, ed. *The Versatile Defoe.* Totowa, N.J.: Rowman and Littlefield, 1979.

Daiches, David, ed. *The Penguin Companion to English Literature.* New York: McGraw-Hill, 1971.

Davis, Thadious M., and Trudier Harris, eds. *Dictionary of Literary Biography: Afro-American Fiction Writers After 1955.* Detroit: Gale Research, 1984.

Dennis, Everette, ed. *The Magic Writing Machine: Student Probes of the New Journalism.* Eugene: University of Oregon School of Journalism, 1971.

Dennis, Everette E., and William L. Rivers. *Other Voices: The New Journalism in America.* San Francisco: Canfield, 1974.

Downie, Leonard. *The New Muckrakers.* Washington: New Republic Books, 1976.

Evory, Ann, ed. *Contemporary Authors: New Revision Series.* Vol. 2. Detroit: Gale Research, 1981.

Fast, Howard, ed. *The Selected Work of Tom Paine: Set in the Framework of His Life.* New York: Duell, Sloan and Pearce, 1945.

Filler, Louis. *The Muckrakers.* University Park: Pennsylvania State University Press, 1976.

Flippin, Charles C., ed. *Liberating the Media: The New Journalism.* Washington, D.C.: Acropolis Books, 1974.

Frankfort, Ellen. *The Voice: Life at the Village Voice.* New York: William Morrow, 1976.

Garraty, John A., ed. *Dictionary of American Biography: Supplement Six 1956–1960.* New York: Charles Scribner's Sons, 1980.

Gornick, Vivian. *Essays in Feminism.* New York: Harper and Row, 1978.

Graham, Otis L., Jr. *An Encore for Reform: The Old Progressives and the New Deal.* New York: Oxford University Press, 1967.

Harris, Richard. *Decision.* New York: E. P. Dutton, 1971.

Harrison, John M., and Harry H. Stein. *Muckraking: Past, Present and Future.* University Park: Pennsylvania State University Press, 1973.

Hellman, John. *Fables of Fact: The New Journalism as New Fiction.* Urbana: University of Illinois Press, 1981.

Hentoff, Nat. *The First Freedom: A Tumultuous History of Free Speech in America.* New York: Delacorte, 1980.

Hoftman, Frederick J., Charles Allen, and Carolyn F. Ubrich. *The Little Magazine: A History and a Bibliography.* Princeton, N.J.: Princeton University Press, 1947.

Hollowell, John. *Fact and Fiction: The New Journalism and the Nonfiction Novel.* Chapel Hill: University of North Carolina Press, 1977.

Hynds, Ernest C. *American Newspapers in the 1980s.* New York: Hastings House, 1980.

Irwin, Will. *The Making of a Reporter.* New York: G. P. Putnam's Sons, 1942.

Johnson, Michael L. *The New Journalism: The Underground Press, the Artists of Nonfiction, and Changes in the Established Media.* Lawrence: University Press of Kansas, 1971.

Josephson, Matthew. *The Robber Barons: The Great American Capitalists, 1861–1901.* New York: Harcourt, Brace, 1934.

Kibler, James E., Jr., ed. *Dictionary of Literary Biography: American Novelists Since World War II: Second Series.* Detroit: Gale Research, 1980.

Kiernan, Robert F. *Gore Vidal.* New York: Frederick Ungar, 1982.

Kotz, Nick. *Let Them Eat Promises: The Politics of Hunger in America.* Englewood Cliffs, N.J.: Prentice-Hall, 1969.

Larner, Jeremy, and Ralph Tefferteller. *The Addict in the Street.* New York: Grove, 1964.

Lindsey, Ben B., and Harvey J. O'Higgins. *The Beast.* Seattle: University of Washington Press, 1970.

Lindsey, Ben B., and Rube Borough. *The Dangerous Life.* New York: Arno, 1974.

Locher, Frances Carol, ed. *Contemporary Authors.* Vol. 81–84. Detroit: Gale Research, 1979.

McArthur, Chester. *Henry Demarest Lloyd and the Empire of Reform.* Philadelphia: University of Pennsylvania Press, 1963.

Macdonald, Dwight. *Memoirs of a Revolutionist: Essays in Political Criticism.* New York: Farrar, Straus and Cudahy, 1957.

MacDougall, Curtis D. *Interpretative Reporting.* New York: Macmillan, 1977.

McReynolds, David. *We Have Been Invaded by the 21st Century: A Radical View of the Sixties.* New York: Praeger, 1970.

Marchetti, Victor, and John D. Marks. *The CIA and the Cult of Intelligence.* New York: Alfred A. Knopf, 1974.

Markham, Edwin, Benjamin B. Lindsey, and George Creel. *Children in Bondage.* New York: Arno and the *New York Times,* 1969.

Mills, Nicolaus, ed. *The New Journalism: A Historical Anthology.* New York: McGraw-Hill, 1974.

Moore, Harry T., ed. *Contemporary American Novelists.* Carbondale: Southern Illinois University Press, 1964.

Moritz, Charles, ed. *Current Biography Yearbook 1968.* New York: H. W. Wilson, 1968.

_____. *Current Biography Yearbook 1972.* New York: H. W. Wilson, 1972.

Mott, Frank Luther. *A History of American Magazines, Vol. 4: 1885–1905*. Cambridge: Harvard University Press, 1957.

Newfield, Jack, and Jeff Greenfield. *A Populist Manifesto: The Making of a New Majority*. New York: Praeger, 1972.

Powers, Thomas. *The Man Who Kept the Secrets: Richard Helms and the CIA*. New York: Alfred A. Knopf, 1979.

Regier, C. C. *The Era of the Muckrakers*. Chapel Hill: University of North Carolina Press, 1932.

Riis, Jacob A. *How the Other Half Lives — Jacob A. Riis*. New York: Dover, 1971.

Rood, Karen Lane, ed. *Dictionary of Literary Biography: American Writers in Paris, 1920–1939*. Detroit: Gale Research, 1980.

Ross, Ishbell. *Ladies of the Press: The Story of Women in Journalism by an Insider*. New York: Harper and Brothers, 1936.

Rubin, Steven J., ed. *Writing Our Lives: Autobiographies of American Jews, 1890–1990*. New York: Jewish Publication Society, 1991.

Schudson, Michael. *Discovering the News*. New York: Basic Books, 1978.

Schuyler, Robert Livingston, ed. *Dictionary of American Biography*. New York: Charles Scribner's Sons, 1958.

_____. *Dictionary of American Biography: Supplement Two*. New York: Charles Scribner's Sons, 1958.

Starr, Harris E., ed. *Dictionary of American Biography*. New York: Charles Scribner's Sons, 1944.

von Hoffman, Nicholas. *Left at the Post*. Chicago: Quadrangle Books, 1970.

Weinberg, Arthur, and Lila Weinberg, eds. The Muckrakers: The Era in Journalism That Moved America to Reform — The Most Significant Magazine Articles of 1902–1912. New York: Simon and Schuster, 1961.

Wilson, Edmund. *The Triple Thinkers: Ten Essays on Literature*. New York: Harcourt, Brace, 1938.

Wilson, Harold S. *McClure's Magazine and the Muckrakers*. Princeton, N.J.: Princeton University Press, 1970.

Wolfe, Tom. *The New Journalism*, with an Anthology edited by Tom Wolfe and E. W. Johnson. New York: Harper and Row, 1973.

Wood, James Playsted. *Magazines in the United States*. New York: Ronald, 1971.

NEWSPAPERS

Cherokee Phoenix, October 8, 1830.

ARTICLES

Adams, Samuel Hopkins. "The Great American Fraud." *Collier's*, October 7, 1905, pp. 14–15, 29.

Altbach, Philip G. "Radical Pacifist." *Progressive* (December 1970), pp. 45–46.

Barnet, Richard J. "Killers and Jokers." *New York Review of Books*, October 3, 1974, pp. 29–31.

Christianson, K. Scott. "The New Muckraking." *Quill* (July 1972), pp. 10–15.

"The City That Was." *New York Sun*, April 21, 1906.

Connolly, C. P. "The Story of Montana." *McClure's Magazine* (August 1906), pp. 346–361.

Cowan, Robert C. "Yevtushenko in English-Housewifery — Miss Carson's 'Silent S;pring.'" *Christian Science Monitor*, September 27, 1962, p. 11.

DeMott, Benjamin. "Alone in Cover-Up Country." *Atlantic* (October 1973), pp. 115–119.

Dennis, Everette E. "Journalistic Primitivism." *Journal of Popular Culture* (Summer 1975), pp. 122/24–134/36.

"Editorial Announcements." *McClure's Magazine* (April 1906), p. 675.

"Editorial Bulletin: Patent Medicine Frauds." *Collier's*, September 30, 1905, p. 30.

Ellis, Harry B. "Science and Literature of the World's Vast Seas." *Christian Science Monitor*, July 5, 1951, p. 7.

Elshtain, Jean B. "*Justice* and *The Fear of Crime* by Richard Harris." *Commonweal*, May 29, 1970, pp. 274–276.

Flynt, Josiah. "In the World of Graft." *McClure's Magazine* (February 1901), pp. 327–334.

____, and Francis Walton. "True Stories from the Underworld." *McClure's Magazine* (August 1900), pp. 356–363.

Friedenberg, Edgar Z. "Patriotic Gore." *New York Review of Books*, June 19, 1969, pp. 34–36.

Goldstein, Patrick. "Steal Magnolias." *Los Angeles Times Book Review*, November 24, 1991, p. 2.

Hawkes, Jacquetta. "The World Under Water." *New Republic*, January 23, 1956, pp. 17–18.

Hendrick, Burton J. "The Story of Life Insurance." *McClure's Magazine* (May 1906), pp. 36–49.

Hough, George A. "How 'New'?" *Journal of Popular Culture* (Summer 1975), pp. 114/16–121/23.

Lawson, Thomas W. "Frenzied Finance." *Everybody's Magazine* (July 1904), pp. 1–10.

Lawson, Thomas W. "Why I Gave Up the Fight." *Everybody's Magazine* (February 1908), pp. 287–288, 480–48w.

Newfield, Jack. "Notes on the Art: Is There a 'New Journalism'?" *Columbia Journalism Review* (July-August 1972), pp. 45–47.

Okri, Ben. "Colouring Book." *New Statesman*, June 22, 1984, p. 24.

Perrin, Noel. "Another Sojourner." *New York Times Book Review*, June 5, 1988, pp. 42–43.

Ridgeway, James. "The New Journalism." *American Libraries* (June 1971), pp. 585–592.

Shapiro, Laura. "Little Gloria, Happy at Last." *Newsweek*, January 13, 1992, pp. 64–65.

Shearer, Derek. "George Seldes: Muckraker Emeritus." *Ramparts* 12, mo. 2 (August-September 1973), pp. 16–18, 20.

Smith, Wendy. "PW Interviews: Nicholas von Hoffman." *Publishers Weekly*, September 21, 1992, pp. 72–73.

Stark, Steven J. "Investigating Bob Greene: His Mighty Ax Felled Presidential Timber and Cub Reporters Alike." *Quill* (June 1993), pp. 17–21.

Stoehr, Taylor. "Growing Up Absurd — Again: Rereading Paul Goodman in the Nineties." *Dissent* (Fall 1990), pp. 486–494.

Tonkovich, Nicole. "Traveling in the West, Writing in the Library: Margaret Fuller's *Summer on the Lakes*." *Legacy* (Fall 1993), pp. 79–102.

Turner, George Kibbe. "Galveston: A Business Corporation." *McClure's Magazine* (October 1906), pp. 610–620.

Weeks, Edward. "The Peripatetic Reviewer." *Atlantic* (February 1970), pp. 118–119.

"Whatever Happened to … Eldridge Cleaver." *Ebony* (March 1988), pp. 66–68.

INDEX